Gianluigi Passarelli

Contract Law in Contemporary International Commerce

Considerations on the complex relationship between legal process and market process in the new era of globalisation

Nomos

Die Deutsche Nationalbibliothek verzeichnet diese Publikation in der Deutschen Nationalbibliografie; detaillierte bibliografische Daten sind im Internet über http://dnb.d-nb.de abrufbar.

The Deutsche Nationalbibliothek lists this publication in the Deutsche Nationalbibliografie; detailed bibliographic data are available on the Internet at http://dnb.d-nb.de

ISBN 978-3-8487-6038-1 (Print)
978-3-7489-0158-7 (ePDF)

British Library Cataloguing-in-Publication Data
A catalogue record for this book is available from the British Library.

ISBN 978-3-8487-6038-1 (Print)
978-3-7489-0158-7 (ePDF)

Library of Congress Cataloging-in-Publication Data
Passarelli, Gianluigi
Contract Law in Contemporary International Commerce
Considerations on the complex relationship between legal process and market process in the new era of globalisation
Gianluigi Passarelli
207 p.

ISBN 978-3-8487-6038-1 (Print)
978-3-7489-0158-7 (ePDF)

1st Edition 2019

For the unconditional support of my mother,
for my father's consistency.

"Opus est [...] ad notitiam sui experimento;
quid quisque posset nisi temptando non didicit."
Lucio Anneo Seneca
De Providentia

Preface and Acknowledgments

My interest in the topic peaked in 2009 when the Rome I Regulation determining which countries' laws govern most civil and commercial contracts was entering into force. I was in Vienna working at an international law firm, and the idea presented in this book had its genesis when I started to read the Recital of Rome I, which drastically changed the private international law rules of contractual obligations with hard-and-fast rules in order to benefit the internal market. Consequently, I started thinking about: how the law can better relate to international commerce?

I was admitted to a PhD at Universität Wien, where I attended many seminars and courses. During the years in which I was a PhD student, my research was also conducted in prestigious universities, such as the Institute of Advanced Legal Studies of the University of London and the University of Oxford, and I also was Visiting Researcher at King's College of London. Finally, I completed my PhD thesis entitled "Applicable Law in absence of choice in Rome I Regulation. Legal and political implications on the 'evolution' or 'involution' of EU p.i.l." at the Universität Wien under the supervision of em. o.Univ.-Prof. Dr. Dr. h.c. Hans Hoyer. After obtaining my PhD, I continued to study this topic, dwelling above all on contract law theories. These studies were conducted at the Università degli Studi della Campania Luigi Vanvitelli, where I have been Research assistant in Civil Law. During these studies, I received a scholarship from the "Amerigo Association" to finish my research at Fordham Law School in New York, where as a full-time Visiting Scholar Research I completed the book after long years of research.

The monograph proposes a new approach of contract law in the new era of globalization where the "new" change in economic relationships calls for "new" changes in the law, with the aim of bringing economic benefits to the market. Therefore, this book employs a careful and analytic research method, supported also by many practical implications, to its subject matter. I have tried to be as clear and direct as possible in structuring my hypotheses, collecting the relevant data, and conducting the analysis. My hope is that this research can contribute to the normative debate regarding legal certainty (predictability) or legal congruence (flexibility) of the contract law in international commerce by critically reviewing and discussing some of the propositions in the literature, which contain interesting hypotheses on the economic analysis of law. The objective is to bring economic benefits to the market, answering the above-mentioned question which motivated my study of this topic.

I must express my gratitude to a great number of persons who have assisted in the production of this book. Though it is not possible to acknowledge them all, some are due particular thanks. The distinguished Professors of Universität Wien and Università degli Studi della Campania Luigi Vanvitelli have offered their valuable time to discuss this topic with me. I deeply appreciate the indispensable comments and analysis reported in chapters 1 and 2 of Professor Martin Gelter of Fordham Law School. I am also very grateful for the assistance given to me by the Office of International and Non-J.D. Programs of Fordham Law School directed by Professor Toni M. Jaeger-Fine, whose has offered a lovely academic atmosphere. In this respect, I would like to thank the "Amerigo Association" for providing me the opportunity to live the US research world.

In writing this monograph I was inspired also by the insights and careful scholarship of a large numbers of writers in the fields of civil law, private international law, comparative law and commercial law whose works I have cited. Finally, I also appreciate the support and encouragement of the editorial staff at NOMOS and Vincenzo Contri, who have always offered their professional assistance during the various stages of production of the book, and I wish to acknowledge Ana Ciriani-Dean, who has kindly read some of the manuscript in order to improve the linguistic approach of a non-native English speaker. Any errors or misunderstandings are, of course, entirely my own.

Whether or not you agree with the arguments that this book contains, certainly the analysis is new and tries to create progress in the field. However, my personal outcome there is now, after many years of frantic activity on this topic, there is a short period of respite.

Dr. Gianluigi Passarelli
Caserta, Italy
May, 2019

Table of contents

List of abbreviations

ABGB	Allgemeines bürgerliches Gesetzbuch
AcP	Archiv für die civilistische Praxis
ALI	The American Law Institute
Art.	Article
BGB	Bürgerliches Gesetzbuch
Brussels I	Council Regulation (EC) No 44/2001 of December 22, 2000 on jurisdiction and the recognition and enforcement of judgments in civil and commercial maters [2001] OJ L12/1
Brussels Convention	Convention on jurisdiction and the enforcement of judgements in civil and commercial matters done at Brussels on September 27, 1968 [1972] OJ L299/32
CESL	Common European Sales Law
CIDIP	Inter-American Convention on the law applicable to international contracts
C.U.P.	Cambridge University Press
DCFR	Draft Common Frame of Reference
Dicey & Morris	L. Collins (gen. ed.), Dicey, Morris and Collins on the Conflict of Laws
EC	European Community
ECJ	European Court of Justice
ecolex	ecolex Fachzeitschrift für Wirtschaftsrecht
ed.	editor
EU	European Union
EC Treaty	Consolidated version of the Treaty establishing the European Community
HGB	Handelsgesetzbuch
IPRax	Praxis des Internationalen Privat- und Verfahrensrechts
Austrian IPRG	das internationale Privatrecht Gesetz
O.U.P.	Oxford University Press
PECL	Principles of European Contract Law
PICC	Principles of International Commercial Contracts
P.I.L.	Private International Law

RabelsZ	Rabels Zeitschrift für ausländisches und internationales Privatrecht
Rome I	Regulation (EC) n. 593/2008 of the European Parliament and Council of 17 June, 2008 on the law applicable to contractual obligations (Rome I) [2008] OJ L177/6
Rome II	Regulation (EC) n. 864/2007 of the European Parliament and Council of July 11, 2007 on the law applicable to non-contractual obligations (Rome II) [2007]OJ L199/40
Rome Convention	Convention on the law applicable to contractual obligations opened for signature in Rome on June 19, 1980 [1980] OJ L266/1
Report	Report on the Rome Convention by Professors Mario Giuliano and Paul Lagarde, reproduced in the Official Journal of the Communities of 31 October 1980
UK	United Kingdom
UNCITRAL	United Nations Commission on International Trade Law
UNIDROIT	International Institute for the Unification of Private Law
US	United States
ZfRV	Zeitschrift für Europarecht, Internationales Privatrecht und Rechtsvergleichung
ZVglRWiss	Zeitschrift für Vergleichende Rechtswissenschaft
§	paragraph

1. Introduction and context

1.1 The problem to be examined

Globalisation has directly affected the law at both the international and national level. In fact, the "new" in economic relations calls for the "new" in law, with the aim of bringing economic outcomes to the market whose laws governs it.[1] On the basis of these considerations, this book has attempted to respond to the following question: How does the law better relate to international commerce?

Manne, considered a founder of the law and economics discipline, has notoriously argued: "the first is that an effective rule of law is an extremely valuable, indeed almost essential, complement to a functioning market economy".[2] Therefore, using Manne's line of reasoning it becomes clear that a good relationship between law and market can create opportunities for capturing, creating and distributing wealth. Consequently, a norm that rules a transaction can be wealth-creating or wealth-destroying and therefore can increase or decrease the wealth or utility of the contractual parties who are the principal actors within the market. These are the main reasons for which a legal scholar is obligated to also study economic topics.

Undoubtedly, in globalised economics the world is contracting and these "global distances"[3] demonstrate that, when the interpreter analyses an international business transaction, the distinction between international and domestic law is no longer easy to maintain.

In addition, it should be emphasised that almost all trade and economic relations nowadays are based on private contracts that, as a consequence, assume more often that not an international dimension. Furthermore, Weber has already described modern society as a "contractual society",[4] as

---

1 *N. Irti*, *L'ordine giuridico del mercato*, (Laterza Editore, Bari, 2009), 11 and 112, according to the Author the market is a *locus artificialis* and "consists of the law that governs and constitutes it". (Author's traslation).

2 *H. G. Manne*, "What is the 'law' in law and economics? The judiciary and free markets", in (1997) *Harvard Journal of Law & Public Policy*, XXI, 17.

3 *M. J. Whincop – M. Keyes*, *Policy and Pragmatism in the Conflict of Laws* (Dartmounth Publishing Company, Hants, 2001), 1.

4 *M. Weber*, *Economy and Society*, in G. Roth – C. Wittich (eds.), (University of California Press, Berkley, 1978), 669.

contract law contributes significantly to market activities, thereby facilitating the initiation of international transactions[5] and, in so doing, encouraging private transactions by presuming their legality.[6]

The EU has approached this issue by creating an "internal market",[7] which is perceived as an area without internal frontiers in which there is full mobility of production factors,[8] and, at the same time, through the adoption by the EU institutions of rules which will have a direct impact on the market.[9]

In this regard, it is well known that the EU Commission assumes that legal diversity between the EU legal systems increases the transaction costs of cross-border contracting, and that it discourages consumers and small and medium-sized companies from engaging in such transactions.[10] It is obvious what kind of effect an European unification/harmonization/codifi-

---

5 *R. Cooter - U. Mattei - P.G. Monateri - R. Pardolesi - T. Ulen*, *Il mercato delle regole. Analisi economica del diritto civile*, (Il Mulino, Bologna, 2006), I, 137. According to the Authors "*Il primo scopo del diritto dei contratti è quello di mettere i soggetti in grado di cooperare*".

6 *J. W. Hurst*, *Law and Markets in United States History. Different Modes of Bargaining among interests*, (The University of Wisconsin Press, Madison, 1982), 37.

7 The notion of what constitutes the internal market is well explained in Art. 26 of the Lisbon Teatry on the functioning of the European Union according to which: "The internal market shall comprise an area without internal frontiers in which the free movement of goods, persons, services and capital is ensured in accordance with the provisions of the Treaties". Or, shortly, as defined in Article 199 TFEU "an open market economy with free competition" that takes place through the creation of a common market and an economic and monetary union.

8 See case *Van Gen & Loos* 1963, available at https://eur-lex.europa.eu/legal-content/EN/TXT/?uri=CELEX%3A61962CJ0026.

9 At the same time the TFEU provides for the possibility of harmonizing the laws of the Member States (Positive integration) as well it includes provisions prohibiting obstacles to economic activities between Member States (negative integration). In this way see *R. van Leuken*, *Private Law and Market. Direct Horizontal Effect of the Treaty Provisions on the Free Movement*, (Intersentia, Cambridge, 2017), 152; *G. Comparato – H. W. Micklitz*, "Regulated Autonomy between Market Freedoms and Fundamental Rights in the Case Law of the CJEU", in U. Bernitz - X Groussot - F. Schulyok (eds.), *General Principles of EU law and European Private Law*, (Kluwer Law international, Alphen aan den Rijn, 2013), 126 – 128.

10 O.J. 2001, C 255/1 available at https://eur-lex.europa.eu/legal-content/EN/TXT/?uri=CELEX:52006XX1021(01) ; see also Council Report on the need to approximate Member States' legislation in civil matters, adopted by the Council 16 Nov. 2001, DGH III 13017/01. European Parliament, Committee on Legal Affairs and the Internal Market, Report on the approximation of the civil and commercial law of the Member States, A 5-0384/2001 Final: European Parliament resolution on the approximation of the civil and commercial law of the Member States;

cation of p.i.l. and contract law[11] which already appears surprisingly connected to the internal market, would have on EU business transactions if it were implemented.

In this context, it seems to me that a central point is that in the new era of globalisation[12] there is a strong juncture between p.i.l. of contractual obligations and contract law, at national and supranational level because both are strongly connected to the market and because only through both these rules is it possible to encourage the circulation of wealth and, as a consequence, to guarantee benefits to the internal market. To sum up, what I am saying is that, when the interpreter must analyse an international business transaction, the EU p.i.l. of contractual obligations and contract law, should be considereded as a homogeneous body of laws because they are promoting a common goal, i.e. to regulate international transactions. In other words and from a pragmatic business standpoint, taking into consideration the "international business transaction" as a whole, p.i.l. and domestic private law although interdependent are inseparable.[13] In fact as some commentators have observed "if there is no private law, there

---

Contra, *J. Smits* (ed.), *The need for a European Contract Law. Empirical and Legal Perspectives*, (Europa Law Publishing, Amsterdam, 2005), V, who notes that "the view of the European Commission seems to be that diversity of law stands in the way of a proper functioning of the internal market, but this view does not seem to be shared by business: in the reactions to the Communication on European Contract Law (2001) it was striking to see that most companies do not consider the present diversity for be a true barrier to trade".

11 In fact, in Europe, on one hand, it is continued the formation of study group (PECL, UNIDROIT, European Civil Code and Gandolfi Code) with the intent to discover all the benefits for the internal market.

12 When I talk about "new era of globalisation", what I would like to say is that globalization is changing. What we are witnessing is the emergence of a new global economy, an economy without borders propelled by digital rocket boosters. In fact the structural changes taking place in the world economy, set in motion by various digital technologies, such as advanced digital distribution and global digital platforms (i.e. blockchain) and last but not least by new and complex financial instruments (i.e. swaps or venture capital). The consequence is the creation of a different kind of globalisation, more-fragmented, with decentralized supply chains, new contracts and more countries involved.

13 In this regard *M. J. Whincop - M. Keyes*, *Policy and Pragmatism in the Conflicts of Laws*, (Ashgate Dartmounth, Hants, 2001), 40, continuing they assume that "From a practical and theoretical standpoint, however, it must be recognized that transactions and trade are inseparable". See on a similar way also *P. Perlingieri*, *Il diritto dei contratti tra persona e mercato. Problemi di diritto civile*, (E.S.I., Napoli, 2003), 481 points out that "EU law does not live by independent light but complements and supervises national law" (Author's translator).

can be no private international law".[14] As a consequence, I believe that it is necessary to initiate a new dialogue between contract law and p.i.l. of contractual obligations.

This is the approach that I adopt in this book: contract law and p.i.l. of contractual obligations are analysed togheter due to their strong relationship. In so doing I will demonstrate the benefits to all contractual parties and as a result the consequent gain to the market. These are also reasons for which I believe the economic theories that will subsequently be examined can be used and applied to p.i.l. of contractual obligations.

To summarize, it is my assertion, quite obvious to many but not all academics, that, in our contemporary world, business, as well as all the actors of the market, is increasingly transnational, and contract law is no longer the exclusive product of the nation-state.[15] This observation invites contemporary private law scholars and practioners to "interact" employing this science with an international and comparative approach.[16] On the contrary, the study of contract law alone does not keep up with an increasingly fast-moving business society[17] and runs the risk of remaining in a perfect provincialism that it not useful to the market needs resulting from

---

14 *M. J. Whincop - M. Keyes*, *Policy and Pragmatism in the Conflicts of Laws*, (Ashgate Dartmounth, Hants, 2001), 40. The Authors, continuing, point out "The topic of 'conflict of laws' includes such issues within a divided domestic system, as well as private international law in the international system". It is very interesting also the opinion of *T. Wilhelmsson*, "The Ethical Pluralism of Late Mordern Europe and Codification of European Contract Law", in J. Smits (ed.) *The Need for a European Contract Law. Empirical and Legal Perspectives*, (Europa Law Publishing, Amstredam, 2005), 129. according to which "Private law in risk society is forced to become internationalised".

15 See on this point *M. Smits*, *Contract Law. A Comparative Introduction*, (Edward Elgar, Cheltenhamm, 2014), reprinted 2015, *passim*.

16 *M. Infantino*, "Contract Law in a Global World", in (2018) *European Review of Private Law*, 162, according to the Author: "The urgency of stretching the horizons of legal education beyond national borders, of focusing the legal debate on real-world issues, and of transcending traditional distinctions as state and non-state, public and private, hard and soft law, is before everyone's eyes".

17 *L. Rossi Carleo*, "Diritto del mercato, diritto per il mercato o diritto per i soggetti del mercato?", in (1992) *Rassegna di diritto civile*, 757. As consequence according to the her: "The consequence is that the study of private law must reinvent itself and analyze the possibility of adapting the classical tools to new requirements" (translated by the Author).

EU economics. In my opinion, it is not only an interdisciplinary[18] discussion, it is, genuinely, just a fact of the contemporary law. In other words, the risk is to confirm what R.A. Posner[19] rightly has observed: the general loss of confidence in the ability of legal scholars to solve the problems of modern society.

From this point of view, the US has proved an impressive example for other countries. This claim is corrobated not only by the fact that in US law schools the Professors teach general contracts as if there was one matter[20] but above all that in an always thriving market,[21] as is the US's, flexible and uniform rules govern the market.

---

18 Two distinguished Authors, rightly, notes differences about the EU and US approach and point out: "This purely functional approach distinguishes the US legal academia from scholarship in Europe, including the UK. Especially in German-speaking countries, economic approaches to law have been met with rejection quite frequently; law is not merely seen as a field to be investigated with the methods of any branch of social science, but as a separate academic discipline and with particular "scientific" methods." In this way *K. Grechenig - M. Gelter*, "The Transatlantic Divergence in Legal Thought: American Law and Economics vs. German Doctrinalism", in (2008) *Hastings International and Comparative Law Review*, 297.

19 *R. A. Posner*, "The Decline of Law as an Autonomous Discipline", in (1987) *Harvard Law Rewiev*, 766 – 767.

20 *M.A. Eisenberg*, 'The Unification of the Law', in M. Bussani - U. Mattei (eds.), *Making European Private Law: Essays on the 'Common Core' Project* (Trento: Dipartimento di Scienze giuridiche dell'Università degli studi di Trento 2000), 15 ss. ('if you walk into almost any law school in America [...], you will find that many of the statements that you hear [...] in those forums are neither statements of federal law nor statements of local law, that is, the law of particular states. Rather, statements you will hear [...] will be statements of and about law in general terms, divorced from particular federal or state jurisdictions'. As a consequence, *K. Grechenig - M. Gelter*, in "The Transatlantic Divergence in Legal Thought: American Law and Economics vs. German Doctrinalism", in (2008) *Hastings International and Comparative Law Review*, 330 have observed that "the articles published by American law reviews, other than articles in typical German-speaking journals, are hardly under any pressure to be immediately useful to the practice of judges and lawyers, which facilitates focusing on interdisciplinary and theoretical issues".

21 According to *M. Gelter – K. Grechenig*, "History of Law and Economics", in *Collective Goods Preprint, No. 2014/5.* Available at https://ssrn.com/abstract=2421224 , 5, Preprints of the Max Planck Institute for Research on Collective Goods Bonn 2014/. "In the United States, economic analysis became one of the main methods of legal scholarship – both descriptive and normative – in legal academia. Other than in the early 20th century, and in sharp contrast to continental Europe, law is

These issues are obviously crucial in order to understand which are the real needs of the internal market but also the welfare of the state that the parties belong to.[22] To date, a small, albeit rapidly increasing number of articles have been added both in contract law as well in private international law. In my opinion, as will be clearly explained in the next pages, the issues must be jointly faced and in particular can be transferred to the area of contract law because they are strictly linked to the trans-border bargain and also because the new Rome I Regulation represents, for its connection with the real economic world, the first enacted (enforced) norm regarding cross-border transactions of this EU process of harmonization/codification, among other projects underway.

Critically, the purpose of this book is to confront all the above-mentioned assumptions not only with an economic analysis but also with an analysis of the practical response of the market.

1.II *The central role of p.i.l. of contractual obligations in the new era of globalisation*

As already pointed out in the foregoing pages, in a globalised world characterized by a continuing increase in cross-boarder transactions, it is difficult, in my opinion, to argue that p.i.l. of contractual obligations should be viewed as a scientific model independent from contract law. In fact, globalisation is reshaping the law because a rigorous legal analysis of the transactions cannot be made without the knowledge both of contract law and private international law rules. As a corollary of these assumptions, I reiterate that an analysis of p.i.l. of contractual obligations is not separate from contract law.[23]

---

not recognized as an autonomous discipline, but a field to be studied from various social science perspectives".

22 See *U. La Porta*, *Globalizzazione e diritto. Regole giuridiche e norme di legge nell'economia globale.* (Liguori Editore, Napoli, 2005), 113, according to which: "it is not more public law to weave relations with the economy but it is private law - in particular that of contracts - that has to provide answers to new needs" (Author's translation).

23 According to *J. P. Trachtman*, "The International Economic Law Revolution", in (1996) *University of Pennsylvania Journal of International Economic Law*, 34 – 35 "As many realists and critical legal theorists long ago pointed out, "private law" is an oxymoron" and that "[...] the very term "international law" must be revisited and reevaluated, as the system of law that governs international relations has both states and individuals as its subjects and objects. Increasingly, "international law"

These assumptions impose, inevitably, that a legal scholar who is confronted with a cross-border transaction should interface with p.i.l. studies that address cross-border relationships,[24] although extremely complex.[25] In this way, I should also remember what Pfeiffer has stressed in the definition of "private international law" written in the Max Plank Encyclopedia; the author rightly observes that

> "the principles and rules of private international law ('PIL') determine the applicability of a certain law or certain rules of law in situations involving a choice between the laws of different countries. In this context, the term international does not refer to the internationality of the source of law but to the internationality of the cases covered. As to the civil law distinction between private law and public law, the prevailing viewpoint is that PIL is a part of private law [...]".[26]

Following this brief introduction, in this paragraph some considerations will be made with regard the decisive role that p.i.l. plays especially in the European Union today, famously defined by Basedow as "the cradle of pri-

is taken to mean "transnational law," the term coined by Philip Jessup, the late judge of the International Court of Justice, to include in the scope of study private law and other municipal law that affects relations between different countries and their peoples".

24 *H. G. Maier*, "Extraterritorial Jurisdiction at a Crossroads: An Intersection between Public and Private International Law", in (1982) *The American Journal of International Law*, 76, 287. The Author notes that it represents "how the system's component parts interact with each other".

25 *K. Kagami*, "The Systematic choice of Legal Rules for Private International Law: An Economic Approach", in J. Basedow – T. Kono (eds.), *An Economic Analysis of Private International Law*, (Mohr Siebeck, Tübingen 2006), 18.

26 *T. Pfeiffer*, "Private International Law", in *Max Planck Encyclopedia of Public International Law*, (O.U.P., Oxford, 2008), available also online at http://0opil.ouplaw.com.lawpac.lawnet.fordham.edu/view/10.1093/law:epil/9780199231690/law-9780199231690-e1458?rskey=clLyVb&result=1&prd=EPIL. On this vein see *S. C. Symeonides*, *Codifying Choice of Law Around the World*, (O.U.P., Oxford, 2014), 291, who famously argues "The adjective *international* in PIL describes the cases that fall within the scope of the subject cases that have a significant international (or multistate) dimension. [...] Thus, PIL is very much *national* law".

vate international law"[27] as a result of the diversity of existing systems and legal cultures between Member States.[28]

In this sense, the decisive role attributed to p.i.l. of contractual obligations is also linked to the strong impact that it would have on the EU internal market and its related transactions.[29] In fact, it is known that the contract, as an expression of the party's autonomy to regulate their own interests, is the typical expression of the circulation of "wealth" and as such, in a now economic global context, is increasingly dominated by points of contact with various national legal systems. This situation occurs when the parties to the contract are of a different nationality, residence or place of business, i.e. when the characteristic performance of the contract must be carried out in a different State from the one in which the contract was concluded.[30] Therefore p.i.l. with its traditional purpose to determine the jurisdiction and the applicable law, is the only legal tool that can efficiently navigate the problem of the international transactions[31] that in the EU market are mostly represented by exchanges between SME. In fact, according to some EU Reports,[32] a progressive increase of contracts sales (in particular food, manufacturing, innovative goods), provision of advanced services, distribution and franchising or special financial instruments (i.e.

---

27 *J. Basedow*, *The Law of Open Societies: Private Ordering and Public Regulation of International Relations: General Course on Private International Law*, (Martinus Nijhoff Publishers, Leiden/Boston, 2013), 477.

28 *X. Kramer*, "The interaction between Rome I and Mandatory EU Private Rules", in (2010) *Social Science Research Network*. Available at http://ssrn.com/abstract=1666740, according to whom "Private international law nowadays is an important pillar of EU law, and has in the past decade certainly made more progress than the harmonization of substantive law".

29 *S. Leible*, "The role of private international law in European political and economic integration", in (2008) *Revista de processo*, 242.

30 *F. Sbordone*, *Nozioni di diritto internazionale privato*, U. Villani - M. Di Fabio - F. Sbordone (eds.), (E.S.I., Napoli, 2013), 69.

31 *P. R. Beaumont - P.E. McEleavy*, *Private International Law*, (Thomson Reuters, Edinburg, 2011), 55; *G. Van Calster*, *European Private International Law*, (Hart Publishing, Oxford and Portland, 2013), 1.

32 For more also on statistical data see European Commission, Directorate-General for Economic and Financial Affairs Publications BU1 - -1/13, in steps towards a deeper economic integration: the internal market in the 21st century, in http://ec.europa.eu/economy_finance/publications/pages/publication784_en.pdf
Or also The EU Single Market: Impact on Member States, available at http://www.amchameu.eu/sites/default/files/amcham_eu_single_market_web.pdf according to which the provision of services and international bank contracts have grown steadily almost every year since 1992.

venture capital) is taking place in intra-EU trade. These statistical data verify that, in the "new" era of globalisation, the small transactions[33] represent the "core business" of the EU internal market and are the typical concrete case in which p.i.l. of contractual obligations rules are applied, also because often these transactions are characterized as being without a written contract and as a consequence without a "choice of law" by parties.

Exactly for these reasons, p.i.l. rules of contractual obligations have a significant part to play in the internal market. At the same time, a central role is also that of the interpreter (whether he is a judge, arbitrator, lawyer or notary), who must use the p.i.l. tools in order to identify the jurisdiction and the applicable law, locating the geographical centre of a legal relationship,[34] in particular when it is not contractually determined, without creating unfair prejudice to either party. Nonetheless in this undertaking the role that the interpreter takes on, in particular that of the court, is fundamental and as Cheshire stated

> "its object is to ascertain the true intent and meaning of the parties as expressed by the language of the contract. [...] The meaning of a contractual expression and the legal effect of the expression are different things, which are not necessarily determined by the same law. [...] The true province of interpretation, then, is the exact definition of what the parties meant by the words and expressions used in the contract".[35]

Generally, when the interpreter is charged with the crucial task of identifying the applicable law, the legislative instruments at his/her disposal undoubtedly play a key role and, as a consequence, the flexibility or rigidity

33 Detailed statistical data with the tables for each product is available at https://ec.europa.eu/eurostat/web/international-trade-in-goods/data/main-tables . It is important also to point out that "Intra-EU trade statistics do not cover transactions between private individuals or very small businesses which are not subject to VAT obligations" as clearly stressed in https://ec.europa.eu/eurostat/statistics-explained/index.php/International_trade_statistics_-_background.

34 *J.J. Kuipers*, "Bridging the Gap. The Impact of the EU on the Law Applicable to Contractual Obligations", in (2012) *RabelsZ*, 563.

35 In these words, *G. C. Cheshire*, "*International Contracts: being the fifteenth lecture on the David Murray Foundation in the University of Glasgow*", (Jackson, Son & Company, Glasgow, 1948), 74 – 75.

of p.i.l. rules, as private law rules,[36] greatly impact the functioning of the market.[37]

These considerations have given rise to some economic reflections on p.i.l.[38] In fact Carrosca Gonzáles[39] observes that

> *"La règle de conflit est une règle qui épond à une logique économique en ce sens qu'elle gère le commerce international de biens, de droits et de ressources rares. Elle est nécessaire pour la circulation internationale de la richesse et pour la mobilité internationale des personnes"*.[40]

What is more, as Muir Watt rightly stresses, p.i.l. can be described as a "a tool of political economy".[41]

Starting with this assumption I want emphasise that although p.i.l. has not been completely bereft of depth in its economic analysis,[42] a detailed

---

36 *J. Basedow*, "Conflicts of Economic Regulation", in (1994) *American Journal of Comparative Law*, 446.

37 For more see *G. Rühl*, "Economic Analysis of Private International Law", in J. Basedow - G. Rühl - F. Ferrari - P. de Miguel Asensio (eds.), *Encyclopedia of Private International Law*, (Northampton, Edward Elgar Pub., 2017), 579.

38 *Ex multis* on this theory *L. Kramer*, "Rethinking Choice of Law", in (1990) *Columbia Law Review*, 277; *H. M. Watt*, "Aspects Economiques du droit international privè", in (2004) *Recueil des Cours de l'Académie de la Haye*, 25; *M. Whincop – M. Keyes*, *Policy and Pragmatism in the Conflict of Laws* (Farnham, Ashagate, 2001), *passim*; *J. Basedow – T. Kono* (eds.), *An Economic Analysis of Private International Law*, (Mohr Siebeck, Tüebingen, 2006), *passim*; *G. Rühl*, "Methods and Approaches in Choice of law: An Economic Perspective", in (2006) *Berkeley Journal of International Law*, 801; *R. Michaels*, "Economics of Law as Choice of Law", in (2008) *Law & Contemporary Problems*, 73.

39 *J. Carrascosa González*, "Règle de conflit et théorie économique", in (2012) *Revue critique de droit international privé*, 522.

40 It must be noted, in addition, that Basedow famously assumes that "the concept of economic law, as used in the context of p.i.l., is not a plain legal concept with clear border lines. In the context of private international law, economic law is rather a heuristic concept designed to mark a grey area of the law which lies between traditional private law with its bilateral conflict rules and the core of public policy provisions". On this way see *J. Basedow*, "Conflicts of Economic Regulation", in (1994) *American Journal of Comparative Law*, 446.

41 *H. Muir Watt*, "Choice of law in integrated and interconnected markets: a matter of political Economy", in (2003) *Columbia Journal European Law*, 409.

42 See for more on this argument *R. A. Posner*, *Economic Analysis of Law* (Aspen Publishers, New York, 1998), 645 - 646 (arguing that choice of law should be determined according to each state's comparative regulatory advantage); *B. Hay*, "Conflicts of Law and State Competition in the Product Liability System", in (1992) *Georgetown Law Journal*, 617 (applying public choice to interest analysis); *L.*

study it should start with a focus on the core business of cross border economic transaction.

Summarizing all this, I believe that an economic analysis of the EU reforms of p.i.l. of contractual obligations that have been carried out in an attempt to create benefits for the internal market, should start with an evaluation of the relationship between law and economics that has developed, especially in the US. On this point, I want stress again that contract law and private international law of contractual obligations must be dealt with together in an economic analysis, considering their common final goal to determine the "substantive rights" of the parties in an economic transaction. With this precondition in mind, it is quite natural that the specialty of p.i.l. of contractual obligations is inexorably reabsorbed by the contract law. Consequently, the theories that have always characterized the law of contracts can be applied also to p.i.l. of contractual obligations.

1.III Contracts: between law and economics

I began this book by pointing out that contract law should chiefly serve as a tool to facilitate and increase business transactions and that it plays an essential role in economics. In other words, market regulation, described in terms of organizer of social relations and wealth distributor,[43] is indi-

---

Kramer, "Re- thinking Choice of Law", in (1990) *Columbia Law Review*, 339 ss. positing that a clear and frank identification of state interests will allow jurisdictions to develop a stable and cooperative solution to the prisoner's dilemma common in conflicts law; *M. E. Solimine*, "An Economic and Empirical Analysis of Choice of Law", in (1989) *Georgia Law Review*, 74-89 testing empirically and analyzing differences between Restatement (First) of Conflict of Laws and modem approaches; *E. A. O'Hara – L. E. Ribstein*, "From Politcs to Efficiency in Choice of Law", in (2000) *University of Chicago Law Review*, 1151 ss.; *W. Kerber*, "Interjurisdictional Competition with the European Union", in (2000) *Fordham International Law Journal*, 217 ss.; *A.T. Guzman*, "Choice of Law: New Foundations", in (2002) *Georgetown Law Journal*, 883 ss.. In Europe see *E. M. Kieninger*, *Wettbewerb der Privatrechtsordnungen im Europäischen Binnenmarkt*, (Mohr Siebeck, Tübingen, 2002), *passim*; *C. Kirchner*, "Zur öknomik des legislatorischen Wettbewerbs imeropäischen Gesellschaftsrecht", in A. Fuchs - H.P. Schwintowski - D. Zimmer (eds.), *Wirtschafts – und Privatrecht im Spannungsfeld von Privateautonomie, Wettbewerb und Regulierung, Festschrift für Ulrich Immenga* (Verlag Beck, Munich, 2004), 607 – 625; *J. Basedow – T- Kono, An Economic Analysis of Private International Law*, (Mohr Siebeck, Tübingen 2006), *passim*; *G. Rühl*, *Statut und Effizienz* (Mohr Siebeck, Tübingen, 2011), *passim*.

43 *N. Irti*, *L'ordine giuridico del mercato*, (Laterza Editore, Bari, 2009), 112.

rectly made via contract law. As a consequence it is necessary to find a discipline of (European) contract law[44] that is compatible with the freedom and needs of the market.[45] These are the reasons for which an economic approach to contract law is one of the most ambitious ideas[46] that drives the most important scholars in their research to understand which is the right and appropriate approach to use for the creation of perfect market equilibrium.[47]

It is not surprising, therefore, that modern economic analysis of contract law began a long time ago, and that famous studies have been published (almost exclusively) in the US, which is without a doubt the most profitable market in the world. In general, the economic theories of contract law examine the role of the legal systems in promoting efficient exchange. I hope it won't be considered presumptuous but my goal is to add to these theories and then recommend to lawmakers which approach would be more efficient.

Here I would like not only to illustrate all the most important legal theories but above all understand if, starting from these theories, the recent approach adopted by EU institutions can actually create benefits for the EU internal market. Under this assumption and in order to establish ideas for the purpose of this specific analysis, I will limit my focus to the relationship between economic theories and contract law without taking into consideration the link with other legal sectors.

---

44 Some recent studies note that nowadays the majority of the EU students in the European Universities study contract law above all on their own national legal system. It is little sense in a globalized world that has its roots in the cross-boards transactions. In this way *M. Smits*, *Contract Law. A Comparative Introduction* (Edward Elgar, Cheltenham, reprinted, 2015), *passim*. The book has been recently rewieved by *M. Infantino*, "Contract Law in a Global World", in (2018) *European Review of Private Law*, 157 – 164.

45 *P. Perlingieri*, *Il diritto dei contratti tra persona e mercato. Problemi di diritto civile*, (E.S.I., Napoli, 2003), 467.

46 *U. La Porta*, *Globalizzazione e diritto. Regole giuridiche e norme di legge nell'economia globale.* (Liguori Editore, Napoli, 2005), 99 notes that "the relationship between law and economics has been often seen in antagonistic terms and in order to establish the alleged supremacies on each other" (Author traslator).

47 It should be emphasised that the relation between law and economics, in reference to the effects of an internal market, has already been investigated by economists, adopting a mathematical approach rather than to a careful analysis of the law that governs the contractual aspect of the transaction. This circumstance may create prejudices for the contractual parties, and as a consequence for the market itself.

On this premise, it is not surprising that the starting point is to attempt to answer this question: How might law of contract achieves specified economic ends? In order to reply exactly to this question, it will be necessary to analyse shortly the most famous theories in which the law is – unlike for most economists – the primary field of research. It will not be necessary to examine in great detail all these theories as there have been many notable studies and discussions completed in this area. It is simply my intention to construct an overview in order to attempt a response to the above question.

This analysis must start by the two most famous US theories: "Economic Analysis of Law" and "Law and Economics". On the one hand, "Economic Analysis of Law" is an application of pure economic theory to legal materials and is advocated by Posner, who used economic theory to criticize and correct the law. In particular, according to the supporters of this theory: "If the purpose of the law of contracts is to effectuate the desires of the contracting parties, then the proper criterion for evaluating the rules of contract law is surely that of economic efficiency. Since the object of most voluntary exchanges is to increase value or efficiency, contracting parties may be assumed to desire a set of contract terms that will maximize the value of the exchange".[48]

On the other hand, the "Law and Economics" theory that points out that the market mechanism under general deterrence has the advantage that the decision can be practically made by trial and error. As a consequence, the individuals who make the decision most accurately will benefit most in the market. According to this theory the great advantage of the general deterrence[49] of the market is that it is a very effective "trial-and-error device". The main supporter and pioneer of this theory is Calabresi,[50] who used the law to suggest changes in economic theory.

To these well-known theories can be added others that are entrenched in moral obligations of the parties to keep their promises.[51] In fact, as Kenneth Arrow has explained,

---

48 *R. A. Posner – A. M. Rosenfiel, Impossibility and related doctrines in contract law: an economic analysis*, in (1977) *The Journal of Legal Studies*, 89.

49 *Ex multis G. Calabresi, The Cost of Accidents: A Legal and Economic Analysis*, (Yale University Press, New Haven, 1970), 186 ss., who opposes to general deterrence the specific one that he compares to a "hard choice".

50 See *Ibid, passim*; *Ibid, The Future of Law and Economics: Essays in Reform and Recollection*, (Yale University Press, New Haven, 2016), *passim*.

51 *B. H. Fried, The progressive assault on laissez faire*, (Harvard University Press, Cambridge, 1998), *passim*.

> "[T]here is no general principle that prevents the creation of an economic theory based on other hypotheses than that of rationality... [A]ny coherent theory of reactions to the stimuli appropriate in an economic context [...] could in principle lead to a theory of the economy."[52]

However, many other legal commentators have also observed that the contract is always linked to a particular social context that influences the contractual relation. In fact, Collins gives a brilliant overview, assuming that the contract will normally be less important than the business relation and the particular economic deal.[53] In sum he believes that the contractual aspects of a transaction are usually a relatively minor or perhaps even unwanted part of that transaction because "contractual relation always remains 'embedded' in the social practices and norms from which they arise". Therefore, with these considerations, Collins points out two types of "embeddedness":

- market conventions or better "unwritten laws" that are accepted by both sides of transaction, but which are rarely incorporated formally into the written contract because are based upon routine practices and expectations in that line of business;
- embeddedness derived from the identity and past relations of the parties to the contract. According to Collins, this type has its roots in "the identity of the other person as a friend, a fellow member of a kinship or business association, or a person sharing ties of religion".[54]

Similarly, Corbin[55] suggests the idea that contract law is the product of human efforts and society. He believes that in resolving contract disputes, judges should examine not just the "four corners" of the legal document itself, but the intention of the parties, as evidenced by the course of dealing and performance between the parties, as well as the customs of the trade and business community. Corbin, therefore, claims that the main purpose of a contract is to protect the reasonable expectations of each party.

---

52 *K. J. Arrow*, "Rationality of Self and Others in an Economic System", in R. M. Hogarth - M. W. Reder (eds.), *Rational choice: the contrast between economics and psychology*, (University of Chicago Press, Chicago, 1987), 202.

53 *H. Collins*, *Regulating Contracts*, (O.U.P., Oxford, 1999), 130 ss.

54 *Ibid*, 26- 28.

55 *A.L. Corbin*, "The Interpretation of Words and the Parol Evidence Rule", in (1965) *Cornell Law Quarterly*, 188 - 189. See for a detail focus on this theory *A. L. Corbin*, "Corbin on Contracts", (West Publishing Company, St. Paul Minesota, 1982), *passim*.

More importantly, Malloy notoriously points out that common concepts and terms that are useful in understanding the relationship between law and market analysis, strictly connected also to the contractual parties' behaviour. Therefore, in his rigorous analysis Malloy argues that there are some central market concepts used in legal reasoning, among many: "rationality", which means that contractual parties will act in a way that guarantees the best combination of desirable results;[56] "opportunity cost", meaning that "we make a choice, and when we make choices we must give up some opportunities";[57] "competition" which represents the idea that in the market context, as in politics, it is believed to be advantageous to have multiple decision makers and decentralized power;[58] and "risk and return", a concept according to which "the more risk a seller takes on in a contract the higher will be the price, and likewise the more risk assigned to the buyer in a contract the lower will be the price".

In this scenario, I believe that it is also important take into consideration the writing of the American sociologist Suchman, who in his deep analysis has argued that

> "to economists, contracts are agreements that impose tangible costs in exchange for tangible benefits, regardless of whether or not the agreements enjoy legal recognition. To business lawyers, contracts are written instruments formalizing agreements that their clients believe themselves to have made-as well as addressing various remote contingencies that their clients should have considered but probably overlooked. To trial lawyers, contracts are evidence, either to be invoked as proof of agreements willingly made, or to be dismissed as ambiguous, inequitable, or not reflecting actual events. To lay people, contracts are simply pieces of paper that one signs in the course of commerce, often with an un sense of finality, but rarely with a comprehensive understanding of the relevant scholarly doctrines, economic exchanges, contingents claims, or evidentiary implications".[59]

Suchman's and other scholar's conclusion is that "contractual languages create not the rules that the parties want to apply to the ongoing relation-

---

56 R. P. Malloy, *Law in a Market Context. An Introduction to Market Concepts in Legal Reasoning*, (C. U. P., Cambridge, 2004), 144.

57 *Ibid*, 148.

58 *Ibid*, 161.

59 In these words, *M. C. Suchman*, "Contract as Social Artfact", in (2003) *Law & Society Review*, 92

ship", but rather the rules that the party wants a third-party adjudicator to apply if their relationship breaks down.[60] From this widely held view, I would like to assume that the corollary of this analysis in all likelihood is that when a party decides to conclude an economic transaction with a contract containing specific legal conditions, it is the proof that the parties (or one of them) fear that his contract will provide the basis for a future dispute that could bring them create harm, economically and otherwise.

To sum up, and as I will discuss in the next pages, the foregoing theories have been an effort to prove that the concept of economic relationship prevails over the contract concept. Therefore, it is essential that the legal scholar should not focus so much merely on contract but rather on the "economic transaction" that, according to some of the above-mentioned theories, is no longer easily attributable to the single contract but often emerges from a series of interconnected factors.

In the light of the above-mentioned considerations and different thoughts, this book will attempt to reflect on the EU legislative policy in contractual matters of the last years. This policy was ratified with strong actions and developed with inflexible rules created only to guarantee the long-hoped harmonization and uniformity (that are designed as a "need of the internal market"), are supposed to reassure the interpreter, and to offer economic benefits to the needs of the EU market.

In my opinion, as I will try to emphasise in the next pages, the foregoing theories and considerations can be used to demonstrate that contract law, in all its ramifications, must have the purpose to enhance the efficiency of bargains. I have reasoned that in the European Union it is important to create a new legal analysis of contract law – influencing p.i.l. of contractual obligations - that can generate economic benefits for the EU market. It could be called theory of "contract efficiency", and should focus on the examination of the real intentions of parties in order to create benefits for the market, whose principal players are contractual parties.

60 *Ibid*, 107.

2. International Business Transactions

Introduction

Before proceeding any further, it is important to point out that this section takes as its starting point the analysis of international business transactions from both a legal and economic perspective. Therefore, this chapter identifies and analyses in more depth the most famous theories, and tries to explain the importance of realising the will of the contractual parties as well as of drawing up reasonable contract law rules in order to meet the real demands of the market.

By way of conclusion, this chapter points out that the EU needs to modernize contract law, in all its ramifications, and that an important aspect of modernization would be to develop a more integrated view of rules in market transactions as well as to focus on the real economic intentions of contractual parties.

2.1 The eternal battle between legal certainty (predictability) vs. legal congruence (flexibility)

The eternal battle between, on one hand, the need of predictability and uniformity and, on the other, the desire for flexible and individualized solutions is old as law itself,[61] and it assumes still more relevance in the new era of globalisation. In practice, the former limits the power of the court, by imposing rules that reinforce "legal certainty", often disregarding objective connection criteria; the latter compels the court to carry out a careful analysis of the case ensuring "legal congruence".

The usual argument employed by European institutions is that the lack of uniformity of the decisions and private law systems of Member States represents a hindrance to the establishment of a well-functioning internal

61 *S. C. Symeonides, Private International Law at the End of the 20th Century: Progress or Regress?*, (Kluwer Law International, The Hague, 2000), 21. The Author observes also that not only was Aristotle first that spoke on the role of equity as a corrective of the written law but also recent commentators as Resé David that put it that "the law must be certain and predictable on the one hand, it must be flexible and adaptable to circumstances on the other".

market because of the resulting transaction costs.[62] In particular, the EU bodies are convinced that predictability and legal certainty would bring about harmonisation of the rules and decisions that would greatly benefit for the European economics.[63] In practice, the EU Commission maintains that legal diversity increases the transaction costs of cross-border contracting, and discourages small and medium-size enterprises from engaging in such transactions in the first place.[64] In contrast, the USA adopts quite vague standards and flexible rules.

In this context, the latest EU norms, especially in contract law and private international law,[65] have echoed the same: "harmonisation", "legal certainty", "uniformity" and "predictability".[66]

In the following paragraphs, therefore, I will consider some of the teachings of economic analysis of law in order to test whether it is true that hard-and-fast rules and legal certainty really create benefits for the EU internal market, as opposed to flexible rules and competition between legal

---

62 According to *J. Hage*, "Law, Economics and Uniform Contract Law: a skeptical view", in J. Smits (ed.), *The need for a European contract law: empirical and legal perspecitves*, (Europa Law Publishing, Amsterdam, 2005), 58 "There is nothing wrong with evaluating harmonisation from a purely economic point of views limited to monetary costs and benefits".

63 See *J. Smits*, "Diversity of Contract Law and the Europan Internal Market", in J. Smits (ed.), *The need for a European contract law: empirical and legal perspecitves*, (Europa Law Publishing, Amsterdam, 2005), 177-178. The Author explains, supported by Ribestein and Kobayasky view, the arguments against the harmonisation process. He schematically distinguishes 3 types of harms: exit costs; reducing innovation and experimentation; reducing local variation and finally the costs of political decision making as well those of effective realization of the reform; last but not least the cost to educating lawyers and judges. For this reason, according to the Author, full harmonisation is not recommendable.

64 *G. Wagner*, "The Economics of Harmonisation: the case of contract law", in (2002) *Common Market Law Review*, 995.

65 In this regard *C. Kirchner*, "An Economic Analysis of Choice-of-Law and Choice-of-Forum Clauses", in J. Basedow – T. Kono (eds.), *An Economic Analysis of Private International Law*, (Mohr Siebeck, Tübingen, 2006), 48, according to which "Harmonisation of substantive law can only be protected against such erosion if it is accompanied by respective harmonisation of conflict-of-laws rule and *vice versa*" (emphasis added by the Author).

66 For example the Communication from the Commission to the Council and the European Parliament on European Contract Law of 2001 mentioned 11 times the word "uniformity", 5 times the word "certainty" and 22 times the word "harmonisation"; in Rome I Regulation have been mentioned 2 times the word "uniformity", 2 times the word "certanty", 1 time the word "predictability" and "harmonization".

systems.[67] In my opinion, only by analysing the most important doctrines is it possible to consider a constructive approach to this central topic.[68]

Before starting this analysis, I believe it is important to point out the claims made by the Manifesto for Social Justice in European Contract Law and Comparative Law.[69] In this document, some private law scholars[70] criticize the technocratic approach adopted by European institutions, which have pursued a purely economic agenda, disregarding issues of social justice. In fact, to progress rapidly, the agenda has led to a system exclusively inspired by the idea of efficiency rather than justice and progress for the EU market itself.

In this dispute, to establish the exact impact that diversity of laws and decisions, on one hand,[71] and the other hand by enhancement of the economics through their harmonization, I believe it is necessary to start not by the analysis of well known EU actions but rather of those doctrines that assume harmonisation is not only undesirable and inefficient from econo-

---

67 *S. Leible*, "Kollisionsrecht und vertikaler Regulierungswettbewerb", in (2012) *RabelsZ*, 376. The Author, after a meticouls overwiev, assumes that "*Denn Harmonisierung und Systemwettbewerb sind, so scheint es, Antipoden*".

68 As noted by *H. Buxbaum*, *Confict of Economic Laws: From Sovereignty to Substance*, in (2002) *Virginia Journal of International Law*, 944 "the goal of achieving predictability and certainty in international commerce has historically been viewed as a private-law value relevant more to individuals than to states".

69 Social Justice in European Contract Law: A Manifesto Study Group on Social Justice in European Private Law, in (2004) *European Law Journal*, 653 – 674.

70 According to *G. Wagner*, "The Economics of Harmonisation: the case of contract law", in (2002) *Common Market Law Review*, 1009: "The legislative process of Brussels suffers from a deficit in democratic participation and is much more opaque than the processes at national levels, the final outcome of such process hardly being attributable to one particular political group or government, and the impact of interest groups weighing even heavier".

71 In this regard *J. Smits*, "Diversity of Contract Law and the European Internal Market", in J. Smits (ed.), *The Need for a European Contract Law. Empirical and Legal Perspectives*, (Europa Law Publishing, Amsterdam, 2005), 165, who assumes that "an important part of divergence in contract law rules is created by the European Union itself" also for the many legal words used in the EU rules that not have the same meaning in each single EU country (see for example "usages", "compensation", etc.).

mic perspectives[72] but also radically impossible.[73] In fact, EU goals cannot be achieved just by imposing rules through public policy.[74] On this point, Hage, with specific reference to European contract law, has argued that "the harmonisation is comparable to the long term prediction in detail of the temperature in a particular city: there is relevant information available but there is so much relevant information that is not available, that the value of what is available is limited".[75]

Therefore, a priority argument for this analysis is the conviction that the simultaneous realization of mobility and decentralisation logically implies the existence of productive competition among jurisdictions[76] and legisla-

72 On this point see also *G. Comparato*, *Nationalism and Private Law in Europe*, (Hart Publishing, Oxford, 2014), 161 which assumes that an higly harmonised legal system would produce results that are not only inefficient from an economic perspective but even undesiderable from a viewpoint concerned with different values, like first and foremost social justice. This concern in particular for those who sostains that private law should contribute to establish a society that pursues not only economic affairs but also ideal of justice. On the similar view *H. Wagner*, "Economic analysis of cross border legal uncertainty", in J. Smits (ed.), *The need for a European Contract Law. Empirical and Legal Perspectives*, (Europa Law Publishing, Amsterdam, 2005), 27, which points out "full harmonisation itself tends to imply high economic costs, so that it is not generally recommendable. Nevertheless, a gradual (partial) harmonization process could, in some circumstances, be beneficial in the EU".

73 According to *R. Good*, "Contract and Commercial Law: the logic limits of harmonisation", in (2003) *Electronic Journal of Comparative Law*, VII, 4 "a highly harmonised system of law requires the existence of a common social and cultural background".

74 *H. Wagner*, "Economic analysis of cross border Legal uncertainty", in J. Smits (ed.), *The need for a European Contract Law. Empirical and Legal Perspectives*, (Europa Law Publishing, Amsterdam, 2005), 42; *R. Good*, "Contract and Commercial Law: the logic limits of harmonisation", in (2003) *Electronic Journal of Comparative Law*, VII, 4, which assumes that a highly harmonised system of law requires the existence of a common social and cultural background.

75 *J. Hage*, "Law, Economics and Uniform Contract Law: a skeptical view", in J. Smits (ed.), *The need for a European contract law: empirical and legal perspecitves*, (Europa Law Publishing, Amsterdam, 2005), 64. See also *G. Wagner*, "The Economics of Harmonisation: The Case of Contract Law", in (2002) *Common Market Law Review*, 1012 according to which "The harmonization could destroy the variety of solutions and doctrines, the now existing systems of contract law have been developed for traditional and current legal problems".

76 *W. Kerber*, "Interjurisdictional Competition within the European Union", in (2000) *Fordham International Law Journal*, 222.

tors.[77] In this way, Wagner observes that exaggerated harmonisation would prevent such experiments and learning processes from arising and transaction costs from being lowered; in his words "[…] moreover, dynamic competitive processes between legislators may produce voluntary harmonisation. […]".[78]

With regard to the central economic issue of the balance between costs and benefits, some scholars have also assumed that European contract uniformity and the harmonisation of both rules and decisions have a monetary benefit,[79] because they diminish transaction costs.[80] At this point the question is: how important is the cultural identity that may be disregarded

77 About the benefits of the harmonisation or competition between legal systems, many commentators, both in Economic and Law, argue the topic. From an economic point of view see *F. Daumann*, "Zur Harmonisierung der nationalen Rechtsordnungen in einem Gemeinsamen Markt", in (1994) *Hamburger Jahrbuch für Wirtschafts und Gesellschaftspolitik*, 39, 281; *M. E. Streit*, "Systemwettbewerb im europäischen Integrationsprozess", in U. Immenga - W. Möschel – D. Reuter (eds.), *Festschrift für Ernst-Joacchim Mestmaäcker: zum siebzigsten Geburstag* (Nomos, Baden, 1996), 521. Instead, from a legal point of view see *ex multis S. Leible*, "Kollisionsrecht und vertikaler Regulierungswettbewerb", in (2012) *RabelsZ*, 376; *A. Zoppini, La concorrenza tra ordinamenti giuridici*, (La Terza Editore, Bari, 2004), *passim*; *F. J. Garcimartín Alférez*, "Regulatory Competition, a Private International Law Approach", in (1999) *European Journal of Law and Economics*, 251; *B. Lurger*, *Regulierung und Deregulierung im europäischen Privatrecht* (Peter Lang, New York, 1997), 83 ss.

78 *H. Wagner*, "Economic analysis of cross border Legal uncertainty", in J. Smits (ed.), *The need for a European Contract Law. Empirical and Legal Perspectives*, (Europa Law Publishing, Amsterdam, 2005), 40. The Author also points out that "Competition is the most efficient mechanism to control politicians and to restrain their rent-seeking activities. In contrast harmonisation in an union can be considered as a restriction of competition analogous to a cartel, where non-member countries are outsiders".

79 *G. Wagner*, "The Economics of Harmonisation: The case of contract law", in (2002) *Common Market Law Review*, 1014, The Author points out that "it is no exaggeration to say that legal diversity places a tax on European business, a tax that creates no benefits either for firms or for consumers but only benefits for lawyers". According to *H. Kermeester*, "Uniformity of European Contract Law; An Economic Study Between Logic and Fact", in J. Smits (ed.) *The Need for a European Contract Law*, (Europa Law Publishing, Amsterdam, 2005), "Behavioural law and economic yields more arguments for diversity than for uniformity".

80 On transaction costs see infra § 2.III.

by harmonisation? According to Hage, this factor has a price and can also be expressed in monetary terms.[81]

On this premise, now let us consider the hard-and-fast rules that should guarantee harmonisation and economics benefits. It is well known that putting the legislator at the centre of the choice "centralises" the norm. I, however, believe that this centralisation is not helpful to the market and could be interpreted as a limit to the market itself.[82] This opinion arose by studying the illuminating economic theories of Hayek,[83] who considered that knowledge in society is generally dispersed rather than concentrated. The Nobel Prize winner, therefore, assumed that decentralisation is a more desirable option, as centralisation would not allow its constituents to efficiently harness the knowledge they need to bring about good decisions. Most obviously, rigid "centralised" rules "centralize" do not leave the final decisions up to an interpreter familiar with the contract and case, who would be better able to arrive to an equitable solution of the case. In fact, "decentralised" and reasonable rules allow the interpreter to focus on the case and draw upon his/her close knowledge of it. As a result, geographical vicinity seems to be synonymous with availability of knowledge and benefits for contractual parties, who are the principal players of the market.

In addition to these arguments, it is important to point out that several esteemed scholars, probably also influenced by Hayek's economic theory, have affirmed that competition is seen as a rivalling process in which competitors are constantly searching for better solutions. In particular, Kerber emphasizes the point that "locational competition among jurisdictions may be understood as a constant process of parallel experimentation with economic policies such as new institutional arrangements".[84] The economist also assumes that "if centralization or harmonization of regula-

---

81 *S. Hage*, "Law and Economics and Uniform Contract law: A sceptical view", in J. Smits (ed.), *The Need for a European Contract Law. Empirical and Legal Perspectives*, (Europa Law Publishing, Amsterdam, 2005), 58.

82 See *K. J. Hopt*, "Contract Governance, Disclosure, and Rule-setting between the Market and the Law", in S. Grundmann - F. Möslein - K. Riesenhuber (eds.), *Contract Governance: Dimensions in Law and Interdisciplinary Research*, (O.U.P., Oxford, 2015), 462, whose observe for example that "in Germany, banking contract law is traditionally not a matter for the legislator [...] it is a matter for the banks and the courts".

83 *F.A. Hayek*, "The use of knowledge in society", in (1945) *American Economic Review*, 524; *Ibid*, *New studies in philosophy, politics, economics and the history of ideas* (University of Chicago Press, Chicago, 1978), 179.

84 *W. Kerber*, "Interjurisdictional Competition within the European Union", in (2000) *Fordham International Law Journal*, 225. The Author also assumes that "in-

tions is undesirable because of the lacking regional differentiation among EC regulations, then decentralized forms of regulation and an appropriate form of regulatory competition might be recommended".[85] Therefore, the Author concludes that a centralised norm is not required because it brings bureaucratization, rent seeking, and constituents' unfulfilled expectations. Consequently, "[...] through the establishment of appropriate rules for a competitive system of jurisdictions, [...] an internal market for public goods and services can also develop".[86]

The foregoing economic considerations can be summarized into these legal terms: a limit to the competition between legal orders will centralise economic policy and legal choice. On the contrary, it can be assumed that, as other scholars have observed, the combined effect of deregulation[87] (or better still very flexible rules) and of decentralizing or reinforcing the role of the interpreter leads to competition between Member States that will attract businesses.[88]

In addition to the above cited and well-know theories can be mentioned those commentators[89] according to whom competition among jurisdictions improves the quality of legal rules and as a result satisfies the prefer-

---

terjurisdictional competition may also help to solve rent-seeking problems because losers of rent-seeking games are able to leave their respective jurisdictions and choose jurisdictions with less rent-seeking". See also *G. Wagner*, "The Economics of Harmonisation: The Case of Contract Law", in (2002) *Common Market Law Review*, 1006 and before see *J. A. Schumpeter*, *Theorie der Wirtschaftlichen Entwicklung*, (Duncker & Humblot, 1912), *passim*, who discusses competition as innovation process.

85 *W. Kerber*, "Interjurisdictional Competition within the European Union", in (2000) *Fordham International Law Journal*, 244.

86 *Ibid.*, 249. See also *G. Comparato*, "Nationalism and private law in Europe", (Hart Publishing, Oxford, 2014), 152 according to which the centralization can be justified only when there is a need not common to a particular local community, as in the case of consumers.

87 With reference to the deregulation benefits, interpreted as "the elimination of a type of government intervention that prevents competition from working effectively", see *R.A. Posner*, "The Effects of Deregulation on Competition: the Experience of the United States", in (2000) *Fordham International Law Journal*, S12, according to which: "regulation might induce higher costs, which might take the place of lower profits and leave the price level as high as it would be without regulation".

88 *H. Muir Watt*, "Choice of law in integrated and interconnected markets: a matter of political Economy", in (2003) *Columbia Journal of European Law*, 393.

89 *F. Gomez*, "Some Law and Economics of Harmonizing European Private Law", in A. Hartkamp - M. Hesselink - E. Hondius - C. Mak - E. du Perron (eds.), *Towards a European civil code*, (Alphen aan den Rijn, Wolters Kluwer, 2011), 407.

ences of the clients. In this situation the 'sellers' will be under competitive pressure to adopt "commercial rules" that provide maximum benefits to the clients.

Finally, to complete this analysis, I need to recount the theory of certain scholars who, adopting a soft approach, assume that the success of the harmonisation process depends on the communication between the different actors in the market. According to this view, only in this way can rules be created which are suitable to international business transactions that also reflect a pragmatic morality and are based on the expectations of those engaged in such transactions.[90] In fact, according to this doctrine, the EU lives in the era of globalisation and "the moral communication in various relationships – between the parties and the judge, in relation to other interested parties, in relation to the media as well as to the population as a whole – may be a more important function of a case than the actual solution of the problem". Therefore, in order to achieve the harmonisation process, this doctrine believes it is necessary that "a law that is sufficiently open towards moral assessments and does not close its eyes to the inevitable moral judgments that have to be made. [...] The pragmatic moral learning processes require a sufficiently flexible law".[91]

Summarizing all these theories, it may well be advantageous for transnational transactions to introduce competition between jurisdictions in order to improve their performance and also increase the harmonisation. Certainly, this is not currently an approach adopted by the EU legislation. In fact, as Symeonides has reported, "The new equilibrium between certainty and flexibility is no longer as heavily titled in favour of certainty".[92]

But after this fundamental overview, I believe it is possible to demonstrate that EU institutions have not analysed the above-mentioned theories, preferring to adopt hard-and-fast rules in order to assure legal certainty,[93] hoping to create harmonization of the decisions between Member States, that have been perceived as the needs of the internal market.

---

90 *T. Wilhelmsson*, "The Ethical Pluralism of Late Modern Europe and Codification of European Contract Law", in J. Smits (ed.) *The need for a Europan Contract Law*, (Europa Law Publishing, Groningen, 2005), 135.

91 *Ibid*, 136.

92 *S. C. Symeonides*, *Private International Law at the End of the 20th Century: Progress or Regress?*, (Kluwer Law International, The Hague, 2000), 76.

93 It is well known the idea of Malavries, according to which "*l'attività giuridica di per sé è incerta ed è l'espressione della probabilità, del sentimento e dell'intuizione*", see in *A. Luna Serrano*, *La sicurezza giuridica e le verità ufficiali dei diritti*, (E.S.I., Napoli, 2017), 22-23.

At this point, an important theme of my analysis is also to argue through my own personal observations if the legal certainty and hard-and-fast rules can have a relevant function in the harmonisation process and if both can really create benefits to the EU internal market.

In this context I want remind myself that, as Bobbio notably already observed in the '50's, "the cause of today's many troubles is the legal certainty",[94] which represents a lack of intellectual development of those who make and those who receive the law, especially in the business world.[95] On the same point, Macaulay has also carefully observed from a business point of view that "nonetheless, sometimes legal uncertainty could be a factor provoking parties to spend more effort seeking a settlement".[96] In contrast, I simply believe that the certainty of law is not a priority need of the market actors and that the hard-and-fast rules do not guarantee the harmonisation process and benefits for the market.

My point is that the market is strictly connected to the individual desires and expectations of the contractual parties.[97] In other words, in a globalised world characterized by billions of different economic transactions, flexible legal tools that protect reasonable expectations of the parties, as well guarantee the respect for different national cultures must be a cardinal support to the contemporary market. In fact, I claim that these tools can be fitted to the market's extremely rapid changes as well as to political, economic and social changes that may significantly and negativelly influence the economic success of the business transactions. These, in my opinion, represent an adequate answer to the needs of the market itself and at the same time can create new answers that opens up new possibilities, learning from experience both nationally and across the borders, in particular through national experiments and European learning process. In fact,

---

94 Author's traslation, *N. Bobbio*, "La certezza del diritto è un mito?", in (1951) *Rivista Internazionale di Filosofia del Diritto*, 149. Bobbio held that: "*l'origine di tanti malanni di oggi è la certezza del diritto*".

95 *Ibid*, 147 according to the Author: "*Il diritto non è di per sè certo, anzi in un mondo di uomini maturi, non deve essere certo, bensì adattarsi con la massima elasticità ai casi sempre nuovi ed imprevedibili della vita*".

96 *S. Macaulay*, "Non-contractual relations in business: a preliminary studies", in (1963) *American Sociological Review*, 79.

97 In similar way *N. Irti*, *L'ordine giuridico del mercato*, (Laterza editore, Bari, 2009), 34. The Author notably argues: "*l'identità del mercato si definisce in funzione di beni economici e, dunque, di desideri ed attese individuali*".

I believe that the uniformity of decisions can be achieved also by different "cognitive domestic errors".[98]

Therefore, I think that rigid and complex norms not only create confusion and difficulties resulting in unequitable justice[99] but cannot fit the real needs of the market players because they cannot adapt to the fast dynamic of their commercial life.[100]

To conclude, it is my opinion, as I try to illustrate in this book, that the market does not need harmonisation or the certainty of the law, but rather the certainty of efficient legal and economic policy that has as its aim to increase cross border transactions as well as to support the real needs of contractual parties, the principal players of a very fast and competitive market.

---

98 In these words, *S. Shavell, NBER Working Papers 9696, National Bureau of Economic Research, Inc.*, Chapter 14, 4-5, observes that "Rather than so inducing parties to reduce the likelihood of mistake, it may be preferable for society to harness the information that turns out to exist about the occurrence of mistake, by doing what the law does, refusing to enforce contracts that are mistakenly made."

99 It is well known the idea of Serrano that reports a decision of the Tribunal Supremo and observes that "*la certezza del diritto deve intendersi chiarezza e non confusione normativa*". *A. Luna Serrano, La sicurezza giuridica e le verità ufficiali del diritto*, (E.S.I., Napoli, 2017), 38.

100 *P. Stephan*, "The Futility of Unification and harmonisation in international commercial law", in (1999) *Virginia Journal of International Law*, 4, observes in his analysis that in commerce people often prefer off-the-rack legal regimes, but these regimes work only if they do not cramp the relationships they govern with excessively detailed requirements. Therefore the Author argues: "in commercial law we continually must make trade offs between flexibility and certainty, and business people within reasonable limits seem to want the former".

2.II *The party autonomy and need of protection of the "Supreme Will" of the parties*

Legal scholars have spilled substantial ink on the "party autonomy" principle,[101] which is well known be in the area of contract,[102] as the power enjoined by parties of a legal transaction to regulate the conditions of their binding agreement. This principle assumes certain relevance above all in international contracts in which the parties have the opportunity to write a wide agreement, disciplining aspects of the transaction as the reciprocal obligations of the parties or choosing the applicable law and jurisdiction.[103]

The benefits of party autonomy in an international context have been analysed by many academics both in economic and law terms[104] in order

---

101 The roots of this principle are in the philosophy of Kant and Rosseau. However, the final arrangement of this principle is due to Charles Dumoulin who, for the first time, permitted the parties to be able to conclude a contract in one place and subject it to a different law, and also that in the field of legislative policy, any agreement between the parties about the law that should govern their contract must be taken into account. It was later that P.S. Mancini and his theories, in complete harmony with the individualistic mindset of his time and based on the *principio della nazionalità*, stated the need to safeguard free private initiative in the legal as well as political area, in particular if it affects the economic aspects. On this last point see *P.S. Mancini*, "Utilità di rendere obbligatorie per tutti gli stati, sotto la forma di uno o più trattati, alcune regole del diritto internazionale privato per assicurare la decisione uniforme dei conflitti tra le differenti legislazioni civili e criminali", reprint in (1959) *Rivista di Diritto Internazionale*, 367. According to the Author *"L'ordine giuridico è costituito dalla conciliazione della libertà privata o individuale con l'esercizio della potestà sociale, cioè, dalle reazioni tra la legge dello Stato e le prerogative dell'individuo, tra l'ordine politico e l'ordine civile"*.

102 Hague Conference on Private International Law, Principles on Choice of Law in International Commercial Contracts, approved on 19 March 2015, points out that party autonomy is well-established in relation to commercial contracts.

103 *S. Leible*, "Mecanismos para garantir la seguridad jurídica en los contractos internationales", in (1995) *Cuadernos de la Maestría en Derecho*, 77 – 99.

104 For the central role of the party autonomy in the international commerce see *H. Hoyer*, "Der Anwendungsbereich des Einheitlichen Wiener Kaufrechts", in H. Hoyer – W. Posch (eds.), *Das Einheitliche Wiener Kaufrecht. Neues Recht für den Internationalen Warenkauf* (Orac, Wien, 1992), 41; and in similar way with particular reference to Rome I Regulation see *M. McParland, The Rome I Regulation on the law applicable to contractual obligations*, (O.U.P., Oxford, 2015), 288; *F. Ragno*, "Article 3", in F. Ferrari (ed.) *Rome I Regulation. Pocket commentary*, (Sellier, Münich, 2014), 79, according to whom it is "the primary connecting factor".

to avoid harm to the parties and to improve the efficiency of the market and its transactions.[105]

In economic literature, Grossman, Hart and Moore[106] have notably been the pioneers of "incomplete contract" theory, according to which contracts cannot specify what is to be done in every possible contingency, partially because it is too expensive. Therefore, focusing on the nature of private contracting, this doctrine assumes that an "incomplete contract" is a contract that has gaps and ambiguities and has yet to be completed (by renegotiation or by the interpreter). This analysis assuming that a consequence of this "incompleteness" is the so-called "hold-up problem", which may lead to severe economic costs and underinvestment. However, let me be more precise by noting that, in a recent study, the winner Nobel Price Hart, in his illuminating analysis rightly points out that "contracts are incompleted in the reality and contractual incompleteness underlines numerous significant phenomena, some of which have great policy relevance".[107] More importantly, I believe that Hart expresses a widely held view when he authoritatively hopes that "economists, particularly young ones, will, in spite of the messiness, continue to work on this challenging topic".[108]

On the basis of these arguments, contract scholars broadly define an "incomplete contract" as an unwritten contract or a contract without specific clauses (i.e. without an applicable law). Critically, E.A. Posner argues that the above-mentioned economic literature diverges in its legal approach because the former "was motivated primarily by descriptive curiosity about

105 *W. Lorenz*, *Vertagsschluß und Parteiwille im internationalen Obligationenrecht Englands*, (Heidelberg, 1957), 154; *P. von Wilmowsky*, "EG-Vertrag und kollisionsrechtliche Rechtswahlfreiheit", in (1998) *RabelsZ*, 2-37; *H. L. E. Verhagen*, "The Tension between Party Autonomy and European Union Law: Some Observations on Ingmar GB Ltd v Eaton Leonard Technologies Inc.", in (2002) *The International and Comparative Law Quarterly*, 135-154; *F. Marella*, "Funzione ed oggetto dell'autonomia della volontà nell'era della globalizzazione del contratto", in N. Boschiero (ed.), *La nuova disciplina comunitaria della legge applicabile ai contratti (Roma I)*, (Giappichelli, Torino, 2009), 11

106 *S. J. Grossman - O. D. Hart*, "The costs and benefits of ownership: A theory of vertical and lateral integration", in (1986) *Journal of Political Economy*, 691–719; *O. D. Hart, - J. Moore*, "Property Rights and the Nature of the Firm", in (1990) *Journal of Political Economy*, 1119 – 1158; *O. D. Hart*, *Firms, Contracts, and Financial Structure*, (O.U.P., Oxford, 1995), *passim*.

107 *O. D. Hart*, "Incomplete Contracts and Control", in (2017) *American Economic Review*, 1749.

108 *Ibid*, 1750.

the nature of private contracting, not about contract law".[109] Furthermore, Posner assumes that "the incomplete contracts literature does not provide a promising alternative. The contracts that the models predict do not exist in the world".[110]

On this premise, temporarily setting aside this discussion, just as with the Rome Convention,[111] Rome I Regulation,[112] although with a different approach,[113] gives a central role to the party autonomy principle. In fact, the Recital stresses that

> "The parties' freedom to choose the applicable law should be one of the cornerstones of the system of conflict-of-law rules in matters of contractual obligations".[114]

---

109 See *E.A. Posner*, "Economic Analysis of contract law after Three Decade: Success or Failur", in (2003) *The Yale Law Journal*, 855 ss.

110 *Ibid*, 859.

111 Convention 80/934/ECC on the law applicable to contractual obligations. It should be pointed out that the starting point here is not an analysis of the Rome Convention, which still applies today to any contracts dated prior to December 17, 2009 as well as contracts entered into with Denmark. In fact, Article 1 (4) of Regulation makes a clear distinction between "Member States to the Regulation" and "Member States of the European Union". This clarification is based on the circumstance that Denmark, the United Kingdom and Ireland, by virtue of the *opting out* and *opting in* schemes, agreed upon in the drafting of the Treaty of Amsterdam, may refrain from the automatic application of Community regulations. To date Ireland and the United Kingdom have *opted in*, therefore, only Denmark remains excluded, and has not yet expressed the intention to join the Rome I Regulation. It follows that the Danish courts will still continue to apply the criteria dictated by the Convention, at least until Denmark formally agrees to adhere to the Rome I Regulation. Therefore, the territorial aspect, which has always played a very important role in private international law and has become a very ambiguous term, to date, with Denmark which has not adhered to the Rome I Regulation, could still cause several problems in terms of interpretation.

112 Regulation (EC) 593/2008 of the European Parliament and of the Council, of June 17, 2008 on the law applicable to contractual obligations (Rome I) [2008] OJ L177/6.

113 In fact, in absence of an express choice, Article 3 (1) of Rome I points out that the parties choice not expressed in the contract must be "clearly demonstrated by the term of the contrcat or by the circumstance of the case", whereas Article 3 of Rome Convention differs because with a flexible approach requires the choice to be "demonstrate with reasonable certainty by the terms of the contract or the circumstance of the case". This circumastance reflects that Rome I adopts a restrictive approach to discovery of an implied choice. See on this point *P. Stone*, *Private International Law in the European Union*, (Elgar European Law and Practice, Cheltenham, 2018), 436.

114 Recital § 11 Rome I Regulation.

Actually, the parties, as is prooved by the numerous cases in the EU and national courts, do not often specify the details of contracts in cross-boarder transactions, consequently omitting also to choose the applicable law, especially when the parties are SME.[115] This circumstance, also according to the above-mentioned economics theories, not only could cause harm to the reasonable expectations of contractual parties, which are often faced with unpredictable findings but also imposes on the court to carefully interpret the contract as well to identify the applicable law with not always clear and easy p.i.l. instruments. In fact, the task of the interpreter become particularly crucial in cases when he must identify the applicable law to the contract in absence of *electio juris* by parties. In this context the flexibility or rigidity of p.i.l. rules, as will be seen in detail, can either enhance or hinder this task.

In this context, I have reasoned that, this principle being a "creature of the law of contract",[116] party autonomy[117] is based on mutual intention[118] of the parties to make or not a written and detailed contract. In other words, I do not hesitate to say that this will of the parties – understood as their subjective intention to have a freely negotiated bargain (in the absence of externalities) or one with a tacit choice of law,[119] or to have the

115 See *supra* footnotes nr. 32 - 33. In the same vein see *P. Mankowsky*, "Art. 3", in U. Magnus – P. Manowsky (eds.), "European Commentaries on Private International Law – Commentary, II, Rome I Regulation", (Ottoschmidt, Köln, 2017), 117, according to which: "Major firms express a stronger preference for choice of law that SMEs".

116 In these words, *M. Hook*, *The Choice of Law Contract*, (Hart Publishing, New York, 2016), 2, according to which "It is a creature of the law of contract, placed in the service of the conflict of laws".

117 The term "autonomy" is derived from the Greek and means 'auto-'(self) and 'nomos' (law), and was used in order to describe the freedom that certain businessman to regulate their economic interests through private legislation. See on this point *F.K. Savigny*, *System des heutigen römishen Rechts*, (Veit, Berlin, 1849), 112 -113.

118 See on this point *F. Santoro Passarelli*, "L'autonomia dei privati nel diritto dell'economia", in F. Santoro Passarelli, *Saggi di diritto civile*, (Jovene, Napoli, 1961), 228 who notably notes that "*la potestà di autonomia può definirsi come potesà di regolare i propri interessi, potestà derivante o riconosciuta dalla legge e alla stessa subordinata*". In the same vein see also *U. La Porta*, *Globalizzazione e diritto*. (Liguori editore, Napoli, 2005), 173.

119 For example, in the case *Marubeni Hong Kong and South China Ltd v. Ministry of Finance of Mongolia*, the court held that, in a guarantee contract without an express choice of law, the tacit law can be desumed by the email sent during the negotiation. See the case at https://high-court-justice.vlex.co.uk/vid/2001folio-946-52637508.

contract not governed by any law[120] - can be qualified as "supreme" on the basis of general principle of contract law.[121] In fact, the concept of "contract" should include any behaviour of the parties connected to its,[122] and therefore also the voluntary omission to insert one clause. In fact, the reasons behind this voluntary omission could be many,[123] as to have the possibility of future renegotiation as in the case of particular financial operations (i.e. venture capital),[124] or only to have a flexible contractual structure that could be adaptable to future changes or the preference that some contractual points can be interpreted by a court.[125]

---

120 *P. Nugh*, *Autonomy in International Contracts*, (Clarendon Press, Oxford, 1999), 31.

121 *M. Hook*, *The Choice of Law Contract*, (Hart Publishing, New York, 2016), 42 - 43. The Author points out that "more fundamentally, choice of law agreements shares the same legal and philosophcal underpinnings as the law of the contract. [...] There is no separate regime of rules that deals only with legally binding agreements that are not, strictly speaking, contracts. For these reasons, choice of law agreements are best treated as contracts, and they will be referred to as 'choice of law contracts' in this book. [...] Although it is not a contract of obligation, party choice is firmly grounded in principles of autonomy that permeate much of private law, and the law of contract in particular". Therefore, continuing the author assumes "[...] if choice of law agreements are contracts – or are at least like contracts - then they should be regulated and enforced accordingly".

122 See lastly *E. Hosemann*, "Freedom of Contract", in N. Jansen – R. Zimmermann (eds.), *Commentaries on European Contract Laws*, (O.U.P., Oxford, 2018), 38.

123 See for more also *infra* § 2.IV.

124 See on this recent and widely used financial operation *L. Zingalese*, "Why the Incomplete contract approach is important for finance", in P. Aghion, M Dewartripont, P. Legros, L. Zingales (eds.), *The Impact of incomplete contracts on Economics,* (O.U.P., Oxford, 2016), 146, according to which: "The emphasis on renegotiation that the incomplete contract literature brought to finance is extremely important. In the venture capital world, you write contracts that have basically very little hope of being enforced in the way they are written. For example, a typical clause in venture capital contracts gives the venture capitalist (VC) the right to sell back her shares to the firm at a given price at a predetermined time in the future. [...] It is simply because it sets the stage for future renegotiation".

125 In this context it is interesting also to report Shavell's theory according to which: contracts are incompleted for several reasons, including: 1) the effort and cost of anticipating possible contingencies and describe them adequately; 2) the expected consequences of incompleteness may not be very harmfull to contracting parties and therefore this incompleteness (or gap) would be wanted by the parties also because a court might interpreter an incomplete contract in a better manner. See on this point *S. Shavell*, *NBER Working Papers 9696, National Bureau of Economic Research, Inc.*, 7.

After this overview, practically, the point of my discussion is to focus on how the will of the contractual parties, and as a consequence their real economic benefits, should be interpreted. Therefore, in order to focus on this issue, I would like to answer this question: Is an unwritten contract or a contract that omits applicable legal provisions Pareto inefficient? In my opinion, the intentional choice of contract parties to make a cross-boarder transaction based on an "incomplete contract", can represent an enhancement of their "Supreme Will" and can reflect their economic private interests.[126] As a consequence, I have reasoned that an unwritten or incomplete contract also represents a manifestation of the autonomy of contractual parties.

In order to capture these concerns, I should report some considerations supported by academics that stress that, especially in small business transactions, planning a contract is often unnecessary and may have unpleasant economic consequences.[127]

Firstly, E.A. Posner gives a brilliant overview pointing out that "Law and Economics generally assumes that parties choose simple contracts – contracts with a fixed price and quantity and sometimes a liquidated damages clause – and focuses on the effect of different rules on contractual behaviour".[128] In fact, market actors will often tend to leave the "auxiliary conditions" aside and prefer to concentrate on the proper substance of the

126 In this respect according to G. Cordero Moss the parties be deemed to have tacitly chosen the law applicable by simply haveing filling out a standard contract (lacking an express choice of law clause). In *G. Cordero Moss*, *International Commercial Contracts*, (C.U.P., Cambridge, 2014), 141 - 142.

127 *Ex multis R. P. Malloy*, *Law in a Market Context. An Introduction to Market Concepts in Legal Reasoning*, (C.U.P., Cambridge, 2004), 114 – 115. In the words of the Author it is important to take into consideration not only that a decision made by the parties of a commercial transactions could be taken place within a community context but also that the individual choice (as could be the one to not choose the law applicable) could be influenced by knowledge of social efforts to reduce the impact of bad choices. *P. Mankowsky*, "Art. 3", in U. Magnus – P. Manowsky (eds.), "European Commentaries on Private International Law – Commentary, II, Rome I Regulation", (Ottoschmidt, Köln, 2017), 119, who rightly notes that "negotiations of choice of law (and dispute resolution) clauses even if they are staged at all, are often based on solid legal argument, e.g. a careful balancing of comparative legal options searching for the best possibile and most coherent set of choice of law and choice of the dispute resolution mechanism under circumstances. [...] Furthermore, unsophisticated parties (if such category is recognised) do not truly negotiate choice of law".

128 With these words *E. A. Posner*, *Economic Analysis of contract law after Three decade: Success or Failur*, in (2003) *The Yale Law Journal*, 855.

transaction. In many sales contracts, for example, parties will base their decisions on a comparison of products and other considerations rather than on the formation of the contract.[129]

As a result, the reason for which the parties could decide to write an "incomplete contract" or make the economic transactions with an oral (unwritten) contract could be many, including the following: the future is unpredictable and it is not easy to calculate how this contract could respond to remote contingencies; the parties could intentionally draft certain contract terms ambiguously to avoid contentious issues; the parties may also agree to insert some contract terms *ex post*, because it could be too costly to monitor or enforce them;[130] the parties prefer to concentrate on the economic substance of the transaction, also to maximize their time. But exactly for these reasons, it seems to me that the above-mentioned considerations have a stronger voice in the new era of globalisation where market players face fast transactions characterized by access to global products and services by various digital services, such as advanced digital fornitures, global digital platforms or new financial instruments. In this multi-speed globalisation, it is clear that the parties, intentionally prefer to concentrate on the substance of the bargain rather than draft the "perfect" contract.

In addition, some modern doctrines also assume that nowadays businessmen often prefer to rely on "a man's word"[131] in a brief letter, a handshake, or 'common honesty and decency' even when the transaction in-

129 In this way, see *S. Grundmann - F. Möslein - K. Riesenhuber*, *Contract Governance: Dimensions in Law and Interdisciplinary Research*, (O.U.P., Oxford, 2015), 52; *K. Riesenhuber*, 'Die Inhaltskontrolle von Vereinbarungen über Hauptleistung und Preis im Europäischen Vertragsrecht', in T. Pfeiffer - W. Grunsky - J. Damman (eds.), *Gedächtnisschrift for M. Wolf* (Beck, München, 2011), 124 ss.

130 In this way *G. M. Cohen*, "Interpretation and implied terms in contract law", in G. De Geest (ed.), *Contract Law and Economics. Encyclopedia of Law and Economics*, (Edward Elgar, Northampton, 2011), 129. The Author also has mentioned all the Authors that support this theory.

131 See also in this way *L.M. Friedman – S. Macaulay*, "Contract law and Contract teaching: Past, Present and Future", in (1967) *Wisconsin Law Review*, 816, according to which: "A businessman usually cares about his reputation. He wants to do business again with the man he is dealing with and with others". See also *U. La Porta*, *Globalizzazione e diritto*, (Liguori Editore, Napoli, 2005), 63, according to which "*Nell'esperienza mafiosa come in quella religiosa – peraltro codificata dal diritto canonico – la "parola data" pesa più assai di qualunque vincolo giuridico formale, imponendo comportamenti e azioni che rappresenta la sostanza del rapporto giuridico obbligatorio. La "regola di vita" malavitosa serve a disciplinare in maniera tanto cruenta (ed illecita) quanto efficace*".

volves exposure to serious risks".[132] In this way, Macaulay rightly points out that business seldom needs formal contract law because transactions are based on trust.[133] Continuing, in the words of Cooter and Freedman, in fiduciary relationships

> "the parties are unable to foresee the conditions under which one act produces better results than another. Rather, chance events and unanticipated contingencies require continual recalculation to determine which course of action will be the most productive".[134]

Therefore, the authors in their analysis arrive at the conclusion that fiduciary law creates presumptive rules of conduct briefly described as the strong duty of loyalty.[135] This situation verifies that the actors of the market often prefer to have a loyalty obligation that fits in well with their economic interests.

Another key element behind the choice of the parties to proceed with an "incomplete contract" is, as was also argued from an economic perspective,[136] that the basic characteristics of economic players (specifically the SME) is their attitude toward risk if drafting a contract causes expensive

---

132 In this way *S. Macaulay*, "The Real and the Paper Deal: Empirical Pictures of Relationships, Complexity and the Urge for Transparent Simple Rules", in (2003) *The Modern Law Review*, 58. Summarizing the result of his studies, the Author concludes that people in sales departments oppose contract.

133 *S. Macaulay*, "The impact of contract law on the Economy: Less than Meets the Eye? Paper given at a Conference on Law and Modernization", Lima Peru, July, 1994, at http://law.wisc.edu/facstaff/macaulay/papers.html

134 *R. Cooter Bradley - J. Freedman*, "The fiduciary relationship: its economic character and legal consequences", in (1991) *New York University Law Review*, 1048. See also *S. Deakin - C. Lane - F. Wilkinson*, "'Trust" or Law? Toward an Integrated Theory of Contractual Relations between Firms", in (1994) *Journal of Law and Society*, 329. The Authors stress that contract law plays an important role in fostering trust, but they expand the idea of contract law to include both the legal and the other-than-legal norms external to the contract that create a stable framework for the process of exchange and the presence of a sense of trust between the parties.

135 In my opinion another reason strictly connected to the one of the Authors could be to continue a solid and fiduciary economic partnership with the counter-party.

136 Has cited some economic scholars *M. Kovač*, *Comparative contract law and Economics*, (Edward Elgar, Northampton, 2011), 6.

costs.[137] Practically, it often is better for an entrepreneur to have an "incomplete contract" - because the costs of contractual completeness (e.g. lawyers) require time and effort and would also exceed the benefits of the transaction.[138] In addition, the costs of court—supplied interpretations, in small transactions, could also be lower than the costs of drafting a contract.

More generally, it may be that parties would prefer not to agree with a written contract or not to choose the applicable law when they do not have a good reason to choose a law[139] or, as notably assumed by E. A. Posner, they may want a court to change the price term, or any other contractual term, based on its own judgment about what is *ex post* efficient.[140] What is more, the reason could be that an incomplete contract offers also the possibility to easily renegotiate[141] the agreement if the future circum-

---

137 On this point *J. Gava - J. Greene*, "Do we Need a Hybrid Law of Contract? Why Hugh Collins is Wrong and Why it Matters", in (2004) *Cambridge Law Journal*, 605, according to the authors "indeed, business parties often actively avoid use of law because of its expense, inconvenience and tendency to harm business relationship".

138 For an empty economic analysis on the activity of acquiring information about an agreement see *P. Aghion - N. Bloom - J. Van Reenen*, "Incomplete Contracts and the Internal Organization of Firms", in *The Impact of incomplete contracts on Economics*, P. Aghion – M. Dewartripont - P. Legros - L. Zingales (eds.), (O.U.P., Oxford, 2016), 72. See also on this point *G. Cordero Moss*, *International Commercial Contracts*, (C.U.P., Cambridge, 2014), 137, the author stresses that using an external law firm increases transactional costs.

139 *G. Ruhl*, "Party autonomy in the Private international law of contracts. Transalantic Convergence and Economic Efficiency", in E. Gottschlak, R. Michaels, G. Ruhl, J. Von Hein (eds.), *Conflicts of Laws in a Globalized World*, (C.U.P., Cambridge, 2007), 161; *M. Hook*, *The Choice of Law Contract*, (Hart Publishing, New York, 2016), 60.

140 *E. A. Posner*, "Economic Analysis of contract law after Three Decade: Success or Failure", in (2003) *The Yale Law Journal*, 859 -860.

141 On the importance of a renegotiation clause see *K.P. Berger*, "Renegotiation and Adaptation of International Investment Contracts: The Role of Contract Drafter and Arbitrators", in (2003) *Vanderbilt Journal of Transnational Law*, 1380 who observes "Contract adaptation and renegotiation are consensual procedures. Legal arguments, positions, and principles mostly fade into the background here. Rather, these processes are a matter of genuine economic or even political considerations and estimations, which are closely woven together with the distribution of negotiating power between the parties and which may vary throughout the duration of the contract". In economic literature *contra O. Hart – J. Moore*, "Contracts as Reference Points", in (2008) *The Quarterly Journal of Economics*, 1–48, according to which renegotiation creates hold-up problems.

stances change.[142] Similarly, this both does and does not disclose private business information that could be essential in case of breach of contract. To be slightly more precise, consider the case in which the buyer is an Italian company that sells multibrand cars and the seller is a famous German car manufacturer. The buyer wants to secure a unique franchise of that brand in an Italian region, by drawing up a franchising contract. The seller does not want to take the risk of opening a franchise business in an unknown and undefined territory, under a strong and binding agreement, and thereby reveal private business information. Therefore, the seller prefers firstly to test the reliance of the small Italian company. In this case, it is clear that the seller prefers, after a meticulous study of that market to test the ability of the buyer by selling a number of cars in that Italian region. Only in the case where the cars meet the needs of that regional market, will the German enterprise agree with the Italian company and set up a franchising contract. Therefore, in this example, it is clear that the intention of the parties is to continue business with an "incomplete contract" in order to agree, in their reciprocal interest, on a franchising contract.

In practice, this example also attempts to demonstrate the parties' fear a strong agreement between them[143] and their "supreme will" to make the

142 The importance of the renegotiation is discussed also by *S. Shavell, NBER Working Papers 9696, National Bureau of Economic Research, Inc.*, 18. For a detail and an economic approach to the need of the parties of a renegotiation of the contract and its benefits, see *B. Salanié, The Economics of Contracts*, (The MIT Press, Cambridge, 1997), 161 – 190; *J. Y. Gotanda*, "Renegotiation and Adaptation Clauses in Investment Contracts, Revisited", in (2003) *Vanderbilt Journal of Transnational Law*, 1462 who, supporting the Berger theory assumes: "[…] contracts typically are of long duration, the political, economic and social climate could change radically during this period and dramatically alter the economic benefits that the parties originally envisioned would flow from the agreement".

143 See *S. Shavell*, NBER Working Papers 9696, National Bureau of Economic Research, Inc., 22, according to which "It is a commonplace that the fear of harm to reputation can serve to induce parties to adhere to contracts. In principle, this reputational factor could lead to the same enforcement of contracts that we imagine to occur in courts. However, that is unlikely for two reasons." According to Macaulay "while detailed planning and legal sanctions play a significant role in some exchanges between businesses, in many business exchanges their role is small" continuing "[…] carefully planned arrangements may create undesirable exchange relationships between business". Businessmen may welcome a measure of vagueness in the obligations they assume so that they may negotiate matters in light the actual circumstances". *Ibid*, NBER Working Papers 9696, National Bureau of Economic Research, Inc., 62 – 64.

transaction with an "incomplete contract" for economic reasons.[144] It is clear that in the case in which a few cars are sold and the small Italian company is deemed reliable, the parties will renegotiate the sales in a franchising contract. I believe this example proves that sometimes the renegotiation does not create a hold-up problem but rather could support the bargain and its future development. Certainly, in my opinion, these benefits only occur with a freely negotiated bargain (in absence of particular externalities) and not with a "renegotiation clause". In fact, I think a renegotiation clause is inappropriate not only for the transaction costs that could be charged to draft the contract but also because the clause could tip the scale in favour of the stronger contractual party.

What is more, in other recent studies, one author has pointed out that an agreement is not only a matter between its parties; in fact, in the words of van Leuk

> "society, whether national or 'European' is also involved: it is society that enables the parties to freely make (cross borders) contracts. Undermining the principles party autonomy it will, therefore, eventually also undermine party autonomy itself".[145]

Consequently, the author notes that in the case in which the legitimate expectations of contractual parties are not protected, "this will hamper the contractual freedom of the person who relied on the conduct of the other party who was acting of his own free will".[146]

The lesson to be learned from all the preceding considerations is that in most circumstances it is better, from an economic point of view, not to have a written contract between the parties but to establish the bargain only on the transaction that represents the core process of contractual formulation. Therefore, the assumption that contractual parties choose an "incomplete contract" could also imply, *inter alia*, that they do not want to

---

144 According to Cseres, one of the aim for an effective functioning of the market is to protect the 'economic freedom' of the market actors. The Author notes that "its goal is the protection of the competitive process from private economic power and to enable and maintain individual economic freedom of market partecipants". In this way *K. Cseres*, "Competition and contract law", in A. Hartkamp – C. von Bar (eds.), *Towards a European civil code*, (Kluwer Law International, Alphen aan den Rijn, 2011), 208.

145 *R. van Leuken*, *Private Law and Market. Direct Horizontal Effect of the Treaty Provisions on the Free Movement*, (Intersentia, Cambridge, 2017), 154.

146 *Ibid*, 191 – 192.

apply a specific law or that they assume a particular law will be applied.[147] As a consequence, in my opinion, the law applicable to the contract cannot be chosen by the legislator with hard-and-fast rules. This is the approach I adopt in this book. In fact, I want to stress that the legislators do not have the same opportunities to engage in an economic learning process as the market players.[148] In this context the interpreter has the duty to find the economic intentions of the parties.

Finally, after this overview, I suggest that the "incomplete contract" tends to be legally and economically perfect in its incompleteness. In fact, the "supreme will" of the parties must be perceived not only as the will to regulate their reciprocal obligations or to choose a law applicable to the contract but also as the will of both parties not to regulate the bargain with a written and complete contract. In fact, the parties may want to have the flexibility of contractual agreement, and as a consequence decide jointly to introduce ambiguity in terms of the contract or decide to conclude the bargain without particular externalities.

Importantly, I believe that in the new era of globalisation, in order to create benefit to the market, legislators need to draft norms that enhance the "Supreme Will" of the parties, that is based not only on the party autonomy principle but it is also strictly connected to the commercial function of market mechanisms.

Concluding, I believe that these considerations can be used to demonstrate that from a Law and Economics point view, typically a freely negotiated bargain between two parties will (in absence of externalities) be Pareto efficient.

---

147 *G. Cordero Moss*, *International Commercial Contracts*, (C.U.P., Cambridge, 2014), 148. The Author takes the example of tacit choice of law, already taken by Giuliano –Lagarde Report. It is the Lloyd's policy of marine insurance in which the parties applying this contract form may be deemed to have tacitly chosen English law. See also *P. Mankowsky*, "Art. 3", in U. Magnus – P. Manowsky (eds.), "European Commentaries on Private International Law – Commentary, II, Rome I Regulation", (Ottoschmidt, Köln, 2017), 165 which rightly observes that "in certain market using terminology and contract wording germane to that very market might indicate an implied choice of law".

148 See also on this point *H. Kermenter*, *Uniformity of European Contract Law; An Economic Study Between Logic and Fact*, in J. Smits (ed.) *The Need for a European Contract Law. Empirical and Legal Perspecitives*, (Europa Law Publishing, Amsterdam, 2005), 80.

2.III *The categories of transaction costs*

The EU bodies assume that legal diversity between EU legal systems increases the transaction costs of cross-border contracting, and discourages consumers and small and medium-size companies from engaging in such transactions.[149] Actually, the Commission firmly believes that the perfect market is one that lacks imperfections and that these economic imperfections are called "transaction costs".

In particular, according to the EU Commission's view, in international bargains the costs may not only be multiplied but also have various reasons: language problems; the lack of precision inherent in the foreign legal language; and the difficulty of getting advice on foreign law. Therefore, the reasons behind a greater comprehensive harmonisation of the law across legal areas are based on the assumption that legal diversity results in transaction costs and lowers economic benefits.

This assumption has led some commentators[150] to not only emphasise that the reduction of costs helps to increase efficiency and thereby welfare, but more importantly to maintain that legal uncertainty is a hindrance for cross border transactions because they generate huge costs. These costs are generally identified as: a) cost of collecting information; b) cost of legal disputes; and c) cost of setting incentives for pushing through legal claims.[151]

However according to Nobel Prize winner Oliver Williamson[152] transaction costs can have a broad definition and can be used to explain a number of different behaviours, such as day-to-day emotional interactions, infor-

---

149 O.J. 2001, C 255/1; see also Council Report on the need to approximate Member States' legislation in civil matters, adopted by the Council 16 Nov. 2001, DGH III 13017/01. European Parliament, Committee on Legal Affairs and the Internal Market, Report on the approximation of the civil and commercial law of the Member States, A 5-0384/2001 Final: European Parliament resolution on the approximation of the civil and commercial law of the Member States.

150 *J. Basedow*, "Lex Mercatoria and Private International Law of Contracts", in J. Basedow – T. Kono (eds.), *An Economic Analysis of Private International Law*, (Mohr Siebeck, Tubingen, 2006), 63.

151 *H. Wagner*, "Economic analysis of cross border legal uncertainty", in J. Smits (ed.), *The Need for a European Contract Law. Empirical and Legal Perspectives*, (Europa Law Publishing, Amsterdam, 2005), 31.

152 *O. E. Williamson*, "The Economics of Organization: The Transaction Cost Approach", in (1981) *The American Journal of Sociology*, 87, 548–577; *Ibid*, "The Theory of the Firm as Governance Structure: From Choice to Contract", in (2002) *Journal of Economic Perspectives*, 171–195.

mal gift exchanges, etc. Therefore, in this economic dispute, Schroeder, in her article published in the Harvard Law Review,[153] lists analytically what qualifies as transaction costs.

Quietly definitively, starting from these studies, we can list what transaction costs exist:

1. Cost of information: the cost of perfect information,[154] in particular "our inability to predict future events like: natural disasters, weather, new technologies, etc.";[155]
2. Bargaining costs: the costs required to come to an acceptable agreement with the other party in the transaction, to draw an appropriate contract, to pay lawyer fees, and so on;
3. Time and space: the cost of transportation of contractual parties or goods;
4. Irrationality: an imperfection inherent the nature of the market;
5. Multiple Parties: in a perfect market a party cannot act "as one";
6. Strategic behaviour: the unfortunate result of other transaction costs;
7. Differentiation: all the commodities must be homogeneous and perfectly divisible.

To these, traditional and well analysed transaction costs arising at the time of contracting, I believe that, in the new era of globalisation characterized by social media actions and also transactions on digital platforms such blockchain, other costs can be added that emerge during contractual performance, these are the cost of marketing and communication of a service or product. In sum, transaction costs can include any costs associated with the writing and enforcing of a contract.

After this analytic list, in these pages I do not want dwell on the "transaction cost" theories, as there are Nobel prize winners[156] that have notably argued this economic topic. Here I would like only to focus on economic

---

153 *J.L. Schroeder*, "The End of the Market: A psycoanalysis of Law and Economics", in (1998) *Harvard Law Review*, 112, 534.

154 According to *C. G. Veljanovski*, "The Coase Theorems and the Economic Theory of Markets and Laws", in (1982) *Kyklos*, 59 ss., there is a subtle difference between transaction costs and information costs.

155 *J.L. Schroeder*, "The End of the Market: A psycoanalysis of Law and Economics", in (1998) *Harvard Law Review*, 112, 534. In the opinion of C. G. Veljanovski there is an important distinction between transaction costs and the cost generated by market uncertainty, i.e. the information costs. See *C. G. Veljanovski*, "The Coase Theorems and the Economic Theory of Markets and Laws", in (1982) *Kyklos*, 63.

156 *Ex multis R. H. Coase* (1910-2013) was awarded the Nobel Prize in Economic in 1991 "For his discovery and clarification of the significance of transaction costs

theory from a legal point of view, but above all from a contemporary view. On the basis of these arguments, in this paragraph my starting point is to ask to this question: Is the incompleteness of a contract a "transaction cost"[157] and does it cause harm to the function of the internal market?

In this paragraph, therefore, some general considerations will be made, starting with Calabresi's illuminating analysis, which clearly points out that a "perfect"[158] or better "costless" market is improbable and could also create harms to the market itself[159] because it is logically impossible to exclude some of these costs from the nature of the market. Therefore, an awareness for business people is that business is strictly connected to economic risk, and transaction costs are a large part of this risk. In this context, Miceli assumes that "[…] in a competitive market these costs are assumed to be zero, but in the real world they can often be considerable".[160]

Critically, I believe that, by referring to the above list, it is possible to understand which transaction costs can be decreased.

---

and property rights for the institutional structure and functioning of the economy", in *R.H. Coase*, "The Problem of Social Cost", in (1960) *Journal of Law and Economics*, 19. The Author assumes that the presence of transaction costs actually means that the law's contents can have an effect on overall well-being.

157 In § 2.II I have defined a complete contract as the one in which have been disciplined all the reciprocal legal obligations of both parties and the law applicable and jurisdiction have been chosen by parties.

158 See also on this point *J.L. Schroeder*, "The End of the Market: A psycoanalysis of Law and Economics", in (1998) *Harvard Law Review*, 112, 516. The Author rightly assumes that "to achieve a perfect market would result in the end of all actual market transactions". In particular the Author, in her interesting as particular analysis of the market notes that "the perfect market is an extraordinary world with no differentiation, no time, no space, no desire, no exchange, no objects". As a consequence, continuing, she arrives to the conclusion that "[…] the perfect market it is literally unimaginable and unspeakable, therefore […] a close examination of the perfect market it is not only merely empirical but also theoretically impossible". Finally she concludes the issue assuming that the perfect market is a goal impossibile to achieve.

159 *G. Calabresi*, "Transaction Costs, Resource Allocation and Liability Rules: A Comment", in (1968) *Journal of Law and Economics*, 67 – 73.

160 *T. J. Miceli*, *The Economic Approach to Law*, (Stanford University Press, Redwood, 2009), 90. On this point also Malloy arguing the Coases's Theorem shows that "Life in a world of greater than zero transaction costs. However, is life in a world of personal and subjective experiences that make a difference in the networks and patterns of exchange". See *R. P. Malloy*, *Law in a Market Context. An Introduction to Market Concepts in Legal Reasoning*, (C.U.P., Cambridge, 2004), 184.

Practically, on the basis of these assumptions, I agree with those authors according to whom it is impossible to reduce some costs, such as time and space. In fact, as Schroeder[161] has justifiably assumed, the abolition of these elements from the market is the abolition of its objectivity. Additionally, I believe that it is impossible to have a market with only one contractual party and as a consequence without commercial risks. Finally, I claim that in the new era of globalisation, a marketing and communication investment is a necessary cost.

By contrast, I critically think that the "bargaining costs" that also include the draft of a "perfect" and "complete" contract are unique costs that obviously can be decreased. In fact, the majority of these costs are incurred through legal advice, as lawyer fees are extremely expensive, especially in the handling of international transactions.[162] On this view, in the words of Warren, the transaction costs are higher "when lawyers are involved in routine contract negotiation not only because of the legal fee, but also because of the delay involved as the lawyer takes the time to reflect and to advise on each aspect of the transaction".[163]

After these considerations, let me use an example starting with a practical question: If the law can be chosen by the parties, which is the better law for both parties? It is well known that to respond to this question, it will be necessary for the parties to ensure they have legal advice, and this will entail a transaction cost. Therefore, it would be to the parties' advantage not to have an additional cost, as this would represent an economic reason for which the parties may prefer not to choose an applicable law.[164]

---

161 *J.L. Schroeder, The End of the Market: A psycoanalysis of Law and Economics*, in (1998) *Harvard Law Review*, 112, 536. The Author reports the masterpiece Immanuel Kant "Critique of Pure Reason", (J.M.D., Meiklejohn trans, 1878), *passim*.

162 See in the same vein *G. Cordero Moss, International Commercial Contracts*, (O.U.P., Oxford, 2014), 137.

163 *E. Warren*, "Trade Usage and Parties in the Trade: An Economic Rationale for an Inflexible Rule", in (1981) *University of Pittsburg Law Review*, 543.

164 Kagami has argued from an economic view: "the sophisticated system of private international law inevitably produces large costs". On this point see *K. Kagami*, "The Systematic choice of Legal Rules for Private International Law: An Economic Approach", in J. Basedow – T- Kono (eds.), *An Economic Analysis of Private International Law*, (Mohr Siebeck, Tübingen, 2006), 16.

These considerations can be used to demonstrate that, as notably highlighted by R. A. Posner, the costs of a perfect contract "are prohibitive".[165] In this context, it is well known that usually the big enterprises know how to cope with legal diversity - for example, hiring lawyers as counsel in each case of a cross-border transaction. On the contrary, for SME it is often disproportionate to pay for legal advice compared to the value of the transaction.[166] Therefore, it is reasonable to conclude, also on the basis of this example, that the parties in international transactions (especially when the parties are SMEs), for legitimate economic reasons, might prefer not to write a contract in order to reduce some transaction costs.

Summarizing all this in Coase's words, transaction costs are "the cost of using the price of the mechanism",[167] some of which are intrinsic in the market's nature.

Applying these theories, I claim that an "incomplete contract" adopted in SME bargains, reduces some transaction costs because it creates economic benefits for the parties that are the principal players of the market.[168] In other words, an unwritten contract or a contract without a specific clause may be Pareto efficient.[169]

---

165 *R.A. Posner*, "The Law and Economics of Contract Interpretation", in (2005) *Texas Law Review*, 83, 1582. In this way see also *G. Calabresi*, "Transaction Costs, Resource Allocation and Liability Rules: A Comment", in (1968) *Journal of Law and Economics*, 64, that in his illuminating analysis stress that " 'seem perfection', even if desirable and feasible, may cost so much". On this topic see also *J. Gava – J. Greene*, "Do we Need a Hybrid Law of Contract? Why Hugh Collins is Wrong and Why it Matters", in (2004) *Cambridge Law Journal*, 605, according to which "indeed, business parties often actively avoid use of law because of its expense, inconvenience and tendency to harm business relationship".

166 I have just stressed in § 2.III the costs of contractual completeness (e.g. lawyers) would also exceed the benefits of the transaction.

167 For a deep analysis of this theory see *R. Coase*, *The Nature of the Firm*, (Economica, New Series, 1937), *passim*.

168 *E. Warren*, "Trade Usage and Parites in the Trade: An Economic Rationale for an Inflexible Rule", in (1981) *University of Pittsburg Law Review*, 540 assumes that "No market can function completely free of transaction costs, but all competitive markets will reduce them to the lowest point".

169 See also *B. Hayward*, *Conflict of Laws and Arbitral discretion. The closest connection test*, (O.U.P., Oxford, 2017), 156.

2.IV The interpretation of the contract: an economic analysis

As seen in the previous pages, the flexibility of rules can enhance the task of the interpreter when determining who should take it upon themselves to perform the delicate duty of interpreting the "supreme will" of the parties and identifying the most equitable law to be applied.

As history teaches us, the role of the jurist (in particular the court) is an important one because it gives life to "*ars boni et aequi*", using the single term present in the contract[170] to proceed in searching for a plurality of connecting indices.[171] This work of interpretation and identification becomes greater when the court is faced with an international contract and the parties have different nationalities, and thus different legal traditions.[172] In this case the interpreter should rely on a flexible legal instrument in order to avoid inequitable outcomes and to facilitate adaptation to general tendencies through judicial decisions.[173] This implies that the court holds a moral and professional obligation to take into consideration not only the legal aspects and the language of the contract but also its underlying economic, cultural and inner aspects. At the same time, the court should not forget the importance that some legal systems attribute to trade customs[174] and commercial usages,[175] which more often play a prominent part in deciding the substance of the dispute.

---

170 *P. Perlingieri*, "Interpretazione e qualificazione: profili dell'individuazione normativa", in (1975) *Diritto e Giustizia*, 827. According to the Author "*Il contratto va non soltanto interpretato ma anche qualificato alla luce dei princípi dell'ordinamento. Il problema sta nell'individuazione della funzione pratico-giuridica, socio-giuridica di ogni singolo atto*".

171 *P. Lagarde*, in (2007) *Revue critique de droit international privé*, 602.

172 *G.C. Cheshire*, "International contracts", (Jackson, Son&company, Glasgow, 1948), 76. According to the Author "It must be inferred from the language of the contract and its attendant circumstances what law the parties had in mind when they made the contract".

173 *F. Schwind*, "Problems of codification of Private International Law", in (1968) *International and Comparative Law Quarterly*, 434.

174 On the importance of "commercial usages" in p.i.l. as "alternative to international legislation" see *P. Šarčević*, *International Contracts and Conflicts of Laws*, (Graham&Trotman/Martinus Nijhoff, London/Dordrecht/Boston, 1990), 18.

175 Some legal systems distinguish custom from usage (*usos y costumbres, usages et coutmes*, usages and customs) but the distinction is not supported by an adequate definition. *R. Goode*, *Commercial Law*, London, 1995, 14 at the footnote 44 mentioned Halsbury's Laws of England (4the ed.) according to which "[...] custom is the practice of a particular locality, usage the practice of a trade, profession or vocation. Others considers that usage is merely a pattern of behavior

The foregoing considerations have been an effort to illustrate that a central argument, from an economic point of view, is to interpret *ex post* the "Supreme Will" of the contractual parties in order to reflect their private economic interests and to investigate their mutual intentions. In fact, as seen, party autonomy could also result in an incomplete or different contract. On this point various writers have accepted that the contract is not always the perfect representation of the real and economic will of the contractual parties; in fact, certain formulations are said to be "ambiguous", "indefinite", or the product of a "mistake".[176] In other words, these formulations are not economically relevant to the contract and, more importantly, they are irrelevant to the interpretation[177] of the whole transaction and of the "Supreme Will" of the contractual parties. Only in this way[178] I be-

---

and that custom is the application of the usage from a sense of binding obligation. Others again divide custom into different categories, according to the degree of antiquity or universality. The modern approach is to treat two terms as interchangeable. In transnational commercial law the term "usage" or "usages" is that generally adopted: in international law the reference is usually to custom". According to *O. Lando*, "The role of party autonomy and the relevance of usages", in M.J. Bonell – F. Bonelli (eds.), *Contratti commerciali internazionali e principi Unidroit*, (Giuffre, Milano, 1997), 119 "the period needed to establish a usage does not have to be very long. New trade usages may, for instance, come into existence in a relatively short period".

176 For a discussion on this argument see *C.J. Goets - R. E. Scott*, "The limits of expanded choice: An analysis of the interactions between express and implied contract terms", in (1985) *California Law Review*, 301 according to the authors "Contractual language is subject to ambiguity error to the extent that it lacks pre-established conventions for its interpretation; and in this way also *Macaulay*, that quite definitely concludes observing that "Clearly, contract documents often fail to capture the real deal between the parties". See *S. Macaulay*, "The Real and the Paper Deal: Empirical Pictures of Relationships, Complexity and the Urge for Transparent Simple Rules", in (2003) *The Modern Law Review*, 79.

177 Contract law draws a distinction between interpretation and implied terms. "Interpretation" refers to the process by which the court ascertains the meaning of express term, whereas the "implied terms" are those that courts deem to be part of the contract even though the parties did not expressly agree to them. On this point see *G. M Cohen*, "Interpretation and implied terms in contract law", in *G. De Geest* (ed.), *Contract Law and Economics. Encyclopedia of Law and Economics*, (Edward Elgar, Cheltenham, 2011), 125.

178 In this context I don't want take in consideration the obvious solution in which the parties decide to resolve autonomously the contractual dispute. In this case looked at through both eyes of economists and lawyers, the obvious solution to problems of legal diversity is to let the party make a choice. In particular, the economists also assume that if every individual pursues her own interests, the

lieve that it is possible to guarantee economic benefits to the contractual parties and as consequence to the market.

Broadly, there isn't a large literature on the economic interpretation of the contract, or on the issues of the contract's, formation, validity and remedies both at national and international level.

However, it is well known that the interpretation of the contract has a relevant function, not only for the the efficiency of the norm[179] but also from a economic point of view that can create benefits to the contractual parties who are the principal players in the market. In fact, as the writing of Shavell suggests:

> "the advantage to parties of correct interpretation of their intentions by courts is not only direct -- terms that they leave incomplete will be filled in as they would have wanted. The advantage of correct interpretation is also indirect -- that the parties can then omit more explicit terms and thereby save drafting and negotiating costs".[180]

Therefore, as the Author rightly points out, the expected consequences of an incomplete contract may not be very harmful to contractual parties, and this gap could be wanted by the parties. In summary, a good and loyal *ex post* interpretation of an incomplete contract can also create economic benefits for the principal players of the market.[181]

Starting with these assumptions, Cohen argues very clearly on the topic of the economic approach in the area of contract law, insisting that "court intervention is most justifiable when contracts are efficiently incomplete".[182] In fact, adopting this approach, which I fully support, the inter-

---

result will be excellent not only for the contractual parties but also for the society as a whole. In this regard see *G. Wagner*, "The Virtues of Diversity in European Private Law", in J. Smits (ed.), *The need for a European Contract Law. Empirical and Legal Perspectives*, (Europa Law Publishing, Amsterdam, 2005), 5.

179 In this regard *P. Perlingieri*, *Il diritto dei contratti tra persona e mercato*, (E.S.I., Napoli, 2003), 286, assumes that "*è la teoria dell'interpretazione, l'ermeneutica che realizza il passaggio dalla legge al diritto*".

180 *S. Shavell*, NBER Working Papers 9696, National Bureau of Economic Research, Inc., 8.

181 *Ibid*, 7.

182 *G. M Cohen*, "Interpretation and implied terms in contract law", in G. De Geest (ed.), *Contract Law and Economics. Encyclopedia of Law and Economics* (Edward Elgar, Northampton, 2011), 149.

preter can also understand the economic reasons[183] behind an "incomplete contract".[184] This could also be a virtue of a consistent and long-standing pattern of conduct, and at the same time the parties could create "past practices" that may also be binding[185] or simply reduce the transaction costs.[186] Therefore, without a written contract the interpreter could track down more easily the "Supreme Will" of the parties particularly when it is based on past practices.[187]

Another key element regarding contractual partie's preference for an "incomplete contract" is when they want an *ex post* interpretation of a court "to complete" the contract or also to choose the applicable law. In order to explain more fluently this case let me rephrase the example of Shavell,[188] who takes the case in which

> "a builder and a buyer do not include a term in their contract stating whether the builder is to perform if material prices rise steeply, but had they included the term, it would have relieved the builder of having to perform in that circumstance. The parties would want the courts to interpret the incomplete contract in that way should prices rise steeply".

It is clear that in this case the interpretation of an incomplete contract assumes also an economic function according to the party's intentions.

Notably, the present premise, in which the parties want to appoint the interpreter to resolve some aspects of their contract, also allows the inter-

183 In fact according to *S. Macaulay*, "The Real and the Paper Deal: Empirical Pictures of Relationships, Complexity and the Urge for Transparent Simple Rules", in (2003) *Modern Law Review*, 66 "Products sold in these markets usually are not standardised. Relying on long-term relationships minimises the costs of shopping and trying out products".

184 See *supra* § 2.II.

185 *R. J. Abrams*, *Inside Arbitration. How an Arbitrator Decides Labor and Employment Cases*, (Bloomberg, BNA, Arlington, 2013), 9.

186 For an economic analysis see *ex multis O. Hart – J. Moore*, "Incomplete contracts and renegotiation", in (1988) *Econometrica*, 756.

187 Often in multinational investments, lawyers suggests to conclude the bargain with unwritten regulations. See *R. H. Folsom*, "International Business Transactions. A Problem oriented", (West, Eagan, 2012), 907 that mentions the "Operation Code" that is a "pivotal concept for foreign investor's lawyers to understand. It is important largely because it is not written, or where written is not pubblicly disclosed. [...] The definition of the Operational Code suggests that is limited to formal unwritten regulations".

188 *S. Shavell*, *NBER Working Papers 9696, National Bureau of Economic Research, Inc.*, 7/8.

preter to embody a set of governance technologies or a set of "significant gestures", carrying particular meanings with particular discourses. Moreover, the interpretation of the contract could also discern other symbolic tokens or cultural messages, and an interpreter can gauge the sophistication of any given contract design not only by its efficiency and effectiveness but also by its comprehensibility.[189]

Upon analysis, the foregoing doctrine, seems to me to reflect that with a "perfect" contract,[190] there is no efficiency-enhancing role for a court other than to enforce the contract according to its terms; therefore, an incomplete contract, by these observations, could appear to be a necessary factor in order to give an active and efficient interpretation of the real economic intentions of the parties by the court.

The foregoing considerations have emphasised the central role of the interpretation of the contract from an economic point of view. Therefore, let me end by noting that, with regard to this assumption, the consequence is that adopting hard-and-fast rules, when the interpreter is faced with an "incomplete contract", flags the importance of an economic interpretation of the contract and causes harm to the contractual parties.

2.V *The role of the trade usages in supporting international transactions*

The interpretation of the contract in an international transaction assumes, as seen, a central rule not only from an economic point of view but also because it allows the interpreter to examine the cultural and inner aspects

---

189 With these words *M. C. Suchman*, "Contract as Social Artfact", in (2003) *Law & Society Review*, 100 – 101. On this point see also *P. Perlingieri, Il diritto dei contratti tra persona e mercato*, (E.S.I., Napoli, 2003), 465, according to which "[...] for a true interpretation of the parties will are important, the statements, the expressions, the behaviour with which the parties have extern the will to make an agreement" (Author translation). In addition, according to Smith "Gestures and emblems, less than techniques and devices, emerge and develop as elements of larger social systems, and most studies of conventional symbolic artefacts operate, at least in part, at this macroscopic level. In particular, sociolegal researchers might profitably build on mode of ideology, models of legitimation, and models of communication to explore how contract regimes interact with broader societal beliefs and understandings". In these words, *J.M. Smits*, *Contract Law a Comparative Introduction*, (Edward Elgar, Northampton, 2014), 126.

190 According to *G. M Cohen*, "Interpretation and implied terms in contract law", in G. De Geest (ed.), *Contract Law and NorthEconomics. Encyplopedia of Law and Economics.* (Edward Elgar, Northampton, 2011), 128 "many if not most contracts are incomplete".

of the transaction that may also have strong links with trade customs and commercial usages,[191] which often play a more prominent part in deciding the substance of the dispute. In the US these have always had a particular function. In fact, R.A. Posner has famously argued, some rules can be obtained from the practices of the industry or trade in which the contract was made. In other words, Posner observes that "historically, Anglo-American contract law derived from the law merchant, the set of customary norms created by businessmen; such norms would carry a presumption of efficiency".[192]

Indeed, trade usages have particular relevance also in several EU legal systems, assuming often a function alternative to legislation,[193] and commercial trade practices[194] should be treated as a deed signed by all contrac-

191 Some legal systems distinguish customs from usages (*usos y costumbres, usages et coutmes*, usages and customs) but the distinction is not supported by an adequate definition. *R. Goode*, *Commercial Law*, (Published by Penguin Books Ltd, London, 1995), 14 at the footnote 44 mentioned Halsbury's Laws of England (4the ed.) according to which "[...] custom is the practice of a particular locality, usage the practice of a trade, profession or vocation. Others considers that usage is merely a pattern of behavior and that custom is the application of the usage from a sense of binding obligation. Others again divide custom into different categories, according to the degree of antiquity or universality. The modern approach is to treat two terms as interchangeable. In transnational commercial law the term "usage" or "usages" is that generally adopted: in international law the reference is usually to custom". According to *O. Lando*, "The role of party autonomy and the relevance of usages", in M.J. Bonell – F. Bonelli (eds.), *Contratti commerciali internazionali e principi Unidroit*, (Giuffre, Milano, 1997), 119 "the period needed to establish a usage does not have to be very long. New trade usages may, for instance, come into existence in a relatively short period".

192 *R.A. Posner*, "The Law and Economics of Contract Interpretation", in (2005) *Texas Law Review*, 83, 1588. It is well known that in the early 1950's the Uniform Commercial Code was drafted, and the changes it made in the law of custom have persisted through all versions of the Code since 1952. Therefore, the Code abandoned the high standards for proving custom, and indicated an affirmative policy to use trade usage.

193 Also Kelsen in his famous book "Derogation" points out that the costums have the power to create a new norm and as a consequence it loses its efficacy and validity. Kelsen's thought is rewritten in *G. Gitti*, "Le clausole d'uso come fonti del diritto", in (2003) *Rivista di diritto civile*, 120 according to which the Derogation represents "*l'indice più evidente della pressione o spinta che il diritto materiale esercita da sempre su quello formale*".

194 *A. Giardina*, "L'autonomia delle parti nel commercio internazionale", in *Gli usi del commercio internazionale nella negoziazione ed esecuzione dei contratti internazionali*, (Giuffre, Milano, 1987), 21, according to the Author "*l'indagine circa il*

tual parties.[195] As a consequence, in order to interpret the contract, these rules can be elevated to the status of a legal rule thereby having a strong impact on international cases.[196]

In light of those considerations, it appears necessary to focus on the great importance of usages in international commerce.

At first, according to that literature[197] that examines the relevant function of the usages of the international trade, that are a subset of *lex mercatoria*,[198] these are not developed by any particular legal system but simply by the transformation of standard contracts[199] into transnational customary

---

contenuto delle regole del commercio internazionale dimostra l'esistenza di principi generalissimi e di norme di dettaglio volte alla costruzione e al completamento di istituti tipici del diritto commerciale".

195 According to *V. Gessner*, "Contractual certainty in International Trade", in V. Gessner (ed.), *Towards a Theoretical Framework for Contractual Certainty in Global Trade*, (Hart Publishing, Oxford, 2009), 133 "usages and customs are used to interpreter the contract, and they can also be the source of obligations for the parties".

196 *F. Marrella*, "La nuova lex mercatoria, principi Unidroit ed usi dei contratti del commercio internazionale", in F. Galgano (ed.), *Trattato diritto commerciale e diritto pubblico economia*, (Giuffre, Milano, 2003), 242. According to the Author "*l'arbitro* [...] *potrà attribuire agli usi del commercio internazionale autonoma valenza e quindi valore contrattuale, normativo o interpretativo, in relazione alla fattispecie sottoposta al suo esame, a prescindere dalle vicende della legge applicabile, salva solo l'ipotesi in cui le stesse parti avessero escluso l'applicazione degli usi del commercio internazionale*".

197 *R. Goode*, "Usage and its reception in transnational commercial law", in (1997) *International Comparative Law Quarterly*, 1.

198 *G. Aksen*, "The Law Applicable in International Arbitration. Relevance of Reference to the Trade Usages", in van der Berg (ed.), *Planning Efficient Arbitration Proceedings: the Law applicable in International arbitration – ICCA Congress series No.* 7 (The Hague Kluwer Law International), 471. On this point *V. Gessner*, "Contractual certainty in International Trade", in V. Gessner (ed.), *Towards a Theoretical Framework for Contractual Certainty in Global Trade*, (Hart Publishing, Oxford, 2009), 76, that assumes that in particular market as timber or diamond sale, these rules are mechanism that have been supported strongly the timber transactions, as a consequence the *lex mercatoria* represents an internal mechanism for international commerce, also because often these rules exclude national legislation and courts.

199 According to ICC International Court of Arbitration, Paris of 1997 n. 8873 at http://www.unilex.info/case.cfm?id=641, the principles that usually are inserted in standard contracts can be qualified as commercial usages.

practices[200] that are linked to single economic transactions. Indeed, a reference to trade usages and transnational practices is inserted in art. 1.8 of the UNIDROIT Principles, according to which the contractual parties "are bound by any usage to which they have agreed and by any practices which they have established between themselves" and "[...] by a usage that is widely known to and regularly observed in international trade". Moreover there are "world wide usages", that represent a commonplace,[201] in shipping, banking, franchising, distribution, insurance trade or sales as in specific sectors of the construction,[202] diamond or timber[203] businesses. In addition, it is also important to point out that some trade associations (i.e. FOSFA, GAFTA, etc.) often offer for their associates standard model of

200 *F. Marrella*, "La nuova lex mercatoria, principi Unidroit ed usi dei contratti del commercio internazionale", in F. Galgano (ed.), *Trattato diritto commerciale e diritto pubblico economia*, (Giuffrè, Milano, 2003), 188.

201 *G. Aksen*, "The Law Applicable in International Arbitration. Relevance of Reference to the Trade Usages", in van der Berg (ed.), *Planning Efficient Arbitration Proceedings: the Law applicable in International arbitration – ICCA Congress series No. 7* (Kluwer Law International, The Hague, 1996), 475 according to which the trade usages in contract as shipbulding, charter party, oil and gas, reinsurance, securities, power plant construction, computer technology, commission agents, license and distributionship, technical assistance, transfer of technology, joint ventures have become so "common place that if parties wish to avoid its impact, they must expressely exclude its application from the contract". See also *A. Guarnieri*, "Gli usi e il sistema delle fonti del diritto civile", in (2000) *Rivista di diritto civile*, 29.

202 *H. Collins*, *Regulating contracts*, (O.U.P., Oxford, 1999), 27, clearly notes that "in the construction business [...] general contractors and subcontractors will conduct themself towards each other by reference to the local customs of the trade, therefore their reciprocal commitments will be defined not by their explicity negotiations but also by the routine prectices and expectations in that line of business".

203 *V. Gessner*, "Contractual certainty in International Trade", in V. Gessner (ed.), *Towards a Theoretical Framework for Contractual Certainty in Global Trade*, (Hart Publishing, Oxford, 2009), 75, the Author assumes that "the cross border timber trade works very well on the basis of the established long-term business relationship self-created rules and intra-industry arbitration". The Author reports that there are also several unwritten and codified commercial customs in the international timber trade, as the ones used in field of hardwood trade. See *Ibid*, 60.

contracts[204] (in market areas such as franchising, sale, distribution)[205] and that these are drawn up on their respective trade usages.[206]

These considerations can be used to demonstrate that parties,[207] especially SME, prefer to regulate their transactions with self-made rules adapted to the specific needs of their business community.[208] Likewise, they will generally consider these usages implicit and often, in order to reduce the

---

204 According to *V. Roppo*, "Il contratto, e le fonti del diritto", in (2001) *Politica del diritto*, 531, "*la circolazione dei modelli contrattuali genera un fenomeno «creativo» di norme, perché «il contratto si fa prassi; la prassi genera l'uso; e l'uso crea la norma»*".

205 *P.F. Soleti*, "I contratti del commercio internazionale tra ordinamenti statali e lex mercatoria", in (2017) *Diritto del commercio internazionale*, 62.

206 *F. Sbordone*, "Il diritto applicabile al merito della controversia nell'arbitrato commerciale internazionale", in *L'autonomia negoziale nella giustizia arbitrale in Report of the X International Congress of Società Italiana degli Studiosi del Diritto Civile*, (E.S.I., Napoli, 2016), 149. The Author points out the importance of standard model contract in the international sale ships "*il Saleform 1993 predisposto dalla Norwegian Ship-brokers Association; in materia di countertrade, la Legal Guide on International Countertrade Transactions predisposto dall'UNCITRAL; in materia di engineering, la Guide for drawing up international con- tracts on consulting engineering including some related aspects of technical assistance, realizzata dalla Commissione Economica per l'Europa delle Nazioni Unite (ECE); per i c.dd. turnkey contracts (aventi per oggetto la costruzione e le consegna di impianti industriali «chiavi in mano»), la Legal Guide on Drawing up International Contracts for the Construction of Industrial works dell'UNCITRAL*".

207 How clearly explained by *E. Warren*, "A vast number of parties who litigate the application of trade usage to interpret a disputed term concede, explicitly or implicitly, that they are in the trade and that the trade recognizes a particular usage. They often dispute, however, the question of whether the usage should be used to interpret the instant contract. These cases-the ones in which the parties themselves do not choose to dispute that they are in the trade or that the usage can be established-are the cases that should be routinely decided", See *E. Warren*, "Trade Usage and Parties in the Trade: An Economic Rationale for an Inflexible Rule", in (1981) *University of Pittsburg Law Review*, 524.

208 It is important also remember Robert Gordon's warning about the "dark side" of relational contracting, where dominant market players create an edit business custom in ways that favour their needs, in this way see *R. Gordon*, "Macaulay, Macneil, and the Discovery of Solidarity and Power in Contract Law", in (1985) *Wisconsin Law Review*, 570-571. See also *C. Milhaupt - M. West*, "The Dark Side of Private Ordering: An Institutional and Empirical Analysis of Organised Crime", in (2000) *University of Chicago Law Review*, 67, 41. In the similar vein *G. Cuniberti*, "The Merchant Who Would Not Be King", in H. Muir Watt – D.P. Fernández Arroyo (eds.), *Private International Law and Global Governance* (O.U.P., Oxford, 2014), 142.

transaction costs,[209] not refer to them in their contract,[210] preferring to make the transactions without a written contract,[211] or only with a mere *renvoi* to this “trade linguistic”.[212] In other words, the application of a trade usage to a written contract has strong economic effects on the business parties. In this debate, Warren rightly notes in economic terms and with some clear diagrams, that the impact of transaction costs cannot be overstated by business people and that trade usages translate to lower transaction costs.[213] In fact, as the author suggests,

> “the automatic application of trade usage to those in the trade may be explained by an examination of its economic impact on the distribution of goods and services. The distribution of goods and services is costless only in idealized economic models. Actually, it involves transaction costs which include all costs incidental to the exchange, such as costs of marketing, information gathering, negotiating, and financing”.[214]

Therefore Warres concludes that “trade usage can reduce transaction costs by encouraging extensive use of trade terms, by permitting parties to negotiate routine contracts without lawyers, by reducing the likelihood of liti-

---

209 See *supra* 2.III.

210 *O. Lando*, “The role of party autonomy and the relevance of usages”, in M.J. Bonell – F. Bonelli (eds.), *Contratti commerciali internazionali e principi Unidroit*, (Giuffre, Milano, 1997), 121.

211 *U. La Porta*, *Globalizzazione e diritto*, (Liguori editore, Napoli, 2005), 13 who strongly argues that nowadays the contract is seen as unsuitable legal tool to act as a formal support for the economic relations.

212 These were defined in this way by some Authors in order to point out this specialized language.

213 *E. Warren*, “Trade Usage and Parites in the Trade: An Economic Rationale for an Inflexible Rule”, in (1981) *University of Pittsburg Law Review*, 540.

214 *Ibid*, 535. See also *H. Beale – T. Dugdale*, “Contracts between Businessmen: Planning and the Use of Contractual Remedies”, in (1975) *British Journal of law and society*, 47 – 48. The Authors assume that not every businessman (especially the smaller firms) necessarily "uses" contract law even in the planning sense when making an agreement: within the trade certain terms and certain customs or "unwritten laws" were widely accepted; is that such planning is expensive, while the risk of a serious dispute or loss may be low. Therefore the Authors conclude that the reasons behind this “informal formation process” is into rely either upon trade custom or a "gentlemen's agreement" with the other contracting party.

gation, and by limiting the risk associated with an adverse decision if litigation ensues".[215]

On this basis, although conflicting with my opinion, the interpreter should not be obliged to apply a specific national law but ought to also base a decision on the "rules" of international law.[216]

In order to encapsulate the relevance of trade usages, it is important to point out that in legal doctrine we find two different opinions: some maintain that international usages must be distinguished from national usages because they have a specific and particular locality function for international players; others, believe international usages must be assimilated with the national usages and as a consequence the interpreter must apply a single national provision.[217]

However, in some EU legal systems, in particular those of the highly industrialized countries, usages and trade customs assume more often a progressive and faithful consolidation. In fact, in countries such France and England,[218] it is necessary that the parties display an explicit will, thus showing an awareness of the need to engage with usages and customs; in fact according to art. 1511 France c.p.c., in international arbitration the arbitrator must decide the case by applying *"règles de droit"* chosen by the

---

215 *E. Warren*, "Trade Usage and Parites in the Trade: An Economic Rationale for an Inflexible Rule", in (1981) *University of Pittsburg Law Review*, 545. The author also observes that "Trade usage puts a bound on possible litigation and an adverse decision. By reducing the risk of deviant interpretations, trade usage lowers transaction costs for all contracts, both those negotiated without lawyer assistance and the specialized, heavily negotiated ones in which lawyers have participated extensively as a contract interpretation device".

216 With reference to the arbitration see *M.J. Bonell*, "I principi UNIDROIT dei contratti commerciali internazionali: origini, natura e finalità", in (1995) *Diritto del commercio internazionale*, 19; *G. Cordero-Moss – D. Behn*, "The relevance of the UNIDROIT principle in investment arbitration", in (2014) *Uniform Law Review*, 15; *F. Sbordone*, *Contratti internazionali e lex mercatoria*, (E.S.I., Napoli, 2008), 45.

217 According to Italian Corte di Cassazione "[...] *gli usi del commercio internazionale vengono assunti quali veri e propri usi normativi, vere e proprie fonti di diritto oggettivo; ma di un diritto oggettivo non statuale, bensì sovranazionale: di un diritto oggettivo della societas mercatorum*". In these words Corte di Cassazione February 8, 1982 nr. 722 in *F. Marrella*, "La nuova lex mercatoria, principi Unidroit ed usi dei contratti del commercio internazionale", in F. Galgano (ed.), *Trattato diritto commerciale e diritto pubblico economia*, (Giuffrè, Milano, 2003), 239.

218 *P. Hellwege*, "Handelsbrauch und Verkehrssitte", in (2014) *AcP*, 872-873 and on the principal German theories of interpretation see 880 – 886. In the U.K. the proved trade custom is binding.

parties and in absence of the parties choice with the usages of international commerce.[219]

In other countries such as Austria[220] and Germany,[221] it is not necessary that the parties be aware of usages and customs, and as a consequence an express will for their exclusion is needed. Therefore these observations should impose on the court a detailed investigation of the all the circumstances of the case, especially in countries such as Germany where the interpreter not only must search for the real intention of the parties[222] but must also qualify their legal nature, in particular if they are "*Kaufleuten*", in order to apply § 346 HGB.[223]

Likewise, in Italy, usages and customs assume a relevant role in the interpretation of the contract. In fact, these are expressly referred to in artt. 1340, 1368 e 1374 of the *codice civile*. However, compared to other legal systems, in Italy[224] the legal doctrine has created two different types of us-

---

219 Art. 1511 France c.p.c. hold "*Le tribunal arbitral tranche le litige conformément aux règles de droit que les parties ont choisies ou, à défaut, conformément à celles qu'il estime appropriées. Il tient compte, dans tous les cas, des usages du commerce.*" In the same way art. 1054 Dutch c.p.c. according to *P.F. Soleti*, "I contratti del commercio internazionale tra ordinamenti statali e lex mercatoria", in (2017) *Diritto del commercio internazionale*, 72.

220 § 863 ABGB "(1) *Man kann seinen Willen nicht nur ausdrücklich durch Worte und allgemein angenommene Zeichen; sondern auch stillschweigend durch solche Handlungen erklären, welche mit Überlegung aller Umstände keinen vernünftigen Grund, daran zu zweifeln, übrig lassen.* (2) *In bezug auf die Bedeutung und Wirkung von Handlungen und Unterlassungen ist auf die im redlichen Verkehr geltenden Gewohnheiten und Gebräuche Rücksicht zu nehmen*". See aboit this topic also *B. Verschraegen*, "Austrian Report", in (2012) *European Review of Private Law*, 78 ss.

221 *P. Hellwege*, "Handelsbrauch und Verkehrssitte", in (2014) *AcP*, 855-856.

222 *Ibid*, 860.

223 § 346 HGB "*Unter Kaufleuten ist in Ansehung der Bedeutung und Wirkung von Handlungen und Unterlassungen auf die im Handelsverkehr geltenden Gewohnheiten und Gebräuche Rücksicht zu nehmen*".

224 The Italian *Codice Civile* rules two differents types of "*usi*". In one hand the so called "*usi normativi*" inserted in Article 1374 according to which "*Il contratto obbliga le parti non solo a quanto è nel medesimo espresso, ma anche a tutte le conseguenze che ne derivano secondo la legge, o, in mancanza, secondo gli usi e l'equità*". In the other the so called "*usi negoziali*" inserted in Article 1340 in line with which "*Le clausole d'uso s'intendono inserite nel contratto, se non risulta che non sono state volute dalle parti*". As reported by *C.M. Bianca, Diritto Civile. Il contratto*, (Giuffrè, Milano, 2000), 3, 339 these "[…] *trovano applicazione senza che occorra la prova che le parti li abbiano conosciuti e accettati*".

ages:[225] firstly, the so-called "*usi normativi*", which could be more aptly identified as customs and are commonly qualified as secondary legal rules;[226] secondly, the "*usi negoziali*" or "*clausole d'uso*",[227] which are typical of a specific market area and are inserted automatically in the contract, unless the parties have expressly agreed otherwise.[228] Importantly, only the "*uso negoziale*" prevails as a general rule.[229]

In short, this careful analysis of all the circumstances of the contract and of the real intention of the parties appears incompatible with a "mechanized judgment" or with those rules that limit the power of the interpreter. It is clear, from this outline, that commercial usages create benefits for the internal market, but these are not compatible with hard-and-fast rules.[230]

Concluding, hard-and-fast rules cause harm to the EU internal market and to contractual parties that often specifically fail, within routine contracts, to make reference to trade usages. These considerations demonstrate a tremendous need for enhancing trade usages in commercial contracts, in

---

225 *R. Sacco*, "Il diritto non scritto". *Le fonti del diritto italiano, 2, Le fonti non scritte e l'interpretazione*, in R. Sacco (ed.) *Trattato di diritto civile*, (Giappichelli, Torino, 1999), 14; *E. Del Prato*, "Fonti legali ed usi", in (2002) *Rivista diritto civile*, 515. *Contra P. Perlingieri*, "Fonti del diritto ed 'ordinamento del caso concreto'", in (2010) *Rivista di diritto privato*, 26 according to which "*appare fumosa la distinzione tra usi normativi e negoziali*" that are also incompatible with the *iura novit curia* principle "*che rende inadeguata la distinzione*".

226 *C. Marseglia*, "Usi negoziali e anatocismo", in (2012) *I Contratti*, 54, according to which "*l'uso si considera normativo se un dato comportamento sia ripetuto nella convinzione di uniformarsi ad una norma giuridicamente vincolante*".

227 According to *A. Genovese*, "Gli usi nella disciplina dei contratti commerciali", in (1950) *Rivista trimestrale diritto e procedura civile*, 391 are "*clausole abituali, che presuppongono una prolungata relazione di affari, del medesimo genere, intervenuta fra gli stessi contraenti*".

228 *G. Quadri*, "Gli usi nella disciplina del contratto: spunti per una ricostruzione unitaria", in (2009) *Contratto e impresa*, 1076- 1077.

229 *R. Calvo*, *Diritto civile*, II, *Il contratto*, (Zanichelli, Bologna, 2015), 262 "*Gli usi negoziali – a differenza di quelli normativi- prevalgono sulle disposizioni suppletive di legge. Ciò in quanto l'efficacia dell'uso negoziale è assimilabile a quella riconosciuta alla clausola contrattuale, che può senz'altro derogare la norma integrativa*".

230 On this point see also *H. Dedek*, "Usages and Practices", in N. Jansen – R. Zimmermann (eds.), *Commentaries on European Contract Laws*, (O.U.P., Oxford, 2018), 54 – 55, according to which "usages are perceived as being of vital importance for international trade and are even seen as the very essence of a cosmopolitan, flexible 'law merchant' that serve as a form of self-governance in international commerce".

order to achieve full economic benefits, which accrue only in a developed market[231] and if the court has the power to use flexible rules.

2. VI Tentative conclusion

This chapter has stipulated that the word "globalisation" needs reasonable rules[232] in contract law (in all its ramifications) in order to be adaptable to a fast changing society as well as to the market.[233] On this premise, there is a normative argument in favor of the duty of each legislator to contribute to global regulation.[234] In this respect, my job today is only to suggest that, at this point in time, starting with the US model, European legal and economic theories must be developed in order to support EU institutions in the complex path to creating rules that guarantee real benefits for the internal market.

What is more, the foregoing pages have shown what was notably also argued by Posner, that law is not recognized as an autonomous system, but as an integral part of social life that must be studied from various social science perspectives[235] in order to economically benefit the market players. In fact, it is well known that the market process is a meaningful human expe-

---

231 *R. Calvo*, *Diritto civile*, II, *Il contratto*, (Zanichelli, Bologna, 2015), 578.

232 In this vein *P. Schlesinger*, "I mercati neri", in (1999) *Rivista diritto civile*, 188.

233 Contract law can function as a generator of economic benefits only if it is sufficiently flexible, on this point see *ex multis T. Wilhellmsson*, "The Ethical Pluralism of Late Modern Europe and Codification of European Contract Law", in J. Smith (ed.), *The Need for a European Contract Law. Empirical and Legal Perspecitves*, (Europa Law Publishing, Amsterdam, 2005), 129 who assumes that "adequate learning concerning new risks and their optimal management cannot be gathers within a very rigid and abstract normative structure"; *J. W. Hurst*, *Law and Markets in United States History. Different Modes of Bargaining among interests*, (The University of Wisconsin Press, Madison, 1982), 60 that points out that the market is not a static phenomenon that can be estimated and is subject to variable condition and to be profitable must fit to change social structure, political alignments and cultural values. Finally, *N. Irti*, *L' ordine giuridico del mercato*, (La terza editore, Bari, 2009), 73 has pointed out that "It is not the right that presupposes the economy, but the economy that presupposes the right, a determining condition of its structure" (Author translator).

234 *H. Muir Watt*, "Choice of law in integrated and interconnected markets: a matter of political Economy", in (2003) *Electronic Journal of Comparative Law*, 402.

235 *R.A. Posner*, "The Decline of Law as an Autonomous Discipline", in (1987) *Harvard Law Review*, 766 – 767. See also *J. S. Kraus*, "Legal Design and the Evolution of Commercial Norms", (1997) *The Journal of Legal Studies*, 381.

rience and not merely an exercise in "scientific" calculation.[236] Consequently, according to Malloy, "the process is not one of calculating efficiency but mapping and representing alternative cultural-interpretive understandings of the market as a human exchange process capable of continuously generating and transforming meanings and values".[237] In this regard, Malloy suggests, an "exchange relationship" among law, culture and markets[238] can create greater benefits for market actors. Therefore, from the previous analysis, and as will also be pointed out in the next pages, it seems inconvenient for the market to have rigid or complex rules because they can be extremely harmful to the above-mentioned "exchange relationship" and as a consequence to economy.[239]

In this context, the EU needs to modernize contract law, in all its ramifications, primarily by developing a more integrated view of regulation in market transactions and focusing on the real economic intentions of contractual parties. In fact, I argue that the EU bodies should conceptualize trading between private persons for profit not as product of law but, as emphasided by Hurts in one of his last monographs, as

> "primarily the product of goals set and means fashioned by industrialists, merchants, bankers, lenders and borrowers, employers and employees, and ultimate consumers. [...] Relative to the whole play of factors that produced the market, the law was marginal".[240]

The corollary, in my opinion, of this significant theory is that the market can be modified by it own players. It does not mean that the law is not important; the point is that the law does not create or modify the market, but instead must increase the vitality of the market itself, supporting all of those involved in the market. What constitues the nature of the market are only the bargains that must be supporterd by a law adaptable to their case-by-case needs.

---

236 *R. P. Malloy*, *Law in a Market Context. An Introduction to Market Concepts in Legal Reasoning*, (C.U.P., Cambridge, 2004), 70.

237 *Ibid*, 75.

238 *Ibid*, 62 ss. Therefore, the Author points out that "economics can help us understand law in a market context but economics can not eliminate the need to engage in the exploration of the meanings and values of worthy human values".

239 *L. Rossi Carleo*, "Diritto del mercato, diritto per il mercato o diritto per soggetti del mercato", in (1992) *Rassegna di diritto civile*, 764.

240 *J. W. Hurst*, *Law and Markets in United States History. Different Modes of Bargaining among interests*, (The University of Wisconsis Press, Madison, 1982), 9.

To sum up, it is clear that a legislative intervention in an exchange, will not protect all the economic choices made by the parties or guarantee the good functioning of the market.[241] In fact, as already seen,[242] the rigid rules could also be interpreted as a limit to party autonomy.

More generally, some modern doctrines assume that, in a global context, contract law rules have "the duty to disclose relevant matters at each important juncture of a transaction to avoid making a misleading impression or misrepresentation; the duty to renegotiate with the possibility of the adaptation of a contract, and the importance of customs and usages", as well as "the need to protect the parties' intentions, reasonable reliance, and reasonable expectations arising from a particular contractual context".[243] In addition, Stephan assumes that a "better rule" is one that improves on the *status quo* with respect to some normative social goal, such as redistributive justice or enhancing economic welfare.[244] In accordance with this theory, I believe that hard-and-fast rules are capable not only of generating problems of efficiency for market goals but also of creating issues of social welfare not measurable by a market calculus, as the economic inequality between the different actors may be possible.

Starting with these considerations, it seems to me that the EU needs a new economic theory of contract law, even more than the US, which does not have strong cultural diversity, since the American people share a common language and (in spite of regional differences) a homogeneous culture supported by common media. We need to modernize contract law and implement a new legal theory in the EU that we can call theory of "contract efficiency".[245] This theory should start from the assumption that economic transactions are self-sufficient and independent of any formal

---

241 *U. La Porta*, *Globalizzazione e diritto*, (Liguori editore, Napoli, 2005), 150.

242 See *supra* § 2.II.

243 *K. Sono*, "The Rise of A National Contract Law in the Age of Globalisation", in (2001) *Tulane Law Review*, 1189. See also *M. J. Whincop - M. Keyes*, *Policy and Pragmatism in the Conflicts of Laws*, (Ashgate Dartmounth, Hants, 2001), *passim*, according to the authors the benefits will be with an approach boosted on two main pilasters: (1) policies that underlie substantive private law should generally inform conflict of laws rules; (2) parties and their interests should be enhanced, not the interests of states or other entities.

244 *P. Stephan*, "The Futility of Unification and harmonisation in international commercial law", in (1999) *Virginia Journal of International Law*, 5.

245 See also *supra* § 1.III.

constraint that may come from politics.[246] In fact, some Authors have pointed out that business culture prefers the "neutrality" of the legal norm of contract law[247] with respect to economic phenomena, confident of the market's ability to self-discipline and protect the best economic interest of market actors.[248] I would like, once again, to emphasize that legislators should understand that, in the new era of globalisation, market players do not have need of a rigid norm but rather of a legal instrument which can mold quickly to the fast global society, and which allows the court an *ex post* reasonable interpretation of the bargain.

I propose that a better way is to fully enhance the real economic intention that has led the market players to make that bargain. Therefore, a change in contractual matters should allow a creative capacity for party autonomy and its case-by-case interpretation. This, in my opinion, is the best solution to carve the pathway for a future EU contract law than can seriously fit with the market and its real economic needs. In fact, I believe that only the contractual parties, not the legislatures, should weigh their economic interests. Therefore, in order to enhance these parties' interests, legislatures at national and international level, should create reasonable legal tools that the court must apply to interpreter the economic interests of contractual parties for any specific case, as well as rules that can adapt to the continuous and fast changes of international commerce.[249] In practice, adopting this approach we shall face an improvement in the economic in-

246 In order to capture those I should say that law derives from the culture of a given society and not by the power of the lawmakers which have the duty to draw only general principles.

247 Collins, although in my opinion not clearly explain what mean, push for an "hybrid" contract law. For a critical analysis of Collins approach, see *J. Gava – J. Greene*, "Do We Need a Hybrid Law of Contract? Why Hugh Collins is wrong and why it Matters", in (2004) *Cambridge Law Jorunal*, 630. "His claims that a hybrid law would have the capacity for reflexive learning and that the results of case law can be disseminated widely enough to influence market players are also unpersuasive. While none of these criticisms is necessarily fatal for his project, the cumulative effect is to raise serious dubts about the plausibility of a hybrid law. […] Collins' project fails because it demands of judge's skills and knowledge that no human could muster. Judges will not be able to do what he wants of them".

248 *N. Irti*, *L'ordine giuridico del mercato*, (Laterza, Bari, 2009), XI.

249 *T. Wilhellmsson*, "The Ethical Pluralism of Late Modern Europe and Codification of European Contract Law", in J. Smith (ed.) *The Need for a European Contract Law. Empirical And Legal Perspecitves*, (Europa Law Publishing, Amsterdam, 2005), 128 according to the author "the risk society needs a law that can adapt quickly to new experiences".

tentions of the parties, regardless of specific rules but on the condition that, through legislation, a collapse of the business system will be prevented.[250] This would allow a correct and detailed analysis of the specific case,[251] inserted in the socio-economic reality and reasonable expectations of contractual parties.

In addition, it should be emphasised that the market needs a "dynamic jurisprudence",[252] one that has the competence to adapt to the fast changes of the globalisation era and one that contributes to improve the market by participating in the "informal economy".[253] Importantly, in order to see a "dynamic jurisprudence", intended as co-actors of the change of the market, it needs flexible rules that can allow it to make informed decisions.

These foregoing considerations have given me the opportunity to reflect on those rigid rules, as we will see also in Rome I Regulation,[254] that could frighten the market players (especially SME) to build up business abroad and thereby leading to the seemingly paradoxical conclusion that the rigid rules represent a brake also for the development of the small transactions that represent a great market share.

As mentioned, the US market, known to be the most profitable commerce, has adopted a very flexible approach on contract law and conflict of laws. As Macaulay clearly has observed, "nonetheless, even with this kind of uncertain contract law in action, America has enjoyed great economic success"[255] and "as I have emphasised, despite, or because of, the imprecise

---

250 *U. La Porta*, *Globalizzazione e diritto*, (Liguori Editore, Napoli, 2005), 140.

251 *E. A. O'Hara – L. E. Ribstein*, "From Politcs to Efficiency in Choice of Law", in (2000) *University of Chicago Law Review*, 1191, according to which: "One might argue that a precise policy match on a case-by-case basis is more important than clarity when the transaction costs of choosing are so high that even a clear rule is unlikely to guide the parties' choice".

252 *J. Jacobson*, "The Other Path of the Law". "Symposium: The Informal Economy", in (1994) *Yale Law Journal*, 2213 – 2214. The Author uses this term as opposed to the state-oriented, "static jurisprudence" of the formal economy.

253 *Ibid*, 2237. According to the Author "the informal economy is one that enhances our power as citizens, that cultivates personality instead of suppressing it, that puts its persons, not the state, at the center of jurisprudence". In order to the effects, the Author assumes that "[...] Static jurisprudence can create a boundary. Dynamic jurisprudence always breaches it".

254 See *infra* § 3.III

255 *S. Macaulay*, "The Real and the Paper Deal: Empirical Pictures of Relationships, Complexity and the Urge for Transparent Simple Rules", in (2003) *The Modern Law Review*, 58.

and often conflicting nature of our contract law, the American economy has been successful".[256]

In addition, it seems to me that the inflexible approach of the rules of contract law not only, as seen, cause harm to SME transactions, which constitute a big market share, but also creates an increase in the phenomenon of populism, which are nowadays experiencing in Europe. The economic damages that this type of movement can cause should not be underestimated. In fact, as some Americans authors have reported in reference to populist governments:

> "any suggestion that the government should intervene in response to people's mistakes raises the question whether the government will be able to avoid such errors. The prospects for productive and useful intervention may be smallest in the case of populist government; the actions of such a government, based heavily on pressures coming from citizens, may tend to be subject to the very same biases and errors that afflict citizens [and businessman]".[257]

However, the foregoing discussion has been an effort to illustrate that legislators at the nation and EU level have the potential and the viable opportunity, especially during this particular time, to benefit the market with a contract law reform without falling victims to it. In a practical approach, the adaptation of the contract to the global market society, means rethinking a form of contract far from traditional schemes and based on reasonable rules. This legal need should urgently be made in order to avoid huge prejudices to the market itself.

Indeed, although I do not want to dwell on the numerous and well-known works on contract law across the European Union, I think that the foregoing pages could represent a starting point for national legislators and EU institutions to reflect on solutions to guarantee economic benefits to market players. In light of the critiques that have been done, I do not hesitate to say again that the starting point is to enhance the "Supreme Will"

256 *Ibid*, 63.

257 Brackets from the Author. In these words, *C. Jolls - C. R. Sunstein - R.H. Thaler*, "A behavioural Approach to Law and Economics", in (1998) *Stanford Law Review*, 1543. The Authors, continuing, assume that "thus behavioral analysis complements existing accounts of the problems with populism. An example of the effects of populism is the Superfund statute, discussed in Part III.C; irregular perceptions of risk by ordinary people may tend to produce irregularities in regulation, as the cognitive errors that ordinary people make are replicated in statutory and administrative law."

of the contractual parties and to create reasonable rules that support economic interpretation by the court especially when it is faced with bargains concluded in the absence of externalities. Only in this manner can the economic interests of all the parties be balanced.

The recent Hague Principles on Choice of Law for International Contracts[258] and PECL were surely a positive step. In fact, PECL with a flexible approach exclude the *causa* and form, which limit party autonomy, from the essential elements of the contract. But, as is obvious, these principles cannot to be applied by the court if there is no specific reference to them in a clause contract. So why not directly apply the Principles in case of "oral" or "incomplete" contracts? This could be an idea that EU institutions could seriously take in consideration, but nowadays I believe that it is yet impossible.[259] In my opinion, a court cannot apply an uncodified law or principle in absence of an explicit reference by the parties,[260] as in the case of a bargain concluded absent externalities. This rule could also contrast with basic national legal principles or with the "supreme will" of contractual parties.

Overall, at the national level an important step has recently been made in France's legal system that has deleted the "causa" as an essential element

---

258 For a comment to these recent principles see *S. Symeonides*, "The Hague Principles on Choice of Law for International Contracts: Some Preliminary Comments", in (2013) *The American Journal of Comparative Law*, 873 ss.

259 In contrast, there are EU court decisions that have applied soft law instruments as UNIDROIT Principle governing the contract although the contractual not have made an express choice. It is the case of the Belgian Court de Cassation in 2009 and two French decisions (Court d' Appel of Reims of 2012 and Court de Cassation 2015), defining them as "code of international contracts containing general principles governing the law of international commerce. All the above decisions have been reported in *M. J. Bonell*, "The law governing international commercial contracts and the actual role of the Unidroit Principles", in (2018) *Uniform Law Review*, 28.

260 The *Bundesgerichtshof* (BGH), 28 February, 1975, *Neue Juristische Wochenschrift* (NJW) 1975, 1597 - 1598 held that "in interpretation of international conventions which regulate private law relations between the citizens of contracting States, it must be kept in mind that domestic concepts and principles cannot indiscriminately be considered as underlying the convention", the translation is made by *J. Basedow*, "International economic law and commercial contracts: promoting cross-border trade by uniform law conventions", in (2018) *Uniform Law Review*, 6. The Author also made explicit reference to Belgian *Court de Cassation*, 27 January, 1977 and translates the Belgian court decision in this way: "would be futile to elaborate a convention designed to establish an international statute if the court of each State interpreted it in line with the concepts of their own law".

of the contract from the civil code. This circumstance allows to the court to have a flexible legal tool in order to examine all the economic circumstances of the case.

To summarise, this reasonable approach, which enhances the role of the interpreter and create benefits to contractual parties, clashes with hard-and-fast rules such as Rome I Regulation[261] that should be applied especially in case of a freely negotiated bargain or "incomplete" contracts between EU entrepreneurs.

261 See *infra* § 3.III.

3. The rules of p.i.l. of contractual obligations nowadays

Introduction

It is clear that, from a practical point of view, the benefits of the abovementioned theories, as well as the flexibility or rigidity of a norm can be measured when the contractual parties break the law or fail to mention specific contractual clauses regarding which law may be applied to the contract. In this case, the interpreter has the power to examine the case and use a legal instrument to resolve the dispute. Overall, the flexibility or rigidity of the norm can enhance or not her/his decisive role. Most obviously, p.i.l. rules such as the Rome Convention or the recent Rome I Regulation will be applied to EU transactions, while nowadays in US transactions the Second Restatement of Conflicts of Laws is applicable.

From the perspective just outlined, this chapter analyses the p.i.l. instruments that the interpreter can use in order to find the law applicable to the contract. This chapter's focus is more pragmatic. In doing so, the chapter proves that the Rome Convention, Rome I Regulation and Second Restatement of Conflict of Laws have different approaches and, as a consequence, also a different impact on the market. In this regard, this chapter also critically examines all the principal innovations introduced by the Rome I Regulation, with the aim of evaluating many practical issues of its rigid rules.

3.1 Analysis of the Rome Convention

In order to draw conclusions on the main innovations introduced by the Rome I Regulation, it is necessary to begin by including a footnote concerning the rules of the Rome Convention and in particular the instruments that it uses to identify the applicable law.

In absence of an *electio juris* by the parties, Article 4 of the Rome Convention states that the governing law shall be the law of the country with which the disputed matter has the closest connection (or subjective connection).[262] Nonetheless, the Convention does not contain a specific definition of the principle of closest connection and only lists in paragraphs 3 and 4 some "presumptions", as in the case of contracts relating to a right *in rem* or contracts for the carriage of goods.[263]

This is identified by ECJ as "the general principle"[264] of Article 4 of the Convention, and it stands to reason that this is an undetermined criterion where the court must consider many connecting factors[265] between contract and countries. In other words, the identification of the circumstances of contact, necessary for subjecting the contract to a specific law, moves from the sphere of the lawmaker to that of the interpreter, and in particular of the court.[266]

This principle is reaffirmed in line with the U.S.'s "most significant relationship doctrine"[267] or "centre of gravity method", or the long-standing

---

262 *P. Volken*, "How Common are the General Principles of Private International Law? America and Europe Compared", in (1999) *Yearbook of Private International Law*, 85 ss.; *L.F. Kuyven*, "Convention de Rome du 19 juin 1980 sur la loi applicable aux obligations contractuelles - Article 4 (5) sur la loi applicable à défaut de choix - Note sur la décision de la Cour de Cassation (France) du 19 décembre 2006", in (2007) *Uniform Law Review*, 382.

263 *F. Ferrari*, "From Rome to Rome via Brussels: Remarks on the Law Applicable to Contractual Obligations Absent a Choice by Parties (Art. 4 of the Rome I Regulation)", in (2009) *RabelsZ*, 154. In line with the Author's opinion "the Convention gave rise only to an "empty formula" that was "devoid of any innate, objectively ascertainable meaning".

264 ECJ C-133/08, *Intercontainer v Interfrigo*, § 26.

265 *R. Baratta*, *Il collegamento più stretto nel diritto internazionale privato dei contratti*, (Giuffrè, Milano, 2001), according to whom "*il fattore che "localizza" fattispecie all'interno dell'uno o dell'altro ordinamento statale, non è rappresentato dal collegamento più stretto in sé considerato, ma dal punto o dai punti di contatto che, a loro volta, esprimeranno il collegamento rilevante nel singolo caso*".

266 See *T. Ballarino*, *Manuale breve di diritto internazionale privato*, (Cedam, Padova, 2008), 217 ss.; *U. Villani*, *Nozioni di diritto internazionale privato*, U. Villani - M. Di Fabio - F. Sbordone (eds.), (E.S.I., Napoli, 2013), 39. The Author notes that this principle "[…] *non costituisce una circostanza stabilita, in via generale ed astratta dal legislatore, idonea a collegare automaticamnente la fattispecie a un dato Stato; esso, al contrario, implica il riferimento a una pluralità di elementi di un contratto e comporta per il giudice (e in generale per l' interprete) un' opera delicata di accertamento e di ponderazione della rilevanza di tali elementi nella ricerca della più generale e significativa connessione tra la fattispeciè ed uno Stato*".

267 *W. L.M. Reese*, "Conflict of Laws and the Restatement Second", in (1963) *Law and Contemporary Problems*, 699.

English notion of the proper law of the contract,[268] which delegates to the court the delicate task of identifying and framing those elements determining the centre of gravity of the case in point. Therefore, according to Lando,[269] the interpreter, via the "centre of gravity method", should aim to find the country with which the contractual subject matter has the closest connection (or relationship).[270] In particular, the interpreter must use this technique to localize "the law which on policy ground, seems to have the most significant connection with the chain of acts and consequences in the particular situation".[271] In contrast, some Authors[272] identify the most relevant contacts via the *principle of proximity*,[273] which allows the interpreter to analyse an individual contract with respect to the fundamental principles of each legal system.[274]

---

268 See *F.A. Mann*, "The proper law of contracts concluded by International Arbitration", in (1987) *International and Comparative Law Quarterly*, 437; *J. O'Brien*, *Conflict of laws*, (Cavendish Publishing Limited, London, 1999), 339. The Author, in reference to the search of the law, points out the approach of the English Court that "was to have regard to all the connections such as: (a) the place of contracting; (b) the place of performance; (c) the language of the contract; (d) the money of the account; (e) the personal law of the parties; and (f) all circumstances surrounding the contract".

269 *O. Lando*, "New American Choice of Law Principles and the European Conflict of Laws of Contracts", in (1982) *American Journal of Comparative Law*, 21.

270 *L. Di Donna*, "La scelta della legge applicabile ai contratti internazionali in difetto di determinazione delle parti", in (2004) *Nuova Giurisprudenza Civile Commentata*, 360.

271 *J. Morris*, "The proper law of tort", in (1951) *Harvard Law Review*, 881 ss.

272 *L. Di Donna*, "La scelta della legge applicabile ai contratti internazionali in difetto di determinazione delle parti", in (2004) *Nuova Giurisprudenza Civile Commentata*, 360.

273 In these words *P. Lagarde*, "Le principe de proximité dans le droit international privé contemporain", in (1986) 1 *Recueil des cours*, 13 ss. According to the Author *"principe exprime simplement l'idée du rattachement d'un rapport de droit à l'ordre juridique du pays avec lequel il présente, sinon le lien les plus étroits, du moins ou lien étroit, enfin d'une subordination de l'efficacité d'une décision à l'étroitesse des liens qui la rattachent a l'autorité qui l'a prise*'. For more see *P. Picone*, "Caratteri ed evoluzione del metodo tradizionale dei conflitti di legge", in (1998) *Rivista di diritto internazionale*, 63. In line with the Author's opinion the characteristic element of the *principe de proximité "è dato dal fatto che in esso è il giudice ad essere sempre investito del potere di determinare la legge applicabile, facendo uso di valutazioni in larga parte discrezionali*".

274 *T. Ballarino – G.P. Romano*, "Le Principe de Proximitè chez Paul Lagarde - Mélanges en l'honneur de Paul Lagarde", in B. Ancel - B. Audit - T. Ballarino - G.P. Romano (eds.), *Le droit international privè : esprit et methodes,* (Dalloz, Paris, 2005), 53.

To summarise these interpretations of the closest connection principle as the "centre of gravity contract", illustrate that the interpreter, in the task of individualising the applicable law, uses a flexible tool that can allow her/him to analyse all the circumstances of the contract and apply the most equitable law.

3.I.A The characteristic performance rule

The Rome Convention introduces another important instrument to identify the applicable law in the absence of parties choice: the characteristic performance.[275] Article 4 (2) stresses that the contract is most closely connected with the country where the characteristic performer (or debtor obliged to provide the characteristic performance) has maintained, when concluding the contract, his habitual residence or, in the case of a corporate or unincorporated entity, its central administration.

Therefore, the concept of characteristic performance presupposes the possibility of reconstructing the "identity" of the contract. In particular it has a feature that could be defined as a "skill to identify",[276] with the result that the interpreter is obliged to search within the contract for an element that distinguishes it from others.

However, it should be remembered that characteristic performance is not defined by the Rome Convention and a definition may itself be problematic considering that even the Giuliano – Lagarde Report itself fails to

---

275 There is abundant literature on the characteristic performance, *ex multis H. U. Jessurun d'Oliveira*, "Characteristic Obligation in the draft EEC Obligation Convention", in (1977) *American Journal and Comparative Law*, 303 ss.; *F. Vischer*, "The Principle of the typical performance in international contracts and the draft Convention", in K. Lipstein (ed.), *Harmonisation of Private International Law by the E.E.C.*, (Institute of Advanced Legal Studies, London, 1978), 25 ss.; *M. Magagni*, *La prestazione caratteristica nella Convenzione di Roma del 19 maggio 1980*, (Giuffrè, Milano, 1989), *passim*; *U. Villani*, "Aspetti problematici della prestazione caratteristica", in (1993) *Rivista di diritto internazionale privato e processuale*, 514 ss.; *M. Virgòs Soriano*, "La ley aplicable a los contratos internacionales: la regla de los vinculos estrechos y la presuncion basada en la prestaciòn caractieristica del contrato", in *Estudios juridicos en homenaje al profesor Aurelio Menèndez*, (Civitas, Madrid, 1996), 5289 ss.

276 *P. Franzina*, "Struttura e funzionamento del foro europeo della materia contrattuale alla luce delle sentenze Car Trim e Wood Floor della Corte di Giustizia", in (2010) *Rivista di diritto internazionale privato e processuale*, 663. In the Author words it has a "*identificatrice*" function.

proffer a definition. In addition to the work of several scholars,[277] this "technical term"[278] was coined in Swiss doctrine, specifically by Schnitzer,[279] and was soon adopted and applied by the Swiss courts. Furthermore the characteristic performance, also known as *"unterscheidendes Merkmal"*,[280] was thus used in Swiss doctrine and jurisprudence to fulfill the legal-technical requirements typical of that p.i.l. system.[281]

According to Schnitzer's formulation and subsequent development by Vischer,[282] any type of contract would be characterised by its performance,

---

277 During the Florence meeting 1908, *Annuaire de l' Institut de droit international, 5* (Edition nouvelle abrégée), 409-475, for which the applicable law in absence of choice by parties *'sera déduite de la nature du contrat, de la condition relative des parties ou de la situation de la chose'*.

278 *K. Lipstein*, "Characteristic performance – A new Concept in the conflict of laws in matters of contract for the EEC", in (1981) *Northwestern Journal of International Law & Business*, 405.

279 *A.F. Schnitzer, Handbuch des Internationalen Handels-Wechsel-und Checkrechts*, (Zürich-Leipzig, 1938), 203; *Ibid, Handbuch des internationalen Privatrechts*, (Vlg f Recht u Gesellschaft, Basel, 1958), 639; *Ibid*, 'Les contracts internationaux en droit international privè Suisse', in (1969) *Recueil des Courses de l'Académie de Droit International*, 579. According to whom "*En effet, la prestation qui caractérise le contrat vise la fonction du rapport juridique, voire du contrat, dans la vie économique ou sociale de l'homme*"; *Ibid*, 'Die Zuordnung der Vertrage im internationalen Privatrecht', in (1969) *RabelsZ*, 23. In line with the Author's opinion "*Die charakteristische Leistung einer jeden Vertragskategorie weist nämlich darauf hin, in welcher Sozialsphäre ein Vertagsverhaltnis jeweils verankert ist*".

280 *A.F. Schnitzer, Handbuch des Internationalen Privatrechts*, (Vlgf Recht u Gesellschaft, Basel, 1958), 643.

281 *A. Giardina*, "Volontà delle parti, prestazione caratteristica e collegamento più significativo", in T. Treves (ed.), *Verso una disciplina comunitaria della legge applicabile ai contratti*, (Cedam, Padova, 1983), 15-16. The Author assumes that the characteristic performace was used *"per rispondere ad esigenze tecnico-giuridiche tipiche del sistema internazionalprivatistico di quel Paese"*, because "[…] *una volta effettuata la distinzione tra validità del contratto ed i suoi effetti (grosse Spaltung), ma, soprattutto, una volta effettuata la distinzione fra le obbligazioni dei contraenti (kleine Spaltung), l'individuazione della prestazione tipica si rilevava necessaria al fine di sottoporre l'intero contratto ad una sola legge*".

282 *F. Vischer*, in his course for the *Hague Academy of international law Collected courses* (1974) seems to have diluted the theory of the typical performance with pragmatic fluids. While maintaining the demand that one law be selected to cover, in principle, the whole contract, the emphasis is shifted to combining a "private law approach which puts the interest of the individual in the first rank […] the social demands of the States involved". In line with the Author's opinion is applicable "in the social order of which the economically or socially most essential obligation is carried out". In this way see also *L. De Winter*, "Considerazione sulla legge della prestazione caratteristica", in (1971) *Diritto Internazionale*, 227 ss.

which would distinguish it from all other contracts. However, as we will see below,[283] it is not possible to identify the characteristic performance in all contracts. To specify Schnitzer's assessment, the characteristic performance should be the counter-performance of the payment of a sum of money, also called the "*typische Leistung*".[284] This factor should be inherent in every contract as it distinguishes one contract from another. These considerations are based on the concept that in modern economies, as a general rule, performance in exchange for a fee (monetary performance) always exists and, consequently, cannot be deemed a characteristic that distinguishes one contract from another. In this way, characteristic performance would thus coincide with the non-monetary nature (*Nicht-Geldleistung*) of the transaction, by means of which the interpreter can establish, for example, whether he is dealing with a sales or transport contract, etc.

Therefore, the interpreter, after localizing the transaction's characteristic performance, must identify the applicable law that does not coincide with the place of effective performance but rather with Schnitzer words, "*Schuldort des charakteristichen Leistung*",[285] i.e. the centre of activity of the debtor owing the specific characteristic performance.

As a result, the characteristic performance not only anchors the contract to a country where it expresses its economic and social function,[286] but also generates the practical advantage of simplifying the connection to the country whose law shall be applicable, thereby eliminating the problem of identifying the place where the contract has been negotiated or concluded.

The previous analysis suggests that this legal instrument, as the closest connection, values the task of the interpreter who is required to evaluate carefully all the circumstances of the contract for the purpose of recon-

---

283 See for example barter transactions, joint venture or exchange contracts *infra* § 3. IV.

284 *A. F. Schnitzer*, *Handbuch des internationalen Privatrechts*, (Vlgf Recht u Gesellschaft, Basel, 1958), vol 2, 644.

285 *Ibid*, 647. In line with the Author's opinion "*Schuldort*" should not be confused with the "*Erfüllungsort*", i.e. the place where, from the analysis of the will of the parties or the circumstances of the actual case, the provision must effectively be supplied, not with the "*Abschlussort*", i.e. the place where the contract was concluded. See also *U. Villani*, "Il ruolo della prestazione caratteristica dalla Convenzione di Roma al regolamento Roma I", in (2010) 3 *Studi sull'integrazione europea*, 580, who suggests "*con la sede del debitore della stessa prestazione*".

286 *A. F. Schnitzer*, *Handbuch des internationalen Privatrechts*, (Vlgf Recht u Gesellschaft, Basel, 1958), vol. 2, 645. According to Schnitzer "*Die Obligation ist vielmehr dort innerlich verankert, wo sie eine Funktion im Dasein der Menscheit ausübt*".

structing the "identity" of the contract in order to localize the applicable law.

3.I.B *The "escape clause"*

The flexibility of the Rome Convention instruments and therefore the central role of the interpreter are also corroborated by the presence of an "escape clause"[287] in Article 4 (5), according to which "if the characteristic performance cannot be determined" or "if it appears from the circumstances as a whole that the contract is more closely connected with another country",[288] the law of the country with the closest connection to the contract shall apply. As a consequence, quite often the concept of characteristic performance is abandoned, in particular when the intricacy of a transaction's contractual ties produces a complex contract[289] for which it is difficult to identify the characteristic performance.[290] In these cases, as I will ex-

287 In GIULIANO – LAGARDE Report not was called as an exception clause contrary. For more on this topic, that was done for the first time by Swiss legislator in Article 15 (1) of the Federal Statute of 1987 on private international law, see *ex multis D. Kokkini-Iatridou, Les Clauses d' Exception en matière de Conflits de Lois et de Conflits de Juridictions – ou le principe de proximité*, (Martinus Nijhoff Publishers, Dordrecht/Boston/London, 1994), 15 - 20; *J. O'Brien*, *Conflict of Laws*, (Cavendish Publishing Limited, London, 1999), 345 according to whom this clause "might be used by English courts to continue the common law approach of seeking the objective law of the contract". For more on this clause see *C.E. Dubler*, *Les clauses d'exception en droit international privé*, (Genf, Genève, 1983), *passim*; *K.H. Nadelmann*, 'Choice of Law Resolved by Rules or Presumptions with an Escape Clause', in (1985) *American Journal of International Law*, 297 – 309; *F. Mosconi*, 'Exceptions to the Operation of Choice of Law Rules', in (1989) *Recueil des Cours 217*, 188 ss.; *C. Campiglio*, 'Prime Applicazioni della Clausola d' Eccezione 'europea' in materia contrattuale', in (1992) *Rivista di diritto internazionale privato e processuale*, 241 – 254; *D. Kokkini–Iatridou*, *Le Clauses d' Exception en mateère de Conflits de Lois et de Juridictions – ou le principe de proximité*, (Martinus Nijhoff Publishers, Dordrecht/Boston/London, 1994), 10 – 29.

288 Article 4 (5) of the Rome Convention.

289 For example, in barter or exchange transactions. See for more *infra* § 3. IV.

290 *Court of Appeal Civil Division*, April 27, 2005, *PT Pan Indonesia Bank Ltd TBK v Marconi Communications International Ltd* [2005], which examined the problem of the applicable law to a credit letter issued by a bank with registered address in a different State respect to the confirming bank and payable in a further State where the beneficiary had his business address. The Court attached importance to the closest connection between the letters of credit issued and confirmed by the banks, placing the emphasis on the obligation upon the beneficiary and

pand upon below, the escape clause can be applied when the contract is more closely connected with another country.

In this context, it is easy to understand that this "*clause d'exception*" was created for the intention of addressing these deficiencies filling any gaps of a rule which, by its nature, is not adaptable to all types of contract and, as a result, can never be perfect. In fact, some scholars assume that the escape clause could be defined as:

> "a provision inserted in a legal instrument to supplement or cure the defect in the main rule, especially where the main rule has little or no connection with the issue to be resolved before the court. *This instrument* [...] honour[s] the claim that no legal instrument is perfect *and* [...] this feature in an escape clause makes it deserving of special attention".[291]

By adding this type of clause, the framers of the Rome Convention deemed it necessary to provide greater flexibility in the interpretation of Article 4 thereby facilitating an easier verification of the country with the closest connection to the contract whilst at the same time attributing greater value to the role of the interpreter in the task of identifying the most equitable law.

However, the "escape clause" has been widely criticized in regard to its excessive use and, in light of the above-mentioned considerations, it might appear that this clause can be applied only in certain circumstances. Moreover, considering that not all the escapes are born equal,[292] all scholars admit to the easy application of the escape clause.[293] These issues have opened one of the most bitter p.i.l. debates of recent years and have given life to a number of different opinions which can be divided as follows:

---

finding in favour for application of the law of the State in which the latter would have had to request the payment. For more see http://westminsterresearch.wmin.ac.uk/4730/.

291 In these words, *C. S A. Okoli - G. O. Arishe*, "The Operation of the escape clauses in the Rome Convention, Rome I regulation and Rome II Regulation", in (2012) *Journal of Private International Law*, 513.

292 In this regard *S. C. Symeonides*, *Codifying Choice of Law Around the World*, (O.U.P., Oxford, 2014), 201.

293 *Ibid*, 190. According to the Author "[...] it is an open question whether escape clauses are a bolder step toward flexibility than rules containing flexible connecting factors [...], much depends on the language, number, and especially the breadth of the escape clauses".

Weaker presumption approach

The first approach, defined as the "*weaker presumption approach*", is supported by those academics[294] for whom the clause was inserted within the Convention for the purpose of compelling the interpreter to study all the circumstances of the case more carefully in order to apply the law closest to the contract.[295] In particular, the English courts have identified specific connection factors that the interpreter can take into consideration, thus dismissing the characteristic performance rule: the country's currency of payment; the place of negotiation or conclusion of the contract; the place of residence of the parties and object of the contract; the place of payment in disregarding the presumptions;[296] etc.

In this sense, the supporters of this legal doctrine have shown their endorsement by stating that the Convention made the escape clause "a strong tool in addressing choice of law problems in commercial transactions by flexiblity locating the law that is most closely connected to the contract in question".[297] North,[298] who is one of the most important supporters of this theory, observes that "they are not likely significantly to affect the determi-

---

294 Labelled as English and French approach. See for more *S. Atrill*, "Choice of law in contract: The missing pieces of the article 4 Jigsaw?", in (2004) *International and Comparative Law Quarterly*, 549 ss. The Author talks about a "wider considerations" than presumed intention of the parties.

295 In doctrine see *U. Villani*, *Il ruolo della prestazione caratteristica dalla Convenzione di Roma al regolamento "Roma I"*, in (2010) 3 *Studi sull'integrazione europea*, 587. In line with the Author's opinion "*Le indicazioni relative, rispettivamente, alla prestazione caratteristica e alle circostanze che colleghino il contratto con un Paese diverso si pongono, a nostro avviso, su due binari distinti: la prima riguarda il tipo contrattuale, la categoria astratta; la seconda, al contrario, concerne il concreto, specifico contratto, il quale viene in rilievo con tutte le sue particolari circostanze. Il par. 5, pertanto, non va visto come una clausola eccezionale rispetto ad una presunta regola generale risultante dalla prestazione caratteristica, ma piuttosto come espressione della esigenza di calare nel concreto la valutazione dei collegamenti che il contratto presenta con uno o più Paesi*".

296 In these words, *C. S. A. Okoli - G. O. Arishe*, "The Operation of the escape clauses in the Rome Convention, Rome I regulation and Rome II Regulation", in (2012) 8 *Journal of Private International Law*, 518. The Authors mentioned cases as *Definitely Maybe v. Marek Lieberberg*; *Samcrete Egypt Engineers v. Land Rover Exports Limited*; *Opthalmic Innovations Limited (U.K.) v. Opthalmic Innovations International Incorporated (U.S.A.)*.

297 In these words, *Ibid*, 518.

298 In these words, *P.M. North*, "Contract conflicts: the E.E.C. Convention on the Law Applicable to Contractual Obligations: a comparative study", (North-Holland Pub. Co., Amsterdam/New York/ Oxford, 1982), 22.

nation of the law applicable in any particular case". Continuing, in reference to the presumptions, he rightly points out:

> "The more certainty you have, the less flexibility there will be in the general rule and common lawyers have traditionally seen great merit in flexibility and little virtue in presumptions. So it is not surprising that the other element of compromise in the use of presumptions is that they are rebuttable, thereby of course diminishing a good deal of the certainty which they would appear to provide".

What is more, this approach, which commends the interpreter's task allowing him to apply the most equitable law, has been strongly criticized because, as has been claimed, it would undermine legal certainty and allow excessive discretionary powers,[299] which, as a consequence, may lead to unpredictability and lack of uniformity of the decisions.

Strong presumption approach

In contrast to the "weaker presumption approach" is the theory called the "strong presumption approach",[300] according to which the "escape clause" of Article 4 (5) constitutes a mere exception.[301] In particular, the supporters of this doctrine maintain that providing certainty and uniformity in de-

---

299 *P.A. De Miguel Asensio*, "Applicable law in absence of choice to contracts relating to intellectual or industrial property rights", in (2008) *Yearbook of Private International Law*, 203.

300 Labelled also as Dutch, Italian and Scottish approach. For more about Italian doctrine see *U. Villani*, "Aspetti problematici della prestazione caratteristica", in (1993) *Rivista di diritto Internazionale Privato e Processuale*, 534 or also *O. Lopes Pegna*, "Il Rilievo del collegamento più stretto dalla Convenzione di Roma alla Proposta di Regolamento 'Roma I'", in (2006) *Rivista di Diritto Internazionale*, 771.

301 See also cases like *Hoge Raad Société Nouvele dea Papéteries de l' Aa v. Machinefabriek BOA*, September 25, 1992, with reflections of *T.H.D. Struycken*, "Some Dutch Judicial Reflections on the Rome Convention, art. 4 (5)", in (1996) *Lloyd's maritime and commercial law quarterly*, 18 – 24. According to the Author "Both the uniformity of result in similar cases and the predictability of the law that will govern a contractual relationship are enhanced by such a general use of the presumptions. A wide use of the rebuttal clause would reduce the value of a conflicts rule based on presumptions, a danger against which several commentators have warned".

termining the applicable law, in absence of choice, is inherent to the aim of Article 4.[302]

In light of these considerations, the courts should apply the escape clause only in specific circumstances, such as, when there is an absence of the characteristic performance in the contract or when the choice of the characteristic performer is "*inapropiada*".[303] Thus, the "strong presumption approach" not only gives life to total rigidity and lack of adaptability in providing solutions for conflicts of laws in a constantly evolving international market[304] but it also "demeans" the crucial task of the interpreter in his effort to identify the law that has the closest connection with the contract.

The conclusion reached by the extreme supporters of this doctrine[305] thus is the elimination of the escape clause altogether.

It is my contention that this theory can be criticized, given that from a detailed analysis of Article 4 of the Rome Convention it is clear that the "escape clause" must not be deciphered as the *extrema ratio* to which the interpreter must adhere if he/she has not found different points of contact with other countries. On the contrary, on the basis of the flexibility that characterizes the Rome Convention, it must be qualified as the clause that the interpreter shall use in order to apply the most equitable law in cases where the contract appears to have more important points of contact with other legal systems.[306]

---

302 *C. S. A. Okoli - G. O. Arishe*, "The Operation of the escape clauses in the Rome Convention, Rome I Regulation and Rome II Regulation", in (2012) *Journal of Private International Law*, 518. The Authors have mentioned cases like *Societé Nuovelle des Papeteries de l' AA SA v. BV Machinefabriek BOA*; *Caledonia Subsea Ltd v. Microperi S.r.l;* See also *O. Lopes Pegna*, "Il Rilievo del collegamento più stretto dalla Convenzione di Roma alla Proposta di Regolamento 'Roma I'", in (2006) *Rivista di Diritto Internazionale*, 771, according to which "*sarebbero preferibili quelle interpretazioni delle disposizioni della Convenzione che, in ossequio al principio dell' effetto 'utile', risultano maggiormente funzionali ad una applicazione uniforme dei criteri di collegamento e quindi al perseguimento di una maggiore prevedibilità e certezza del diritto applicabile*".

303 *W. F. Martínez Luna*, "El articulo 4.3 del Reglamento Roma I. Una verdadera clàusola de excepciòn", in (2012) *Revista Electrònica de Estudios Internacionales*, 14.

304 *Ibid*, 15.

305 *O. Lopes Pegna*, "Il Rilievo del collegamento più stretto dalla Convenzione di Roma alla Proposta di Regolamento 'Roma I'", in (2006) *Rivista di Diritto Internazionale*, 774.

306 For more on the national courts that have tended to favour this interpretation see *P. A. De Miguel Asensio*, "Applicable Law in the Absence of Choice to Con-

Theory of Commercial Expectations

Alongside these two discordant schools of thought, a third one emerges which has been developed in recent years: the so-called "Theory of Commercial Expectations" supported by Fentiman. This approach starts with the assumption that the main purpose of Article 4 of the Convention is to identify "the commercial gravity of a contract". Fentiman takes an inclusive approach which looks into the socioeconomic function of the contract and considers it not a "mere accumulation of connection factors" or "an arithmetical preponderance of elements" or "simply a matter of judicial intuition".[307]

In this regard, Fentiman notably assumes that the escape clause in Article 4 (5) is

> "intended to capture a contract's commercial context and presumably thereby to ensure its commercial effectiveness. [...] The animating principle is that the significance of the relevant connecting factors should be assessed in commercial terms".[308]

Based on this concept, Fentiman[309] disregarding the presumptions regulated by Article 4 of the Convention states:

> "the Article 4 (2) presumption is not universal. By Article 4 (4) the Article 4 (2) presumption does not apply to contracts for the carriage of goods. Such contracts are presumed to be most closely connected with the country in which, at the time of contracting, the carrier has his principal place of business, where that country is also the country of loading, or of discharge, or the country where the consignor's principal place of business is situated. In some cases the Article 4 (2) presumption does not determine the contractual law". [...] "The obligation characteristic of a contract between bank and consumer is the provision of banking services; that between a confirming bank and beneficiary pursuant to a letter of credit is the payment of money; and under

---

tract Relating to Intellectual or Industrial Property Rights", in (2008) *Yearbook of Private International Law*, footnote nr. 13. In particular the Author makes deals with Dutch and German decisions.

307 *C. S. A. Okoli - G. O. Arishe*, "The Operation of the escape clauses in the Rome Convention, Rome I regulation and Rome II Regulation", in (2012) *Journal of Private International Law*, 521, have rewritten the Fentimans words.

308 *R. Fentiman*, *International Commercial Litigation*, (O.U.P., Oxford, 2010), 216.

309 *Ibid*, 210.

a contract of guarantee, there is no room for doubt that obligation characteristic of the performance is the payment of money by the guarantor".[310]

Certainly, this is a pragmatic approach which appears to be based only on commercial expectations[311] the identification of which requires a careful examination of all the circumstances by the court committed to identifying the applicable law on "commercial gravity of a contract". As a consequence, the court takes on the central role of identifying the applicable law on the basis of the commercial and economic characteristics of the contract.

In conclusion, on the basis of the foregoing pages, it is reasonable to conclude that the flexibility that characterizes the Rome Convention, rooted in the US experience,[312] suggests that the "weaker presumption approach" should characterize the escape clause of Article 4 (5). However, the implications of this flexibility are twofold. While on one hand it enhances legal congruence and the task of interpreter in his/her endeavour of identifying the most equitable law, on the other hand, according to the framers of the Rome I Regulation, this flexibility would undermine legal certainty, with the consequence that the uniformity of decisions may not be guaranteed. In fact, according to the Rome I Recital,[313] the uncertainty of the applicable law would contrast with a need of a properly functioning internal market and represents the main criticisms of the flexibility of the Convention.

I believe that these severe criticisms to the flexible approach adopted by the Convention must be supported by statistical data or field studies that demonstrate not only that rigid rules guarantee uniformity of decisions, but most importantly that the lack of uniformity of decisions, compounded by the limits to the courts' discretionary power, in identifying the applicable law, creates substantial prejudices to the internal market. These issues, which, as will be seen, have led to drastic changes in the system of EU p.i.l. of contractual obligations, remain largely uncharted. There seem to

---

310 *Ibid*, 211.

311 *C. S. A. Okoli - G. O. Arishe*, "The Operation of the escape clauses in the Rome Convention, Rome I regulation and Rome II Regulation", in (2012) *Journal of Private International Law*, 522.

312 See *infra* § 3.II

313 Recital 6 of Regulation (EC) 593/2008 of the European Parliament and of the Council, of June 17, 2008 on the law applicable to contractual obligations (Rome I) [2008] OJ L177/6.

be only two certainties. Firstly, the criteria adopted by the Rome Convention lawmakers have been used as a model in other legal situations, as in the following cases of Article 117 of Swiss Federal law; Article 126 of the law on Venezuelan private international law; Article 3112 of the civil code of Quebec; Article 26 in the law on conflicts of the Republic of Korea of 2001;[314] Article 1211 of the Russian civil code of 2001;[315] and contract laws of 1999 Chinese private international law.[316] In addition the approach taken by the Rome Convention, with the enhancement of the closest connection principle, was also incorporated in its entirety by the Mexico Convention.[317] Secondly, flexible criteria, similar to those of the Convention, have been used in the largest trade market in the world - that is the USA.[318] The reasons for this choice are not only rational but also economic.

Lastly, a criticism of the rigid criteria of p.i.l. may even result in censure of theories similar to Fentiman's regarding of the "commercial expectations" of Article 4. However this theory that invites the interpreter to look

---

314 *U. Villani*, "La legge applicabile in mancanza di scelta tra vecchia e nuova disciplina", in (2007) *Quaderni della fondazione italiana del notariato*, in http://elibrar y.fondazionenotariato.it .

315 *M. R. Badykov*, "The Russian Civil Code and the Rome Convention: Applicable Law in the Absence of Choice by the Parties", in (2005) *Journal of Private International Law*, 269 – 289.

316 *Y. Shunhong - X. Yongping - W. Baoshi*, "The Closest Connection Doctrine in the Conflict of Laws in China", in (2009) *Chinese Journal of International Law*, 423 – 439.

317 In particular art. 9 of the Convention held: "(1) if the parties have not selected the applicable law, or if their selection proves ineffective, the contract shall be governed by the law of the State with which it has the closest ties. (2) The Court will take into account all objective and subjective elements of the contract to determine the law of the State with which it has the closest ties. It shall also take into account the general principles of international commercial law recognized by international organizations". See *J. A. Moreno Rodriguez – M. Mercedes Albornoz*, "Reflections on the Mexico Convention in the Context of the Preparation of the Future Hague Instrument on International Contracts", in (2011) *Journal of Private International Law*, 516.

318 *I. A. Caggiano*, "L'uniformazione del diritto contrattuale europeo. American and European Perspectives", in (2013) *Contratto e Impresa / Europa*, 26. The Author also focuses on the aspects that differentiate the legal integration in the United States and points out that these adopt a flexible p.i.l. approach, despite having a common language and a unified training of lawyers in the various federal States.

for the "gravity of a commercial contract" with an economic solution,[319] contrary to the hard-and-fast rules[320] which prevent the court from comprehending the complexity of economic reality and which, I believe, will lead to decisions lacking in equity, detracting focus from the reasons of the transaction.

Notably, almost as if they had been unsuccessful and without a justified reason, the flexible criteria of the Convention, as will be seen below, have been replaced by strict and "untidy"[321] criteria in the Rome I Regulation.

3.II The USA influence

The analysis of the Rome Convention has shown that it operates a flexible approach that enhances the role of the interpreter in order that he/she may find the most equitable law without creating prejudice to the contractual parties.

I do not want to give a definitive explanation of the reasons behind the flexible approach of the Rome Convention, but in this context, it is important to recognize that this "softening process" has its roots in B. Currie's US theory of "datum". According to this theory, the judge has a duty to know not only the law of the forum but also foreign law.[322] In reference to the latter, the court must verify whether or not that law is a mere fact or supplies a datum "which will be relevant in the application of the rule of decision".[323] This theory has been strengthened by the notion of "moral"

---

319 *C. S. A. Okoli - G. O. Arishe*, "The Operation of the escape clauses in the Rome Convention, Rome I regulation and Rome II Regulation", in (2012) *Journal of Private International Law*, 522.

320 See for more § 3.III.

321 *A. Briggs, Private International Law in English Courts*, (O.U.P., Oxford, 2014), 510.

322 *B. Currie*, "On the Displacement of the Law of the Forum", in (1958) *Columbia Law Review*, 983. Before Currie it was Pasquale Stanislao Mancini that used as p.i.l. instrument the so called "*Principio della nazionalità*". According to E. Jayme, a deep scholar of Mancini thinking "*Lo strumento tecnico era costituito dalla norma bilaterale di diritto internazionale privato che utilizzava lo stesso collegamento per i cittadini e per gli stranieri. Per ciascuna persona doveva valere* [...] *la sua legge nazionale*", continuing "*Mancini cercava di determinare la nazionalità precisando alcuni elementi o fatti costanti: La religione, la razza, la lingua, le costumanze, la storia, le leggi, e le religioni*". In these words *E. Jayme*, *Internationales Privatrecht: Ideengeschichte von Mancini und Ehrenzweig zum Europäischen Kollisionsrecht*, (C.F. Muller, Heidelberg, 2009), 95 and 98.

323 *B. Currie*, "On the Displacement of the Law of the Forum", in (1958) *Columbia Law Review*, 1022. For a modern critical approach to B. Currie theory's see *K.*

and "local" data defined by Ehrenzweig. Practically, in line with the "moral" data that are phrased in terms of justice and equity, "the forum law is automatically applied (typically without discussion), notwithstanding the presence of foreign elements which otherwise, under accepted rules of choice, would call for the application of a foreign rule".[324] At the same time the "local" data represent the "awareness of the application, in certain cases, of foreign rules as data of the domestic rule rather than as foreign rules of decision".[325] In light of these considerations, it is clear that these theories place the interpreter at the heart of the choice of the applicable law and that, in the judicial analysis, he/she can be influenced by the datum concept.

Undoubtedly, under the significant influence of these theories, the "softening process" was reinforced by the "conflict of laws revolution" started in the United States (1970s).[326] This "revolution" which could be defined as a "theory revolution", has the merit of resolving doubts over the law regulating the contract, not by rigid criteria of p.i.l. rules but by flexible criteria that dictate that the court examine each individual case carefully.[327] As a consequence, the US revolution has been credited for highlighting that the rules of p.i.l. should not be mechanical or neutral because themselves engage with a variety of "policy considerations".[328]

The most important pioneers of this "theory revolution" were Cavers and D.P. Currie.[329] According to former's theory of "better law or better rule", the interpreter should follow the "result selective method" - i.e., through the weight or assessment of the facts,[330] identify the law that ac-

---

Roosevelt, "Brainerd Currie's Contribution to Choice of Law: Looking Back, Looking Forward", in (2014) *Mercer Law Review*, 501 ss.

324 With these words *A.A. Ehrenzweig*, "Local and Moral Data in the Conflict of Laws: Terra Incognita", in (1966) *Buffalo Law Review*, 56.

325 *Ibid*, 57.

326 As see the data's theory was born in US then has been adopted in Germany.

327 For a comprehensive overview on the American Private International Law theories see *R. Banu*, *Nineteenth-Century Perspectives on Private International Law*, (O.U.P., Oxford, 2018), 155. In particular, the Author, with reference to Currie and Caver's theory, argues that these theories have given life to "a more flexible approach with an eye to the interests and claims to justice of the parties".

328 *A. Mills*, "The Identities of Private International Law: Lessons from the U.S. and EU revolutions", in (2013) *Duke Journal of Comparative & International Law*, 466.

329 This theory, which radically changed the rules of US private international law, follows minor schools of thought such as that of "grouping or weighting of contracts theory" of the Willis Reese.

330 *R. Banu*, *Nineteenth-Century Perspectives on Private International Law*, (O.U.P., Oxford, 2018), 152.

cording to reasons of justice and "social opportunity" appears preferable.[331] Therefore, depending on the circumstances of the case, the judge must choose from the different sets of laws those which best regulate the question connected to the relationship.[332] In particular, the court should be compelled to consider the intensity of the connection, conferring crucial value to the procedure with which the question is regulated in said legislations, upholding, the law that is more suitable to the relationship and the times.[333]

In a similar way, D.P. Currie, according to whom the "governmental interest theory" is necessary, claims the following as a consequence:

> "(i) Even where the parties have chosen a state as the source of law to govern their contract, § 332° (c) may require the forum to determine the state which, absent such a choice, would have had the most significant relationship with the contract since no 'fundamental policy' of that state may be overridden by the law chosen by the parties. (ii) In any case involving one of the particular contracts covered by Title B, a party may contend that a state indicated by the relevant section has in fact a 'more significant relationship' with the contract. (iii) Finally, there remains a residual category of cases: those in which the parties have not made an effective choice, the contract is not one of Title B's eleven types, and the places of contracting and performance do not coincide. For this residual category, the black letter of § 332b simply directs the court to consider 'additional factors' in determining the state of most significant relationship, and Comment b list these factors in terms of the traditional 'contacts' – place of contracting, performance, domicil, etc. – departing from jurisdiction-selecting criteria explicitly in only one instance: the fact that the law of a state upholds a contract will overcome all but 'a considerable majority of the important contacts' ".[334]

331 *D.F. Cavers*, "The Two Local Law Theories", in (1950) *Harvard Law Review*, 822 ss.; *Ibid*, *The choice of law Process*, (Ann Arbor, University of Michigan Press, 1965), *passim*; *Ibid*, *The Choice of Law – Selected essay – 1933 – 1983*, (Duke University Press, Durham, 1985), *passim*.

332 *R. De Nova*, "Le concezioni statunitensi dei conflitti di leggi viste da un continentale", in *Scritti di diritto internazionale privato*, (Cedam, Padova, 1977), 653.

333 *Ibid*, 655.

334 In these words, *L. Kramer - D.P. Currie - H. Kay*, *Conflict of Laws*, (West Publishing Company, St. Paul, Minn, 1976), 66 – 67.

On the basis of these theories the Restatement (Second) of Conflict of Laws, characterised by indeterminacy, flexibility and a multi-faceted nature,[335] outlines in § 6 that the goal of the choice-of-law process is to identify the State that has the "most significant relationship". This condition is confirmed by subsequent sections of the Restatement, which contain specific rules that can be defined in modern terms as an "escape clause",[336] whereby the judge is authorized, under the principles stated in § 6, to apply the law of another State if there is a "most significant relationship".[337] Finally, in the absence of a choice, § 188 provides guidance and in so doing achieves a perfect equilibrium between certainty and flexibility,[338] producing a list of relevant factors that the court must take into consideration viz:

(a) the place of contracting;
(b) the place where the contract is negotiated;
(c) the place of performance;
(d) the location of the subject matter of the contract, and
(e) the domicile, residence, nationality, place of incorporation and place of business of the parties.[339]

The reasons that led to the predicted soft approach of the US and the conflict of laws revolution cannot be summed up in a few lines. Certainly, improved logic, the need to dispense justice by applying good law,[340] the expansion of economic efficiency, and the will to foster international uniformity[341] are the principal reasons. At the same time, the Restatement reflects, as Symeonides has notoriously argued, "a typical American scepticism toward categorical a priori rules and a high degree of confidence in the court's ability to develop appropriate colutions on a case-by-case basis".[342]

---

335 *K. Roosevelt*, *Conflict of Laws*, (Foundation Press, New York, 2010), 85 ss.; *C. R. Calleros*, "Toward Harmonisation and Certainty in Choice-of-Law Rules for International Contracts: Should the US Adopt the Equivalent of Rome I?", in (2011) *Wisconsin International Law Journal*, 671.

336 See *infra* § 2.3.

337 American Law Institute, Restatement (Second) of Conflict of Laws, § 146.

338 *A. Reed*, "The Rome I Regulation and Rapprochement of Anglo American Choice of Law in Contract: a Heralded Triumph of Pragmatism Over Theory", in (2011) *Florida Journal of International Law*, 398.

339 See Restatement (Second) of Conflict of Laws, § 188.

340 *R. Leflar – L. Mc. Dougal – R. Felix*, *Cases and Material on American Conflicts Law*, (The Michie Company Law Publishers, Virginia, 1982), 4.

341 *S. C. Symeonides*, *Codifying Choice of Law Around the World*, (O.U.P., Oxford, 2014), 209.

342 *Ibid*, 164.

In light of this overview of the developments of p.i.l. in US it could be true to say that the Rome Convention was influenced[343] by the flexible criteria of the American Conflicts of Laws Revolution.[344] In fact, the Convention, in particular Article 4, differs completely from the *Rapporteur* Giuliano,[345] which clearly adopted the solution of rigid criteria,[346] and which has already been judged negative in Danish doctrine by Lando,[347] in Italian doctrine by Vitta,[348] and in Belgian doctrine by Hanotiau and Jenard.[349]

343 *P. Hay*, "European Conflict of Laws After the American "Revolution"-Comparative Notes", in (2015) *University of Illinois Law Review*, 2053; *F. K. Juenger*, 'The European Convention on the Law Applicable to contractual obligations', in (1981) *Virginia Journal of International Law*, 130–135 states "The key concept used by the European draftsmen, 'the closest connection', mirrors the 'most significant relationship' idea of the Second Restatement and [...] not only resembles the Second Restatement, but it also contains a number of other 'American' ideas". Within these 'ideas' can also be included the theory of 'data', inserted in Articles 3 (3) and 10 (2) of the Rome Convention.

344 For a critical approach on the American conflicts of law Revolution see *S. C. Symeonides*, "The Judicial Acceptance of the Second Conflicts Restatement: A Mixed Blessing", in (2012) 56 *Maryland Law Review*, 1249 – 1282.

345 *M. Magagni*, *La prestazione caratteristica nella Convenzione di Roma del 19 giugno 1980*, (Giuffrè, Milano, 1989), 45–46 which rewrote the exact wording of the *Rapporteur Giuliano "le lieu d'exécution des obligations issues d'un contrat synallagmatique est le lieu où la prestation la plus caractéristique en nature a été ou droit être exécutée.* [...] *lorsque la détermination du lieu de son exécution est impossible, le contrat est régi par la loi du lieu où il a été conclu.* [...] *dans les contrats conclus par correspondance entre personnes se trouvant dans des Etats différents, il est fait application de la loi du lieu d'où l'offre initiale est partie*'.

346 The document outlines "*le contrat est régi* [...] *par la loi du lieu de son exécution*" but this rule was applied only in the absence of particular contracts, such as a) the buying and selling of corporate property; b) transfer agreements and the sales of goods by auction; c) property contracts; d) banking contracts; e) loan agreements; f) insurance contracts.

347 *O. Lando*, "The E.C. Draft Convention on the Law applicable to contractual and non-contractual obligations", in (1974) *RabelsZ*, 6 - 55.

348 *E. Vitta*, "Influenze americane nella Convenzione CEE sulle obbligazioni contrattuali", in (1983) *Rivista diritto internazionale privato e processuale*, 261 - 278.

349 *B. Hanotiau - P. Jenard*, "Les clauses relatives au contrat dans l'avant-projet de Convention C.E.E. sur la loi applicable aux obligations contractuelles et non contractuelles", in *Le contrat économique international*, (Bruylant, Bruxelles, 1975), 41.

3.II.A Forthcoming Third Restatement of Conflict of Laws

Almost half a century after the Second Restatement of Conflict of Laws, the American Law Institute (ALI) is now engaged in its revision[350] with the intention of adapting it to the "international age".[351]

Although, as seen, the Second Restatement has been selected as an example[352] by other lawmakers, some academics have criticised its lacks of clarity and theory for decades. They heighlight the lack of detail about what exactly it means for a state to have the most significant relationship to an issue and about why that should lead to the selection of the applicable law.[353]

However, a central point is that p.i.l. in the new era of globalisation has an international dimension and a direct impact on economics. As a consequence, all legislators around the world will carefully follow the developments of the Third Restatement.

Without the presumption of being able to advise the distinguished scholars that make up the Participants in the Commitee of the Third Restatement, I believe it may be appropriate, before drafting p.i.l. rules of contractual obligations, to focus on the economic theories previously analysed as well as on the effects of the Rome I Regulation's rigid rules.[354] From the perspective just outlined, it is clear that the Third Restatement certainly represents an important occasion to create a clear economic theory of conflict of laws, as well as a norm that can be seriously taken into consideration by all lawmakers.

I suggest that the Third Restatement should ask the interpreter to determine the scope of the transaction and, as a consequence, draft a norm that allows the court to decide any issue, focusing on the social[355] and economic consequences that are likely to follow from that decision. Finally, I re-

---

350 To follow the work in progress is available at https://www.ali.org/projects/show/conflict-laws/.

351 In these words, *M. Reimann*, *"A New Restatement-Forthe InternationalAg"*, in (2000) 75 *Indiana Law Journal*, 575.

352 See *supra* § 3.I.

353 See *ex multis L. Kramer*, "Rethinking Choice of Law", in (1990) *Columbia Law Review*, 277, 321; *K. Roosevelt – B. Jones*, "Symposium on the Third Restatement of Conflict of Laws what a Third Restatement of Conflict of Laws can do", in (2016) *American Journal of International Law*, 139.

354 See *infra* § 3.IV.

355 See also *supra* "tentative conclusion" and on this topic also *R.J. Weintraub*, "The Restatement Third of Conflicts of Law. An Idea that the time has not come", in (2000) *Indiana Law Journal*, 682.

commend creating a norm that, at the same time, can guarantee a right to protection for weaker parties, such as employees and consumers, that also are important market players.

3.III. Analysis of the Rome I Regulation

The "communitarisation of private international law"[356] started a new phase with the implementation of the Rome I Regulation. In fact, as is known, after six years taken up with various phases of consultations and political debates, the Rome Convention was finally restructured into an EU instrument.[357] In particular the conversion of the Rome Convention into an EU Regulation has been proposed by a Green Paper of 2003[358] and by the Proposal presented by the European Commission in 2005.[359]

This conversion is of considerable importance not only from a practical point of view, but also because it represents an important signal about the intentions of EU bodies in terms of p.i.l. in contractual matter. In fact, the reasons behind this "revolution" are highlighted in the Rome I Regulation Recital, according to which

356 See for more *H. Ofner*, "Rom I, editorial", in (2009) *ZfRV*, 34; *J. Basedow*, "The communitarisation of conflict of laws under the Treaty of Amsterdam", in (2000) *Common Market Law Review*, 687-708.

357 The Rome I will be applied in all the EU countries except Denmark where its predecessor, the Rome Convention is still applicable.

358 See Commission "Green Paper on the Conversion of the Rome Convention of 1980 on the law applicable to contractual obligations into a Community instrument and its modernization", COM (2002) 654 final enter January 14, 2003. The European Commission maintains an extensive list of replies to this Green Paper. For some comments to this paper see *A. Bonomi*, "Conversion of the Rome Convention on contracts into an EC Instrument: Some remarks on the Green Paper of the EC Commission", in (2003) *Yearbook of Private International Law*, 53.

359 Proposal of the Commission of December 15, 2005 (COM (2005) 650 final). For an analysis of the Proposal, see *ex multis C. Kessedjian*, "Party autonomy and characteristic performance in the Rome Convention and the Roma I Proposal", in J. Basedow - H. Baum - Y. Nishitani (eds.), *Japanese and European Private International Law in Comparative Perspective* (Mohr Siebeck, Tübingen, 2008), 123; *A. Bonomi*, "The Rome I Regulation on the law applicable to contractual obligations. Some General Remarks", in (2008) *Yearbook of Private International Law*, 165; *K. Boele-Woelki*, "Where Do We Stand on the Rome I Regulation?", in K. Boele-Woelki - F. Grosheide (eds.), *The Future of European Contract Law*, (Kluwer Law International, Alphen aan den Rijn, 2007), 19 - 41.

> "*The proper functioning of the internal market* creates a need in order to improve the *predictability* of the outcome of litigation, *certainty* as to the law applicable and the free movement of judgments, for the conflict-of-law rules in the Member States to designate the same national law irrespective of the country of the court in which an action is brought".[360]
>
> "To contribute to the general objective of this Regulation, *legal certainty* in the European judicial area, the conflict-of-law rules should be highly foreseeable. The courts should, however, retain a degree of discretion to determine the law that is most closely connected to the situation".[361]

To summarise, in order to ensure predictability and legal certainty, the flexible rules of the Rome Convention, which in absence of partie's choice confer on the interpreter the discretionary power to apply the most equitable law, have been changed to hard-and-fast rules. In particular, these changes are made up of the following: a complete revision of the choice of rules regarding the applicable law in the absence of choice (Article 4); new provisions on transports of carriage; insurance and voluntary assignment (Articles 5, 7 and 14); different and stronger protection regarding consumer contracts (Article 6) and employment contracts (Article 8).

Unquestionably, Article 4 of Rome I includes one of the major changes. In general, certain presumptions inserted in Article 4 (3) of the Convention, became a "rule"[362] in a new Article 4 (1). In fact Rome I presents a list of contracts[363] in relation to which it expressly specifies the applicable law.

In particular, the new Article 4 establishes the applicable law in a series of steps:

Firstly, hard-and-fast rules have been established in order to determine the applicable law in eight categories of contracts, namely contracts for the sale of goods, contracts for the provision of service, contracts relating to a

---

360 Recital § 6 of Regulation (EC) 593/2008 of the European Parliament and of the Council, of June 17, 2008 on the law applicable to contractual obligations (Rome I) [2008] OJ L177/6.

361 *Ibid*, Recital § 16.

362 *P. R. Beaumont - P.E. McEleavy*, *Private International Law*, (Thomson Reuters, Edinburg, 2011), 553.

363 A similar list can be found in article 117 (3) Swiss Act on Private International Law although also in § 12 *RAG Rechtsanwendungsgesetz* – Act on the application of law of the former German Democratic Republic and also in the former Private International Law Acts of other formerly Socialist countries. The Swiss PIL is available at http://www.umbricht.ch/pdf/SwissPIL.pdf.

right *in rem*, or to a tenancy of immovable property, contracts relating to a temporary tenancy of immovable property, franchise contracts, distribution contracts, contracts for the sale of goods by auction, and finally, contracts with subject financial instruments. Secondly, for contracts not appearing in this list, the law applicable to contractual obligation has to be identified on the basis of the principles of the closest connection and characteristic performance. Therefore, the general p.i.l. tools of the Convention have been downgraded by a new catalogue of rules for several categories of contracts based on rigid connecting factors.

This new approach seems to be designed in order to presumably ensure legal certainty, and, at the same time, to ensure an improved high level of predictability,[364] clearly defined by Recital[365] as a necessity for the proper functioning of the internal market. Therefore, the central role of legal certainty, with hard-and-fast rules to the detriment of legal congruence with the principles of the closest connection and characteristic performance, seems motivated by a perceived need for rigid rules inherent in the proper functioning of the EU market.

Nevertheless, in order to understand whether the reasons behind the rigid approach, which have radically changed the system of EU p.i.l. of contractual obligations, have led or may lead to benefits for the internal market, as well as certainly of the applicable law, it is necessary to start with an analysis of the individual contracts listed and the solutions that they offer. Importantly, this new approach has been characterized as having entirely abandoned any degree of flexibility in favour of rigid criteria.[366]

3.III.A The hard-and-fast rules

As already discussed, the wording of Article 4 (1) of the Rome I Regulation aims to provide solutions for disputes that can be readily foreseen by the parties and by third parties, with the goal, according to EU bodies, of en-

364 *U. Magnus*, "Article 4 Rome I Regulation. The applicable law in absence of choice", in F. Ferrari - S. Leible (eds.), *Rome I Regulation: the law applicable to contractual obligations in Europe* (Sellier, Munich, 2009), 29.

365 See Rome I Regulation § 6 Recital.

366 *O. Lando - P.A. Nielsen*, "The Rome I Regulation", in (2008) *Common Market Law Review*, 1687 – 1725; *U. Villani*, "Il ruolo della prestazione caratteristica dalla Convenzione di Roma al regolamento "Roma I" sulla legge applicabile ai contratti", in (2010) *Studi sull'integrazione europea*, 433.

suring legal certainty and predictability. The arguably inflexible lines on which this Article has been drafted came about because the "non-rule-approach"[367] of the Rome Convention would not provide the legal certainty and predictability that are, according to the framers of Rome I, needed for the proper functioning of the internal market.

However, the provision of the new Article 4 constitutes one of the principal changes in the Rome I Regulation because hard-and-fast rules have been inserted to replace the flexible principles of the Rome Convention for eight types of contracts. In fact the drafting technique, where Article 4 is concerned, is the complete reverse of that in the corresponding Article of the Rome Convention, through the adoption of connection criteria that typify the characteristic performance - i.e. the performance in each type of contract is identified.[368]

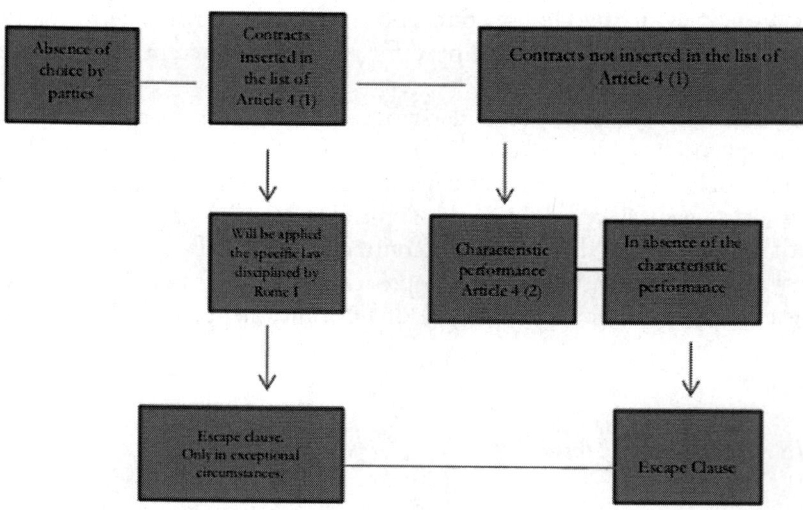

367 In these words *F. K. Juenger*, "The European Convention on the Law Applicable to Contractual Obligations: Some critical observations", in (1981) *Virginia Journal of International Law*, 137. The Author takes in consideration in footnote 92 the opinion of *P. Lagarde*, "The Convention on the Law Applicable to Contractual Obligations", in (1981) *Vanderbilt Journal of Transnational Law*, 93, who argues "[s]ometimes the Convention only indicates to the judge the intellectual step he has to follow rather than dictate the solution to be adopted"

368 *P.A. De Miguel Asensio*, "Applicable law in absence of choice to contracts relating to intellectual or industrial property rights", in (2008) *Yearbook of Private International Law*, 207.

In accordance with the aims of predictability of decisions highlighted by the Recital, the objective of Article 4 would be to assist the court in facilitating the localization of the applicable law by limiting, or cancelling, the interpreter's power in his careful judicial analysis of the contract. In light of the above-mentioned considerations, the natural function of the court is downgraded from an authoritative interpreter of the rules to a mere "machine" that applies the rules "mechanically". In fact, with Rome I in force, the task of the court is limited to analysing only the objective factors.[369] In other words, the court must simply qualify the contract and then, as if it were a "puzzle", add in the "scheme" of the Regulation to identify the applicable law.

Nevertheless, an analysis of the list contained in Article 4 (1) is necessary not only to provide evidence of the technique used by the lawmakers (depending on whether the focus is to be primarily on "characteristic performer" or on the country that the contract has the strongest connection with), but also because it could lead to identify the pros and cons of this rigid approach.

The Article 4 list includes:

Sale of goods: According to Article 4 (1) (a) a contract for the sale of goods is governed by the law of the country where the seller has his habitual residence. The *ratio legis* behind the choice made by the framers of Rome I would appear to be founded on the protection of the seller, considering that in this contract the buyer is only obliged to pay the price and deal with the delivery of the goods, whereas the seller is obliged to confront more hazardous economic uncertainties. As a consequence, by establishing rules governing these proceedings and cushioning the seller against the risks inherent in the international nature of the commercial transaction and in the accrual of costs, it was intended to protect the party who, in the framer's opinion, were deserving of greater legal protection.[370]

I believe that the *ratio legis* behind this step seems devoid of valid legal and economic rationale. In fact, the risks that the seller would face follow-

---

369 *A. J. Bêlohlávek, Rome Convention, Rome I Regulation: commentary, new EU conflict-of-laws rules for contractual obligation,* (Huntington, N.Y., Juris, 2010, 2 v), 789.

370 This theory is confirmed by *P. Franzina*, "Art. 4", in "Legge applicabile alle obbligazioni contrattuali – reg. CE n. 593/2008", in F. Salerno - P. Franzina (eds.), (2009) *Nuove Leggi Civili Commentate,* 677, who in footnotes nr. 35 report also *S. Ota*, "Choice of Law and Economic Analysis: A methodological Introduction", in *J. Basedow – T. Kono* (eds.) "An Economic Analysis of Private International Law", (Mohr Siebeck, Tübingen, 2006), 3 ss.

ing a sale of international goods are not dissimilar to those that may also be faced by the purchaser who is usually a SME and who frequently has to deal with faulty goods or delays in delivery.

Moreover, another problem that could arise within the rule in question is that Rome I does not offer a definition of "sale of goods".[371] According to the Recital § 17 and the opinion of some scholars[372] this could be interpreted in the same way as Article 5 of the Brussels I Regulation,[373] where the sale of goods is in fact catered to.[374] Additionally tools such as a *Draft Common Frame of Reference* may also be relevant.[375] Therefore only by making a comparison with other rules is it possible to identify the concept of "sale".

371 In order to understand the meaning of the "sale of goods", and the wide debate on this topic, is important to point out the definition insert in the Vienna Convention of 1980 «Contracts for the supply of goods to be manufactured or produced are to be considered sales unless the party who orders the goods undertakes to supply a substantial part of the materials necessary for such manufacture or production». The text is available at http://www.uncitral.org . See also *U. Magnus*, "Art. 4", in U. Magnus – P. Mankowsky (eds.), "European Commentaries on Private International Law", (Ottoschmidt, Kölm, 2017), 275, who notes that for the meaning of "goods" the whole body of EU law but also relevant international conventios must be taken into consideration.

372 *P. Piroddi*, "Between Scylla and Charybdis. Art. 4 of the Rome I Regulation Navigating along the cliffs of uncertainty and inflexibility", in G. Venturni - S. Bariatti (eds.), *Liber Fausto Pocar – New Instruments of Private International Law* (Giuffrè, Milano, 2009), 826; *F. Ferrari – J. A. Bischoff*, in F. Ferrari (ed.), "Article 4", *Rome I Regulation. Pocket commentary,* (Sellier, Munich, 2014), 132.

373 Regulation (EC) No 44/2001 of December 22, 2000 on jurisdiction and the recognition and enforcement of judgments in civil and commercial matters. This was replaced by the Brussels I Recast (n. 1215/2012), which extends the protection to transactions with business domicilied in third countries. However according to the Brussels I Regulation, the concept of sale should be understood as an "exchange" and, therefore, all those acts who are intended to provide the exchange of the item with the price should be included in this concept. In this way *P. Franzina*, "Art. 4", in F. Salerno - P. Franzina (eds.), "Legge applicabile alle obbligazioni contrattuali – reg. CE n. 593/2008", (2009) *Nuove Leggi Civili Commentate*, 675.

374 *G.P. Calliess*, *Rome Regulations Commentary on the European rules of the conflict of laws*, (Kluwer Law International, Alphen a/d Rijn, 2011), 90.

375 See *P. Franzina*, "Art. 4", "Legge applicabile alle obbligazioni contrattuali – reg. CE n. 593/2008, in F. Salerno - P. Franzina (eds.), in (2009) *Nuove Leggi Civili Commentate*, 673 footnote nr. 13. It is a Study Group on a European civil code and Research Group on EC Private Law (Acquis Group), Principles, definitions and Model rules of European Private Law – Draft Common Frame of Reference (DCFR), Munich, 2009.

Several problems also arise when identifying the legal concept of "goods", particularly with respect to different languages' versions of this word (German "*Kaufverträge*", Italian "*vendita di beni*", French "*biens*", Spanish "*mercaderias*").[376]

I believe that leasing contracts might be excluded,[377] as contracts completed by a natural person for a use other than for their own business and interests, may concern consumer protection and, as such, should be governed by Article 6 of Rome I.[378] In my opinion, electricity and natural gas contracts can also be excluded, unless they are sold for a set of quantity.

In addition to these observations, which by themselves highlight the complex work required by the interpreter in order to identify the applicable law, it must be remembered that contracts for the sale of goods are also governed by other supranational rules such as the Convention on the law applicable to contracts for the international sale of goods.[379] On this point, Dicey and Morris would welcome an extremely flexible approach to the rule, as in "Free On Board" sales contracts, and also advise the application of the law regulated by the place of delivery. Therefore in contrast to the hard-and-fast rule of Article 4 (1) (a), the learned editors maintain that the law concerning the place of delivery must be applied in situations where "the place of shipment is in the buyer's country, although in such cases there will usually be other connection with that country which will add to the argument for applying the 'escape clause'".[380]

In light of criticism, major inconsistencies and complications of Article 4 (1) (a) emerge. The framers of the Rome I Regulation, using the seller's habitual residence to determine the applicable law, would protect the potentially weaker party in the sale of goods contract. However, in my view,

---

376 In these words, *Ibid*, 677.

377 *M. McParland*, *The Rome I Regulation on the law applicable to contractual obligations*, (O.U.P., Oxford, 2015), 370. According to the Author "these arrangments will probably be considered contracts for the provision of services".

378 See *infra* § 3.III. See *P. Franzina*, "Art. 4 - Legge applicabile alle obbligazioni contrattuali – reg. CE n. 593/2008", in F. Salerno - P. Franzina (eds.), in (2009) *Nuove Leggi Civili Commentate*, 674, according to which the following should be included "*i contratti di scambio cui acceda un facere, a patto che l'operazione programmata dalle parti conservi la funzione 'tipica' della vendita – lo scambio – e non integri una 'prestazione di servizi'*".

379 Hague Convention of December 22, 1986 on the Law Applicable to Contracts for the International Sale of Goods.

380 *Dicey & Morris*, *The conflict of laws*, 15th ed. (L. Collins ed.), (Sweet&Maxwell, London, 2012), no. 33-016, 1887 – 1888, points out the same problems with c.i.f. (Cost, Insurance and Freight) contracts.

the weaker party is most likely the purchaser, usually a SME. Therefore, a rigid p.i.l. rule which imposes the application of the law of the stronger party, who is usually a MNC, does not provide incentives for European transactions and as such contrasts with the objectives of enhancing the proper functioning of the internal market that the Rome I Regulation has set.

Finally, the lack of a clear definition of "sale of goods" contract, rather than simplifing the interpreters task, disorients him/her in the "labyrinth" of rules that govern the sale of goods and in the complex "puzzle" of Article 4 of the Rome I Regulation where it is difficult for the interpreter to connect some contracts to one of those listed in Article 4 (1). It may be the case that the seller also provides the purchaser with certain services, such as a training course on how to use the machinery sold or contracts for the purchase of software including a users licence.[381] Therefore in these particular cases, it is only with the use of flexible connecting factors that the task of the interpreter can be simplified and thereby the most equitable law be applied.[382]

Provision of services: According to Article 4 (1) (b), a contract for the provision of services is governed by the law of the country where the service provider has habitual residence. Habitual residence is deemed to be where the service provider resides at the conclusion of the contract (Article 19 (3). The Rome I Regulation doesn't give a definition of "provision of services" and, according to some scholars,[383] this concept could be interpreted in the same way as Article 5 of the Brussels I Regulation or also Article 4 (1)

---

381 *M. Weller – C. F. Nordmeier*, "Rom I - Art. 4", in G. Spindler - F. Schuster (eds.), *Recht der elektronischen Medien*, (Verlag C.H. Beck, München, 2015), no. 5 – 6, in www.beckonline.beck.de.

382 *P. R. Beaumont - P.E. McEleavy*, *Private International Law*, (Thomson Reuters, Edinburg, 2011), 484 - 485; *Z.S. Tang*, "Law Applicable in the Absence of Choice – The new article 4 of the Rome I Regulation", in (2008) *Modern Law Review*, 794. According to the Author "For example, a company supplies customized software individually to its customers to suit their particular needs. The contract includes the elements covered by the sale of goods and the provision of services. A literal reading of Article 4 (2) might suggest that the elements of this contract are covered by both Article 4 (1) (a) and Article 4 (1) (b), and, as a result, the contract should be excluded from the scope of Article 4 (1) and the characteristic performance rule should apply. It would be helpful in a case where a contract includes elements in both the sale of goods and the provision of services and cannot easily be classified as one instead of the other".

383 *F. Ferrari*, "Art. 4 Rom I-VO", in F. Ferrari – E.M. Kieninger - P. Mankowski (eds.), *Internationales Vertragsrecht, (VO) EG 593/2008*, (Verlag CH Beck, München, 2012), no. 27.

of the Directive 2006/123/EC[384] on services in the internal market. However, contracts for the provision of services (e.g. activities of industrial or commercial character or activities of professions) will generally involve payment although, according to some scholars,[385] unpaid services are not excluded.

The absence of a uniform definition of these contracts in both EU rules and national legislations of the Member States and the similarities that these types of contracts have with others (e.g. franchising contract, financial services,[386] insurance services,[387] commercial agents), makes case law an important tool in identifying the contracts that come under this article. In fact, there are numerous law cases concerning these contracts,[388] highlighting that the "provision of services" concept is very broad and covers a vast range of activities that cannot all be classed as services.[389] On this point the decisions from ECJ[390] and certain national courts have played a significant role, in particular regarding trading contracts,[391] contracts for

384 *F. Ferrari – J. A. Bischoff*, "Article 4", in F. Ferrari (ed.) *Rome I Regulation. Pocket commentary*, (Sellier, Munich, 2014), 139.

385 *G.P. Calliess*, *Rome Regulations Commentary on the European rules of the conflict of laws*, (Kluwer Law International, Alphen a/d Rijn, 2011), 91. See also *P. Piroddi*, "Between Scylla and Charybdis. Art. 4 of the Rome I Regulation Navigating along the cliffs of uncertainty and inflexibility", in G. Venturni - S. Bariatti (eds.), *Liber Fausto Pocar – New Instruments of Private International Law* (Giuffrè, Milano, 2009), 826; *F. Marongiu Buonaiuti*, "Art. 4", "Legge applicabile alle obbligazioni contrattuali – reg. CE n. 593/2008", F. Salerno - P. Franzina (eds.), 691-705.

386 See ECJ C-384/93, *Alpine Investements BS v. Minister Financiën*.

387 ECJ C-118/96, *Jessica Safir v. SkattemyndighetIn I Dalarnas Län, formerly SkattemyndigheIen I Kopparbergs Län*.

388 See *ex multis* ECJ C-381/08, *Car Trim GmbH v. KeySafety Systems Srl* or C-533/07 *Falco Privatstiftung, Rabitsch v. Weller-Lindhorst*. Other cases mentioned in other contributions as *Cour de Cassation* July 11, 2006, in (2006) *Bulletin de la Court de Cassation, Chambres civiles*, n. 373, 320; *Cour de Cassation* October 3, 2006, in (2007) *Journal de droit international*, 132.

389 Significant examples are of course renting and leasing vehicle of moorings for boats are regarded as services within the meaning of article 50 of the European Treaty. About this case see ECJ C-451/99, *Cura Anlagen v. Auto Service Leasing*.

390 ECJ C-533/07, *Falco Privatstiftung and Thomas Rabitsch v Gisela Weller-Lindhorst*, where the ECJ has ruled on some prejudicial matters remitted by the Austrian *Oberster Gerichthof*. See also ECJ C-386/05, *Color Drack GmbH v. Lexx International Vertriebs GmbH*, with reference to asset sale contract.

391 *Cour de Cassation* October 3, 2006, mentioned in (2007) *Journal de droit international*, 132.

advertising consultancy[392] and contracts for various kinds of works and services.[393]

In this context, one scholar,[394] in an attempt to delineate this type of contract as precisely as possible, invites the interpreter to search for the concept of "services" in reference to some EU rules on the freedom of movement of services, therefore providing the relevant interpretation.[395]

Nevertheless, as for contracts for the sale of goods, the work of the interpreter in identifying the applicable law is complicated by the hard-and-fast rule for contract for the provision of services found in Article 4. In fact, a provision of services contract, in some circumstances, could be considered a sale of goods or franchising; therefore, it is difficult[396] to classify it as one of the contract types of Article 4 (1). Furthermore, there are contracts, such as transportation related to package tours,[397] holidays and travel tours, both of which include services and are therefore governed by Article 6[398] or by other EU rules like Directive ECC/90/314. These conditions add to the complications faced by the interpreter in that not only she/he is disori-

392 *Cour de Cassation* November 14, 2007, mentioned in (2008) *Revue critique droit international privé*, 303.

393 *Corte di Cassazione* June 19, 2000 n. 448, in (2001) *Rivista di diritto internazionale privato e processuale*, 415 - 421; *Court of Appeal*, *Ennstone Building Products Ltd v. Stanger Ltd.*, 2002 EWCA Civ. 916, in (2002) *Weekly Law Reports*, 3059.

394 *K.P.E. Lasok*, *Law and Institutions of the European Union*, (O.U.P., London, 2001), 331.

395 Alternatively, another Author says that the interpreter could be faced with "services" when "*si fa riferimento alla prestazione di un'attività di carattere autonomo, resa in uno Stato membro diverso da quello di cui il prestatore è cittadino, ovvero in cui ha la sua sede*". In these words *F. Marongiu Bonaiuti*, "Art. 4 - Legge applicabile alle obbligazioni contrattuali – reg. CE n. 593/2008", in F. Salerno - P. Franzina (eds.), in (2009) *Nuove Leggi Civili Commentate*, 697.

396 Although Rome I Recital 17 also clarifies that Article 4 (1) (b) does not apply in particular cases.

397 According to *M. McParland*, *The Rome I Regulation on the law applicable to contractual obligations*, (O.U.P., Oxford, 2015), 557, this term includes "'pre-packed' contract advertised by travel companies and sold by travel agents of a transport and hotel resort arrangment".

398 *D. Martiny*, "EGBGB" Art. 46b", in *Münchener Kommentar zum BGB*, (Verlag C.H. Beck, München, 2015), no. 65 – 67, in www.beckonline.beck.de. In addition, according to the EC 'Proposal for a Directive on package travel and assisted travel arrangments, amending Regulation (EC) n. 2006/2004, Directive 2011/83/EU and repealing Council Directive 90/314/ECC', consumers are treated as package travelers irrespective of wheather separate contracts for various travel components are concluded.

ented by "labyrinth" of Article 4 (1) of the Rome I Regulation, but she/he is also required to interface with more EU rules.

Finally, invoking the habitual residence of the service provider as a rule to determine the applicable law, the Rome I framers suggest that the service provider is the contractual party that need of more protection.

Indeed, provision of services contracts, as seen, are numerous and different. As a consequence, I have reasoned that to create an *ad hoc* rule is inappropriate and therefore might not ensure the proper functioning of the internal market. To illustrate the reasoning underlying this conclusion, let me raise the case of a multinational Dutch tax consulting firm which, after the payment of expensive fees, provides accounting and tax services for a SME Spanish food company that exports to the Netherlands. The problem that the Spanish company has to face, in addition to the randomness of international transactions and the heavy costs of consulting, is that by applying a law (Dutch law) that is not familiar may create further problems including tax issues. This circumstance certainly does not help to develop the European market. Indeed, the rigid approach probably increases the uncertainty and transaction costs of the business and in so doing hampers the European transactions.

Right in rem to immovable property and tenancy of immovable property: Article 4 (1) (c) establishes that a contract relating to a right *in rem* in immovable property or to a tenancy of immovable property is governed by the law of the country where the property is situated. This point reflects the assumption also enshrined in Article 4 (3) of the Rome Convention.[399] Actually, the only change between the two articles is linguistic, as the expression "right to use immovable property" is simply substituted by "tenancy of immovable property". Certainly, the expression used in the Convention is wider than that used in Rome I, which therefore restricts the field of its application by using the expression "tenancy", instead of "right to use immovable property". As a result, this definition it does not apply, for example, to types of agreements such as "usufructuary lease",[400] a tenancy of im-

399 Also in almost all European legal systems, the conflict of laws are almost always regulated with reference to the law of the country where the immovable property is located, this happens for example in the Italian legal system at art. 51 Law of 31 May 1995 no. 218, and in the Spanish legal system at art. 10.1 *codigo civil.*

400 *R. Plender - M. Wilderspin, The European Private International Law of Obligations*, (Sweet & Maxwell, London, 2009), 180.

movable property concluded for a short time[401] or company lease contracts.[402]

In these contracts I think that the rigid rule does not help the interpreter and in particular circumstances his/her careful analysis of the contract becomes essential. In fact, where the right to use immovable property on a "timeshare"[403] basis is concerned, some issues might arise in identifying the applicable law when, for example, there is a contract that includes a premium for insurance to cover the costs[404] or, as is usual practice, a contract with a bank to finance the acquisition of a timeshare. With reference to the last point, some national courts, such those in Italy,[405] maintain there is a legal connection between a "timeshare" contract and the financial operation. In this situation the hard-and-fast rules do not help the court in the task of identifying the applicable law. In fact, this contract would not only be subject to Article 4 (1) (d) but also to Article 4 (1) (b) or, where one party is also a consumer, to Article 6 (2) of the Regu-

---

401 In these words, *G.P. Calliess*, *Rome Regulations Commentary on the European rules of the conflict of laws*, (Kluwer Law International, Alphen a/d Rijn, 2011), 90.

402 About this topic see ECJ C-73/77, *Sanders v Van der Putte*, from the reading of the judgment it can be seen residually that company lease contracts are excluded from this scope of application given that they would not be part of the granting of a right to use a good, as is the case, for example, in property lease contract, but rather part of the productive needs of the company participating.

403 According to Article 2 of the Directive EC/122/2008, the following definitions shall apply: (a) 'timeshare contract' means a contract of a duration of more than one year under which a consumer, for consideration, acquires the right to use one or more overnight accommodation for more than one period of occupation; (b) 'long-term holiday product contract' means a contract of a duration of more than one year under which a consumer, for consideration, acquires primarily the right to obtain discounts or other benefits in respect of accommodation, in isolation or together with travel or other services; (c) 'resale contract' means a contract under which a trader, for consideration, assists a consumer to sell or buy a timeshare or a long-term holiday product; (d) 'exchange contract' means a contract under which a consumer, for consideration, joins an exchange system which allows that consumer access to overnight accommodation or other services in exchange for granting to other persons temporary access to the benefits of the rights deriving from that consumer's timeshare contract.

404 See ECJ C-8/98, *Dansommer A/S v. Andreas Götz*. *M. McParland*, *The Rome I Regulation on the law applicable to contractual obligations*, (O.U.P., Oxford, 2015), 385 – 386, has reported the case.

405 *Ex multis Tribunale di Busto Arsizio - sezione di Saronno*, decision of May 17, 2011. *Contra Tribunale di Sondrio* decision of January 29, 2015. See also in English doctrine *A. Briggs*, *Private International Law in English Courts*, (O.U.P., Oxford, 2014), 566.

lation,[406] considering that these contracts are defined by Briggs as "quintessential consumer contracts".[407]

In addition, the interpreters task could be complicated even further when he/she is faced with contracts in which a large real estate sale is connected to the restructuring of the property. In this case, the interpreter should identify, within the "puzzle" of Rome I, which law applies among those identified *sub* Article 4 (1) (b), and (c) wherein the characteristic performance might not be the sale but the restructuring.

In conclusion, I would like to consider that the choice of the criterion of *lex situs* certainly aims to ensure a connection between the rule of the mandatory aspects of the operation and that of the *in rem* effects, as well as to guarantee a compromise between the jurisdiction and rules adopted in the field of conflict of laws for immovable property. At the same time, my argument is that this provision does not introduce particular progress, but only a reworking of the equivalent presumptions found in the Rome Convention. Rather, I do not hesitate to say that the Article 4 list could confuse the interpreter and as a consequence would not ensure uniformity of decisions; thus the most equitable law may not be applied. This might well be the case when the interpreter is faced with complex contracts involving a bank loan to finance the acquisition of a timeshare or one in which the sale of a large real estate is linked to restructuring or insurance costs.

Tenancy of immovable property concluded for temporary private use: Article 4 (1) (d) provides an exception to the *lex situs* rule in cases where a tenancy of immovable property has been concluded "for temporary private use for a period of no more than six consecutive months".[408] In these circumstances the contract is governed by the law of the country where the landlord has his/her habitual residence, provided that the tenant is a person and has his/her habitual residence in the same country.

The *ratio legis* behind the provision in question, which makes a clear distinction from the rules governed by Article 4 (1) (c), lies in the fact that, in this contract the tenancy relationship is found to be unconnected to the country where the property is located. Therefore, the connection criteria have a strong legal relationship between the contract and the country of

---

406 *Dicey & Morris*, *The conflict of laws*, 15th ed. (L. Collins ed.), (Sweet&Maxwell, London, 2012), no. 33-049, 1907 – 1908.

407 *A. Briggs*, *Private International Law in English Courts*, (O.U.P., Oxford, 2014), 566 althought § 27 Rome I Recital qualifies timeshare contracts as an exception to the general consumer contracts rule.

408 Rome I Regulation Article 4 (1) (d).

the contracting parties and, in particularly, the country of the landlord which is dominating factor.

This expectation could be vulnerable to a limited number of criticisms. In fact, Rome I does not clarify short-term contracts of immovable property and certainly does not help the court to identify the applicable law. In effect, a short-term contract for tenancy of immovable property not for private use, might take the form of a typical holiday lease for a period of a holiday. To be slightly more precise, let me take the case of an Austrian citizen, whose habitual residence is in Vienna, and who signs a contract for a summer holiday tenancy for a residence on the island of Capri (Italy). The property, owned by a subject whose habitual residence is in Italy, permits a temporary use of less than six months. It is clear that in this case the Austrian citizen is acting as a tourist and furthermore as a consumer,[409] with the result that Article 6 of the Rome I Regulation also may be applied.[410] Furthermore the interpreter could be further disoriented if the tenancy contract had been conducted through a German travel agency operating via the internet. In these circumstances the travel agency provides a service,[411] therefore the interpreter might also choose to apply both by Article 4 (1) (b), and Article 4 (1) (d) followed by Article 6 and then decide whether to apply Austrian, German or Italian law.

Moreover, as this example confirms, Rome I does not provide a clear definition of "temporary private use", and the reference to a period of time would only complicate further the interpreter's already difficult task. Let's take another example, this time of an Italian PhD student who during his years of enrolment at the university, leases an apartment in Vienna for interrupted periods of time, when he undergoes courses or seminars. In this example, the sum total of time recorder over the years may vary and as a consequence the interpreter could mistakes due to his/her difficulty choosing to apply the law of Article 4 (1) (c) or (d).

Overall, the lesson to be learned from the preceding analysis is that providing an *ad hoc* rule in the list of Article 4 for short tenancy of immovable

---

409 On this point see *L. Rossi Carleo, Il turista come consumatore speciale*, in G. Alpa – S. Patti (eds.), *Le clausole vessatorie nei contratti con i consumatori*, (Giuffrè, Milano, 1997), 811.

410 *F. Ferrari – J. A. Bischoff*, "Article 4", in F. Ferrari (ed.) *Rome I Regulation. Pocket commentary*, , (Sellier, Munich, 2014), 147; *A. Briggs, Private International Law in English Courts*, (O.U.P., Oxford, 2014), 566.

411 *D. Martiny*, "Art. 4 Rom I –VO", in *Münchener Kommentar zum Bürgerlichen Gesetzbuch*, (Verlag C.H. Beck, München, 2010), no. 115.

property does not help the interpreters task[412] and at the same time does not guarantee the predictability of the outcome of litigation, or the certainty of the applicable law.

Franchising contracts: The Rome I Regulation is concerned with regulating the franchising contracts, the structure of which is "somewhat complex" and makes it "complicated to determine the applicable law in absence of choice [...]".[413] In particular, Article 4 (1) (e) hold that these contracts are governed by the law of the franchisee's habitual residence. The *ratio legis* behind this choice seems clear and was already been declared by the Commission in the Proposal from 2005: to protect the weaker party in the relationship (the franchisee) to avoid the huge problems encountered by the interpreter when working with the Convention, and to localize characteristic performance.

In order to carry out a detailed analysis on the choice made by the EU lawmakers on Article 4 (1) (e), as well as to identify the pros and cons of the hard-and-fast rules for these type of contracts, it would appear appropriate also to quote, verbatim, the words of Tang, according to whom:

> "It does not separate industrial franchise contracts from other franchise contracts, and it should be understood that this rule applies to both. However, industrial franchise contracts have different characteristic, which raises a question as to whether the same rule should apply. In an industrial franchise contract, the manufacturer, who is the franchisee, acquires manufacturing licenses based on patents and or technical no patented practical information, combined with trade mark licenses to market products. It is clear that the franchisee is the characteristic performer of this type of contract. In other franchise contracts, a franchisor grants a franchisee the right to exploit a franchise for the purpose of marketing goods or services. The franchisee has the obligation to use the franchisor's trade mark, trade names, shop signs, utility models, designs, and copy rights to market the franchisor's goods or services. The franchisor should provide the franchisee commercial or

412 *Contra M. McParland, The Rome I regulation on the law applicable to contractual obligations*, (O.U.P., Oxford, 2015), 393. According to the Author "the provision clarifies that the existence of a shared habitual residence between landlord and tenant, when combined with the temporary period of letting, justifies a choice of law other than the country where the property is situated".

413 With these words, *L. G. Gutierrez*, "Franchise contracts and the Rome I Regulation on the law applicable to international contracts", in (2008) 10 *Yearbook of Private International Law*, 233.

technical assistance and may subject the franchisee to periodic or spot checks. The franchisee should pay the franchise fee, ongoing royalties and advertising contributions. This contract includes a bundle of obligations and it is hard to tell who the characteristic performer is. The *ratio legis* for connecting such a contract to the habitual residence of the rule consistent for all types of franchise contract: first, it is convenient to keep the rule consistent for all types of franchise contracts; second, franchisees in the second type of contract are usually the weaker party to have the law of the franchisee applies; third, the habitual residence of the franchisee usually is coincident with the place of performance of the main of both parties, and has close connections to the contract".[414]

My argument is that the decision of the framers of the Rome I Regulation to insert this contract in Article 4's list and ensure the protection of the franchisee is vulnerable to strong criticism.[415] In fact, in a typical franchise contract, the party that assumes more obligations is the franchisor, who "creates loyalty" and gives important business information (advertising and supporting materials) in favour of the franchisee allowing him/her to take advantages of its trade name, copyrights, know-how and continuing technical assistance, in a country familiar to the franchisee and unfamiliar to the franchisor, who shoulders the risk of investing in a "foreign" territory.[416] Additionally, depending on the type of franchising contract, the characteristic performer might change or might even be impossible to

414 In these words, *Z. S. Tang*, "Law Applicable in the Absence of Choice – The New Article 4 of the Rome I Regulation", in (2008) 71 *The Modern Law Review*, 788-789.

415 *L. G. Gutierrez*, "Franchise contracts and the Rome I Regulation on the law applicable to international contracts", in (2008) 10 *Yearbook of Private International Law*, 238.

416 According to *A. J. Bělohlávek*, *Rome Convention, Rome I Regulation: commentary, new EU conflict-of-laws rules for contractual obligation*, (Huntington, N.Y., Juris, 2010, 2 v), 922, "the opinions which hold that the performance of the franchisor is the characteristic performance and, thus, regard the objective determination of applicable law on the basis of this performance as a principle that has been established over the years by case law as to the definition of the distribution contractual type and the characteristic performance provided within that framework, and the opinions, which only vaguely take into account the fundamental economic differences between the franchise and the relationship based on a distribution contract, or do not take these into account at all, are built on the assumption that a truly dominant performance is present here".

identify, as one scholar has suggested,[417] thereby producing an extremely restrictive interpretation.

Likewise, for some types of contracts such as *master franchising agreements*,[418] there could be a different position than the one indicated in Article 4 (1) with the result that only the provisions of Article 4 (2) or (3) of Rome I could ensure the application of the most equitable law. Therefore, given the various types of franchising contracts, it is essential that the interpreter study carefully the contents of the contract in order to check whether there is a provision that characterises that contract more than another, to avoid applying an inexact and inequitable law.[419]

Moreover, it must be added that a franchising contract is a typical "innominate contract" and according to Šarčević,[420] "in view of the great variety […] and their complexity, a general theory of innominate contracts is still in a *statu nascendi*. A legal analysis of such contracts should also take account of the economic and geographic factors involved as these are the underlying causes of diversity in some areas".

Starting with these observations, it is likely that the court, in undertaking the avoidance of unreasonable harm to a party, would achieve its goal by applying the principle of "closest connection", therefore rejecting hard-and-fast rules whilst considering all the individual characteristics of the franchise contract in detail. These observations could be supported also by some national cases[421] which acknowledge the importance in franchising

---

417 *P. A. De Miguel Asencio*, *Contratos internacionales sobre propiedad industrial*, (Civitas, Madrid, 2000), 305 – 307. In line with the Author's view "*es no posible identificar la prestaciò caracterìstica de el contrato de franquicia*". Furthermore, the Author has suggested the application of the rule of the closest connection.

418 This type of contract is often used by producing companies to organise their distribution network abroad, for one or more main affiliates which in turn will use these goods, rights and know-how to conclude further franchise agreements with other affiliates. See also *A. Bonomi*, "The Rome I Regulation on the law applicable to contractual obligations. Some General Remarks", in (2008) 10 *Yearbook of Private International Law*, 185.

419 See also Dutch Tribunal Hof Arnhem March 4, 2003. In this judgement the subject is a dispute over a franchising contract between a German company and a Dutch one where the court applied Dutch law using the "escape clause". In particular, the court stressed that a franchising contract is specific and needs to be carefully evaluated in order to determine the connecting factors between the various countries.

420 *P. Šarčević*, *International Contracts and Conflicts of Laws*, (Graham&Trotman/Martinus/Nijhoff, London/Dordrecht/Boston, 1990), 21.

421 *Ex multis* Austrian case law Judgment OGH (A) 4Ob 321/87 of 5 May 1987 available at http://www.franchise.at/files/seiteninhalt/faq-pdfs/rechtsurteile.pdf.

contracts of assessing the primary factors at play, with emphasis on the use of license or other rights.[422] For example under Austrian jurisdiction, essentially it is the law in force in the place in which these rights are exercised (or where any infringement of such rights is committed) that applies. Using this concept as a basic premise, one scholar[423] has been predominantly in favour of applying the law depending on the licence provided for the use of intangible assets. This opinion suggests that in a franchising contract it is important to consider the set of intangible assets and rights within each individual contract that links them to the location of their use.

In light of these considerations, Article 4 (1) (e) does not allow the court to apply the most equitable law case-by-case and at the same time creates an imbalance in favour of the franchisee resulting in the undermining of the franchisor who is not only the party that holds the trade mark, trade names, shop signs, license and know-how but also the one who takes on most risks in the contract.

Summarizing all the previous considerations, I believe that the approach adopted for this type of contract, which is a vital part of the internal market,[424] definitely does not improve "a cross-border impact to the extent necessary for the proper functioning of the internal market", as hoped for in the Recital of the Rome I Regulation.[425] For example, if in a litigation case the law of the Ukrainian franchisee is applied, creating substantial harms to the Spanish franchisor who is the holder of an international brand, certainly the latter will re-assess the opportunity to invest more in that country or at least break all franchising contracts in Ukraine.

Distribution contracts: According to Article 4 (1) (f), distribution contracts are governed by the law of the habitual residence of the distributor. According to some Authors, EU lawmakers wanted to regulate these con-

---

422 Academics opinions had differed whether it was the franchisee or the franchisor who were undertaking the characteristic performance of the contract. For the literature see that cited in *F. Ferrari*, "From Rome to Rome via Brussels: Remarks on the Law Applicable to Contractual Obligations Absent a Choice by Parties (Art. 4 of the Rome I Regulation)", in (2009) *RabelsZ*, 769 footnote 104.

423 *A. J. Bělohlávek, Rome Convention, Rome I Regulation: Commentary, new EU conflict-of-laws rules for contractual obligation,* (Huntington, N.Y., Juris, 2010, 2 v), 923.

424 *M. McParland, The Rome I regulation on the law applicable to contractual obligations,* (O.U.P., Oxford, 2015), 394.

425 Report § 1.

tracts not only to assist the court in the complex task of identifying the applicable law but also to protect the "weaker" party of the contract.[426]

Before endorsing or not the EU lawmaker's decision in my opinion it is necessary to start from some observations on the different location of the "centre of gravity of the distribution contract" for adoption by the EU national legal system. In fact, in Italy,[427] France[428] and England[429] the manufacturer is the characteristic performer because in these legal systems the distribution is seen as irrelevant without the manufacture of goods. In contrast, other countries, such as Austria, Germany and Spain, take the opposite view; that is, the manufacturer is not the characteristic performer be-

426 *P. Lagarde*, "Remarques sur la Proposition de Règlement de la Commission Européenne sur la loi applicable aux Obligations Contractuelles (Rome I)", in (2006) *Revue critique de droit international privé*, 339, according to whom *"parait bien hâtive, quand on connait la puissance économique de certains distributeurs"*. See also *I. Fiorelli*, "Contratti internazionali di distribuzione: problemi di legge applicabile e di giurisdizione", in (2007) *Rivista di diritto internazionale privato e processuale*, 633.

427 *Corte di Cassazione* June 11, 2001 n. 7860, better known like *Otto Kogler* case, where an Italian manufacturer filed suit in Italy because its Austrian distributor failed to pay for some orders. The *Corte di Cassazione* held that the contract at issue fulfilled two functions: exchange and collaboration. The court went on to state that the characteristic performance should be identified through the peculiarities and circumstances of the contract at issue, as opposed to abstract contractual classifications. Holding that the contract's exchange function was essential and linked with the provision of goods, the *Corte di Cassazione* concluded that the contract was governed by Italian law. In this case, the importance given to the provision of goods may be explained by the fact that the contract described at length all the obligations assumed by the Italian manufacturer, whereas it was apparently more ambiguous on the role of the Austrian distributor. The *Corte di Cassazione* also expressed the general view that the distribution activity would not have existed without the provision of goods. In these words, *M.E. Ancel*, "The Rome I Regulation and Distribution Contracts", in (2008), *Yearbook of Private International Law*, 225.

428 For more on the France jurisprudence on this topic see *Court de Cassation* May 15, 2001, mentioned in *O. Lopes Pegna*, "Il Rilievo del collegamento più stretto dalla Convenzione di Roma alla proposta di regolamento "Roma I"", in (2006) *Rivista di diritto internazionale*, 763.

429 *M. E. Ancel*, "The Rome I Regulation and distribution contracts", in (2008) *Yearbook of Private International Law*, 225. With reference to the approach given by the English law see *infra* chapter "case law", in particular the case of English Court of Appeal - *Print Concept GmbH v. GEW (EC) Ltd.* March 2, 2001.

cause this is seen as extraneous to the whole point of a distribution agreement.[430]

In addition to these differences, according to one view,[431] the characteristic performer in a distribution contract is the manufacturer, because there is no distribution without a supply of goods. In contrast, other academics[432] argue that the distributor is the characteristic performer because the distribution is the "real meat" of the contract. However, it can also be advocated that no characteristic performer can be identified and that the habitual residence of the distributor, in most cases, will be the place where the goods are delivered to or where the resale occurs.

In light of these considerations, I do not hesitate to say that the distributor's habitual residence should not have a direct relationship with the contract itself[433] and, as a consequence, the most equitable law may only be identified with an analysis of all the circumstances of the contract, starting with all mutual obligations of the parties. Therefore, only the use of flexible connecting tools can guarantee the application of the most equitable law, thus avoiding unfair harm to either party.

These arguments already corroborate that the choice of a fixed rule of the Rome I Regulation is inappropriate and does not guarantee the appli-

430 In these words, *M. E. Ancel*, "The Rome I Regulation and distribution contracts", in (2008) *Yearbook of Private International Law*, 226 who at footnote 16 has mentioned the following cases law: Austria, *OGH*, 20.01.1999, *ÖJZ* 1999.504; Germany, *OLG München*, 26.9.1995; Spain, *Audiencia Provincial Barcelona*, 28.4.2000.

431 For more on the differences between distribution contracts and sale of goods contracts see *J. Fawcett*, "A United Kingdom Perspective on the Rome I Regulation", N. Boschiero (ed.), *La nuova disciplina comunitaria della legge applicabile ai contratti (Roma I)*, (Giappichelli, Torino, 2009), 218 – 220.

432 *M. E. Ancel*, "The Rome I Regulation and distribution contracts", in (2008) *Yearbook of Private International Law*, 226; *R. Plender - M. Wilderspin*, *The European Private International Law of Obligations*, (Sweet & Maxwell, London, 2009), 184.

433 In this regard also *H. Gaudemet–Tallon*, "Le principe de proximitè dans le Règlement Rome I", in (2008) *Revue Hellènique de droit international*, 193. According to the Author '*On peut discuter pour savoir si le contrat de distribution a des liens plus droits avec le pays de la résidence habituelle du distributeur ou avec celui dans lequel le fournisseur a sa résidence habituelle*'. *Contra Z. S. Tang*, "The new article 4 of the Rome I Regulation", in (2008) *Modern Law Review*, 788-789; *M.E. Ancel*, "The Rome I Regulation and distribution contracts", in (2008) *Yearbook of Private International Law*, 227 according to the Author "there are several advantages in choosing the law of the distributor over that law of the manufacturer. The main advantage is that the distribution agreements are generally more closely linked with the country where the distributor has its habitual residence and operates".

cation of the most equitable law. In addition, it should be pointed out that, rather than try to identify the characteristic performer, it is necessary to more important to qualify the category of distribution contracts.[434] Considering that it's definition currently remains unclear and nonspecific under domestic law,[435] but also that contracts such as franchising[436] or provision of services[437] which already appear in Article 4 (1),[438] could be included in this category. Furthermore complex contracts such as commercial agency contracts, may be qualified not only as provision of services[439]

434 *G. Ruscalla*, "The harmonisation of international commercial contract law: the case of international distribution agreements", in (2011) *Bocconi Legal Papers*, in www.bocconilegalpapers.com. According to the Author, " [...] a definition of distribution contracts has been provided by the practice. First of all such contracts are 'bilateral enterprise contracts'; they are characterized by obligations carried out in a constant, continuous and periodical way; they are exchange contracts and cooperation contracts at the same time, depending on which relation one looks at".

435 In Spain *El Tribunal Supremo* held that the distribution contracts are "mixed" contract, resulted from the sale contract. See *Tribunal Supremo* decision November 2000 RJ 9339.

436 *F. Ferrari*, "Art. 4 Rom I-VO", in F. Ferrari – E.M. Kieninger - P. Mankowski (eds.), *Internationales Vertragsrecht, (VO) EG 593/2008*, (Verlag CH Beck, München, 2012), no. 48; *A. Nervi*, *I contratti di distribuzione tra causa di scambio e causa associativa*, (E.S.I., Napoli, 2011), 14. *Contra* ECJ C-9/12, *Corman- Collins SA v. La Maison du Whisky sa*, Opinion of Advocate General JÄÄskinen, [30] held "Those agreements clearly differ from franchise agreements in that the distribution agreement is not based on the grantor making his technical or administrative know-how available to the distributor".

437 In certain circumstances the distribution contract could be connected with a provision of a service.

438 See for more *supra*.

439 *M. McParland*, *The Rome I regulation on the law applicable to contractual obligations*, (O.U.P., Oxford, 2015), 401. The Author relating the opinion of some academics, underlines that "where a 'distribution' agreement is to be sulfilled by individual contracts of sale and purchase of goods, such an agreement will likely not constitute a 'distribution contract' for the purpose of Article 4 (1) (f), but may fall within the operation of Article 4 (2) of the Regulation because it involves elements of both Article (1) (a) and Article 4 (1) (f)".

or sales of goods contracts,[440] but also as distribution contracts[441] or in certain circumstances as employement contracts.[442]

Importantly, in many distribution contracts the habitual residence of the distributor has no direct relation to the contract,[443] and this situation creates a strong contractual imbalance that is unlikely to improve international transactions.

Finally, I have reasoned that the introduction of *ad hoc* rules for distribution contracts, adds further muddle to the already murky "labyrinth" of Article 4. As a consequence, the interpreter, rather than being assisted, becomes disoriented in his/her task of identifying the applicable law. On the basis of this argument, I think that the court could apply the most equitable law and avoid unfair harm to any party only with an autonomous interpretation employing the closest connection principle.

Sale of goods by auction: Article 4 (1) (g) also contains a special rule for the sale of goods by auction and holds that these contracts shall be governed by the law of the country where the auction takes place. The *ratio legis* behind the Rome I Regulation framer's choice to regulate these contracts with a rigid rule can be explained by the fact that these overrule other personal or party connections[444] at the place of the auction.[445] This analysis suggests that the EU lawmakers probably have chosen to adhere to

---

440 *F. Ferrari – J. A. Bischoff*, "Article 4", in F. Ferrari (ed.) *Rome I Regulation. Pocket commentary*, (Sellier, Munich, 2014), 153. According to the Authors the commercial agency contract is not governed by Article 4 (1) (f) because "the commercial agent does not at all bear the risk of distribution, but is merely an aide to the entrepreneur and merely acts as intermediary in the distribution of the goods. Since, however, the commercial agent is a service provider, the commercial agency contract falls within the sphere of application of Article 4 (1) (b) Rome I".

441 *Contra* ECJ C-9/12, *Corman- Collins SA v. La Maison du Whisky sa*, Opinion of Advocate General Jääskinen, [30] held "Those agreements clearly differ from commercial agency contracts in that the distributor does not have the power to represent the grantor".

442 *U. Magnus*, "Article 4 - Rome I Regulation", in S. Leible - F. Ferrari (eds.), *Rome I Regulation the law applicable to contractual obligation in Europe*, (Sellier, Munich, 2009), 375. The Author points out the some national law treats agents as employees.

443 *H. Gaudemet – Tallon*, "Le principe de proximitè dans le Règlement Rome I", in (2008) *Revue Hellènique de droit international*, 195.

444 *A. Briggs*, *Private International Law in English Courts*, (O.U.P., Oxford, 2014), 552.

445 *Z. S. Tang*, "The new article 4 of the Rome I Regulation", in (2008) *Modern Law Review*, 790; *F. Ferrari – J. A. Bischoff*, 'Article 4', in F. Ferrari (ed.) *Rome I Regulation. Pocket commentary*, (Sellier, Munich, 2014), 152.

Schnitzer's theory,[446] reflecting the Convention's approach to the international sale of goods.[447]

However, the wording of Article 4 (1) (g) "if such place can be determined" – suggests the difficulty of determining where the sale has taken place, as in the case where the buyers attend in person or by telephone. Still, in these cases, the law of the country where the auction takes place will be applied. Therefore auctions conducted online (e.g. by e-mail or in general by computer), which are a relatively new but increasingly popular feature of internet sales[448] or auctions for specific financial operations (e.g. the case of the so-called "smart contract" in blockchain platforms)[449] and where it is difficult to identify the country hosting the auction[450] or the location of the bids, according to some Authors[451] could be excluded from the application of Article 4 (1) (g). Actually, not all internet auctions should be excluded from the scope of sale "by auction". Therefore, the interpreter should consider if the place can be determined by the physical location of the computer servers that host the auction.[452] In fact, for example, blockchain based smart contract, usually is composed of the adreess of

---

446 *A. Schnitzer*, "La Loi Applicable aux contracts", in (1955) *Revue critique de doit international privé*, 596. According to the Author the contracts concluded at auctions, fairs, markets and stock exchanges, are respectively subjected to the law of the place of the auction, trade fair, market or stock market.

447 In particular, see article 3.3 of the Hague Convention of June 15, 1955 and article 9 of the Hague Convention of December 22, 1986.

448 For more on "online contracts" see *G. Perlingieri*, "La contrattazione online", in D. Valentino (ed.), *Manuale di diritto dell' informatica*, (E.S.I., Napoli, 2011), 303 – 320;.

449 Consider the case of buying the so-called "token" shares of a German multinational corporation on the famous Estonian blockchain platform "Ethereum" by an Italian investor. It will be not easy for the interpreter to qualify the contract and choose the applicable law in the list of Art. 4 of Rome I.

450 *A. Briggs*, *Private International Law in English Courts*, (O.U.P., Oxford, 2014), 552; *R. Catalano*, "Le aste online", in D. Valentino (ed.), *Manuale di diritto dell'informatica*, (E.S.I., Napoli, 2011), 369, according to whom "[…] *i siti di* on line auction *non sempre svolgono le funzioni di un vero e proprio banditore. In queste ipotesi le aste* on line *non sono qualificabili come incanti in senso stretto* […]".

451 *A. Spickhoff*, in H.G. Bamberger – H. Roth (eds.), *Beck'scher Onlinekommentar BGB*, "VO (EG) 593/2008 Art. 4", (Beck, München, 2013), no. 46, in www.beck-online.beck.de; *A. Briggs*, *Private International Law in English Courts*, (O.U.P., Oxford, 2014), 552. In line with the Author's opinion "for auctions conducted by e-mail or otherwise by computer, the place where the seller receives and processes the bids will have a strong claim to be decisive".

452 *M. McParland*, *The Rome I regulation on the law applicable to contractual obligations*, (O.U.P., Oxford, 2015), 407.

auctioneers, the auction start time and the deadline. In this case I believe that the contract can be located where the auction takes place that is, where the auctioner has habitual residence or where the blockchain platform is located.

Furthermore, according to several Authors,[453] judicial sales might also be excluded, as they are unconnected to the civil and commercial matters that the Regulation is concerned with. In fact, I think this type of auction could also find itself covered by Article 4 (1) (g), especially when it comes to court-ordered auctions relating to a bankruptcy. In this last case, the "civil and commercial matters" covered by the Rome I Regulation are still relevant, given that in bankruptcy proceedings, the commercial interests of the company will continue with the judicial authorities of the bankruptcy proceedings.

In addition, I note that the fixed rule of Article 4 (1) (g) has the same connecting factor appointed through the Rome Convention. Therefore, an interpreter with a flexible rule would have reached the same result, without the added complications such as when he is faced with auctions conducted by email or otherwise by computer.

Contracts concluded within a multilateral system: Finally, in contrast to the Commission's Proposal, Article 4 (1) (h) stipulates a specific rule governing financial markets, typically stock exchanges.[454] According to the Article,

> "a contract concluded within a multilateral system which brings together or facilitates the bringing together of multiple third-party buying and selling interests in financial instruments, as defined by Article 4(1), point (17) of Directive 2004/39/EC, in accordance with non-discretionary rules and governed by a single law, shall be governed by that law".

The *ratio legis* behind the focus of the framers of Rome I and the introduction of these contracts in Article 4 (1), can be explained not only by the difficulties faced by the interpreter with the Rome Convention in using the characteristic performance rule to identify the applicable law, but also

453 *F. Ferrari – J. A. Bischoff*, "Article 4", in F. Ferrari (ed.) *Rome I Regulation. Pocket commentary*, (Sellier, Munich, 2014), 155; *P. Franzina*, "Art. 3 - Legge applicabile alle obbligazioni contrattuali – reg. CE n. 593/2008", in F. Salerno - P. Franzina (eds.), (2009) *Nuove Leggi Civili Commentate*, 689.

454 *F. J. Garcimartin Alférez*, "New issues in the Rome I Regulation: the special provisions on financial market contracts", in (2008) *Yearbook of Private International Law*, 246.

by the significance and complexity of stock exchange transactions.[455] Carried out in a stock market or other such multilateral trading system, these transactions obviously have the closest connection to the market in question "which is similar to the sale by auction",[456] and therefore the related contracts will be governed by that law.

However, what Rome I does not make clear is the meaning of "financial instruments" and "multilateral system". As regards the former, it is important to point out that Recital § 30 of the Regulation refers to Article 4 of Directive 2004/39/EC. The result is that according to some scholars[457] contracts such as swaps, bonds,[458] options, venture capital, financial derivatives for transferral of credit risk or differential financial contracts, should be covered.

Furthermore, the Recital § 26 applies to

> *"[...] financial services such as investment services and activities and ancillary services provided by a professional to a consumer" or "contracts for the sale of units in collective investment undertakings, whether or not covered by Council Directive 85/611/EEC of 20 December 1985 on the coordination of laws, regulations and administrative provisions relating to undertakings for collective investment in transferable securities (UCITS)".*[459]

Recital § 26 thus makes express reference to "ancillary services" but does not actually make clear what is meant by "ancillary". This category may

---

455 *A. Briggs*, *Private International Law in English Courts*, (O.U.P., Oxford, 2014), 554 according to which "the common sense of it is that those who enter into transactions within the framework of such system, of which the most obvious example will be a stock market, will not be taken by surprise to learn that the single law which regulates that system also governs the contracts entered into within it".

456 *R. Plender - M. Wilderspin*, *The European Private International Law of Obligations*, (Sweet & Maxwell, London, 2009), 185.

457 *U. Magnus*, "Article 4 Rome I Regulation. The applicable law in absence of choice", in F. Ferrari - S. Leible (eds.), *Rome I Regulation: the law applicable to contractual obligations in Europe* (Sellier, Munich, 2009), 49; *F.C. Villata*, "La legge applicabile alla negoziazione di strumenti finanziari nel regolamento Roma I", in N. Boschiero (ed.), *La nuova disciplina comunitaria della legge applicabile ai contratti (Roma I)*, (Giappichelli, Torino, 2009), 422 - 423.

458 *Contra R. A. Schütze*, "Internationales Privatrecht", in H. D. Assmann – R.A. Schütze (eds.), *Handbuch des Kapitalanlagerechts*, (Verlag C.H. Beck, München, 2015), no. 49, according to the Author "*Bei fehlender Rechtswahl kommt Art. 4 Rom I-VO zur Anwendung. Es ist nach Art. 4 Abs. 2 Rom I-VO auf den gewöhnlichen Aufenthalt bzw. Sitz der Hauptverwaltung des Anleiheschuldners abzustellen*".

459 Rome I Regulation § 26 Recital.

also include the hire of safety deposit boxes, the administration of financial instruments on behalf of clients, advice to companies in relation to capital structure, and business strategy services and investment work.[460] Surely, if "ancillary services" are interpreted in this way, the work of the interpreter will be more complex, as multiple rules could be applied. Indeed, these contracts could well be included in the provision of Article 4 (1) (b).[461] At the same time, these contracts could also fall under Art. 4 (1) (g) as blockchain based smart contracts, for which it is not easy to locate where the auction takes place, usually where the blockchain platform has its habitual residence or also where the auctioner has his/her habitual residence.[462] However, when in these contracts one of the parties is a consumer Art. 6 could also be applied.

Therefore, the numerous difficulties in interpreting this provision, defined by McParland as "the most obscure provision"[463] of Rome I, do not help the interpreter in the task of identifying the most equitable law. In light of these considerations, establishing rigid rules dictating the contracts that could fall within this category, does not guarantee legal certainty. In fact, in many contracts on financial markets, such as the very common venture capital or swaps,[464] it may not always be easy to localize characteristic performance or to decide whether to describe these as sale of goods, and so it could become subject to another rule laid down by Article 4 of the Rome I. This analysis proves that all these circumstances and different types of contracts create particular difficulties in identifying the applicable law.[465]

---

460 *F.C. Villata*, "La legge applicabile alla negoziazione di strumenti finanziari nel regolamento Roma I", in N. Boschiero (ed.) *La nuova disciplina comunitaria della legge applicabile ai contratti (Roma I)*, (Giappichelli, Torino, 2009), 430 – 431.

461 In reference to deposit contract as banking contract see *F. Ferrari*, "Art. 4 Rom I-VO", in F. Ferrari – E.M. Kieninger - P. Mankowski (eds.), *Internationales Vertragsrecht, (VO) EG 593/2008*, (Verlag CH Beck, München, 2012), no. 126.

462 See supra "sale of goods by auction".

463 *M. McParland*, *The Rome I Regulation on the law applicable to contractual obligations*, (O.U.P., Oxford, 2015), 407. According to the Author "Pheraps inevitably in these troubled times, the City of London has been blamed by some Europeans for the lack of clarity in this provision".

464 *R. A. Schütze*, "Internationales Privatrecht", in H. D. Assmann – R.A. Schütze (eds.), *Handbuch des Kapitalanlagerechts*, (Verlag C.H. Beck, München, 2015), no. 94.

465 *Dicey & Morris*, *The conflict of laws*, 15th ed. (L. Collins ed.), (Sweet&Maxwell, London, 2012), no. 33-324, 2072.

In light of the criticisms that have been made, I believe that the principle of "closest connection" could have a stronger role in localizing the most equitable law when the interpreter is faced with these e-commerce activities or transactions[466] and could thus protect investors and shareholders/savers. It should be emphasized that this e-commerce transactions are now very common among investors and that, therefore, investors themselves as shareholders who invest via intermediaries,[467] can be included in the broader category of consumers.[468] As a consequence, for the investor/consumer the law of Article 6 of Rome I[469] would ensure greater protection than that of Article 4 (1) (h) and that which would be applied according to the Recital.[470]

In conclusion, for this category of contracts, a rigid connecting rule as that identified by Article 4 (1) (h) further impedes the already complex task of the interpreter who could well find the most equitable law based on the principle of the closest connection or *lex specialis* on consumer contracts.

---

466 *C. Kessedjian*, "Party Autonomy and characteristic performance in the Rome Convention and the Roma I Proposal", in J. Basedow - H. Baum - Y. Nishitani (eds.), *Japanese and European private international law in comparative perspective*, (Mohr Siebeck, Tübingen, 2008), 122 - 125. In the Author's opinion "[...]in complex contracts, a better approach is the proper law or a center of gravity approach for, by definition, those contracts may very well cover several characteristic performances".

467 *J. Borg-Barthet*, *The Governing of Companies in EU Law*, (Hart Publishing, Oxford, 2012), 22 – 23. According to the Author "shareholders who invest via intermediaries are also consumers – of financial services, namely the services of advisers, brokers, dealers, managers, etc, while shareholders generally are view in a similar light through the prism of company law".

468 *Ex multis U. Magnus*, "Article 4 Rome I Regulation. The applicable law in absence of choice", in S. Leible - F. Ferrari (eds.), *Rome I Regulation the law applicable to contractual obligation in Europe*, (Sellier, Munich, 2009), 416; *E. Graziuso*, *La tutela del consumatore contro le clausole abusive*, (Giuffrè, Milano, 2010), 160.

469 *R. A. Schütze*, "Internationales Privatrecht", in H. D. Assmann – R.A. Schütze (eds.), *Handbuch des Kapitalanlagerechts*, (Verlag C.H. Beck, München, 2015), 35; *D. Martiny*, in *Münchener Kommentar zum Bürgerlichen Gesetzbuch*, "Art. 4 Rom I –VO", (Verlag C.H. Beck, München, 2010), no. 134. In line with the Author's opinion "*Gleiches sollte bei den multilateralen Systemen, die von Art. 4 Abs. 1 lit. h erfasst werden, gelten, in Bezug auf die gewährleistet sein sollte, dass das Recht des Staates des gewöhnlichen Aufenthalts des Verbrauchers nicht die Regeln berührt, die auf innerhalb solcher Systeme oder mit dem Betreiber solcher Systeme geschlossene Verträge anzuwenden sind*".

470 Rome I Regulation Recital § 28 – 29.

3.III.B The downgrade of the characteristic performance and closest connection principles in Rome I

On the basis of the previous pages, it is clear that the intention of the framers of Rome I in drafting the framework of Article 4 was to increase legal certainty and to limit the discretionary courts' power in the task of identifying the applicable law. However, Article 4 (2) of Rome I preserves the concept of "characteristic performance"[471] that comes into force when the list in Article 4 (1) does not indicate the applicable law. Indeed, at the same time, the Rome I framers fail to provide a definition of this "technical term", thus perpetuating the same problems of the Rome Convention and making a *renvoi* to the old school of thought[472] by the interpreter necessary.

In light of these observations, an important instrument for the interpreter in the crucial task of identifying the applicable law will remain the closest connection principle. As mentioned *supra*,[473] this is one of the basic underlying principles of the Convention, founded on the idea that the applicable law should be identified on the basis of the "most significant relationship".

As noted, this principle, albeit from a completely different perspective, is also inserted in Article 4 of Rome I, thereby establishing that the closest connection is usually best determined on the basis of the concept of characteristic performance.[474] However, the process of reaching this solution was not smooth. In fact, the attempt to eliminate the problematic implications in applying the connection criteria, established in the Rome Convention was undertaken by the Commission's Proposal and by the Green Paper of January 14, 2003. These instruments assumed that, with the simple insertion of objective and rigid criteria and by abolishing any degree of flexibility, the many problematic aspects that had arisen with the Convention would be resolved.

---

471 See for more *supra* § 3.I.

472 More on the different schools of thought see § 3.I.

473 See *supra* § 3.I.

474 *U. Magnus*, "Article 4 Rome I Regulation", in S. Leible - F. Ferrari (eds.), *Rome I Regulation the law applicable to contractual obligation in Europe*, (Sellier, Munich, 2009), 28.

The proposed solutions raised many doubts and criticisms,[475] in particular for their inflexible approach.[476] However, in the end, contrary to the suggestions in the Commission's Proposal (defined as "monument of rigidity"),[477] an extremely restrictive *clause d' exception* was formulated with the goal of ensuring that the closest connection principle applies only where the rigid criteria laid down Articles 4 (1) and (2) could not operate.

Therefore, it follows that, although with a completely different framework compared to the Rome Convention, the Rome I rules contain the "closest connection principle" with an "escape clause",[478] which can be applied only in circumstances in which the governing law cannot be determined under Article 4 (1) and (2), and "where it is clear from all the circumstances of the case that the contract is manifestly more closely connected with a country".[479]

This overview confirms that the closest connection criterion has lost the central role that it held in the Rome Convention. This approach, in my opinion, represents a failure of Rome I, given that this principle is proba-

---

475 The 2005 Proposal of the Commission, that had not been based on a proper academic study, had totally abandoned the escape clause. It only addressed choice of law and fixed rules as means to determine the applicable law abolishing what it called "escape clause". For more details on this proposal or for further comments and criticism see *S. Dutson*, "A Dangerous Proposal: The European Commission's Attempt to Amend the Law Applicable to Contractual Obligations", in (2006) *Journal of Business Law Review*, 610-614; *P. Lagarde*, "Remarques sur la proposition de règlement de la Commission europèenne sur la loi applicable aux obligations contractuelles (Rome I)", in (2006) *Revue critique de droit international privé*, 338; *O. Lando - P.A.Nielsen*, "The Rome I proposal", in (2007) 3 *Journal of Private Internazional Law*, 35; *Max Planck Institute for Comparative and International Private Law*, "Comments on the European Commissin's Proposal for a Regulation of the European parliament and the Council on the law applicable to contractual obligations (Rome I)", in (2007) *RabelsZ*, 225; *P. Piroddi*, "Between Scylla and Charybdis. Art. 4 of the Rome I Regulation Navigating along the cliffs of uncertainty and inflexibility", in G. Venturni - S. Bariatti (eds.), *Liber Fausto Pocar – New Instruments of Private International Law* (Giuffrè, Milano, 2009), 824.

476 *D. Martiny*, "The applicable law to contracts in absence of choice (Art. 4 Rome Convention)", in A.L. Calvo Caravaca - J. Carrascosa González (eds.), *Estudios sobre contratacìon international* (Editorial Colex, Madrid, 2006), 23.

477 *P. Piroddi*, "Between Scylla and Charybdis. Art. 4 of the Rome I Regulation Navigating along the cliffs of uncertainty and inflexibility", in G. Venturni - S. Bariatti (eds.), *Liber Fausto Pocar – New Instruments of Private International Law* (Giuffrè, Milano, 2009), 824.

478 For more see *infra* § 3.I.

479 Rome I Regulation Article 4 (3).

bly the most important instrument when localizing the country that, in practice, the contract actually has the most contact with. Therefore, the narrow and unclear clause of Rome I allows the courts to set aside the rigid rules only in exceptional circumstances.

Compared to the Rome Convention there are three important differences to note. Firstly, the provision establishes the circumstances in which it is appropriate to depart from a hard-and-fast rule.[480] Secondly, Article 4 (3) of the Rome I requires that the contract must to be "manifestly"[481] more closely connected to another country in order to disregard the applicable law designated under Article 4 (1) and (2). In choosing this specific word, the EU lawmakers probably wanted to indicate that the connecting factors of Article 4 (1) and (2) should not be disregarded easily, and are definitely not a "tiebreaker"[482] as one scholar[483] has suggested in respect of the position of Article 4 (2), (3) and (4) of the Rome Convention. Thirdly, the Convention's expression "the circumstances as a whole" has been substituted by "all the circumstance of the case", in order to handle the escape clause with more caution.[484]

However, to dispel any doubt about the limited use that the court can make of this principle, one simple question must be asked: What does "*manifestly closer connection*" mean? Its preamble also points out the connection to the idea that account should be taken of whether the contract in question has a very close relationship with another contract.

In general terms, probably a single aspect cannot in itself be decisive and a wide range of factors must be taken into consideration; as a consequence, the use of the escape clause would be "exceptional".[485] Therefore the word "manifestly" means "obvious"[486] or as in the opinion of Calvo Caravaca and Carrascosa Gonzàlez, when there is "*a vinculaciòn purament formal,*

---

480 *R. Plender - M. Wilderspin*, *The European Private International Law of Obligations*, (Sweet & Maxwell, London, 2009), 195.

481 By some Authors it is defined as "key change", see *P. R. Beaumont - P.E. McEleavy*, *Private International Law*, (Thomson Reuters, Edinburg, 2011), 480.

482 *Queen's Bench Division* (Commercial Court) September 16, 1996 *Credit Lyonnais v New Hampshire Insurance*, in (1997) *Lloyd's Law Reports*, 191 – 194.

483 See also *R. Baratta, Il collegamento più stretto nel diritto internazionale dei contratti* (Giuffrè, Milano, 1991), 135 – 142.

484 *R. Plender - M. Wilderspin*, *The European Private International Law of Obligations* (Sweet & Maxwell, London, 2009), 195.

485 For more see *infra*.

486 *P. R. Beaumont - P.E. McEleavy*, *Private International Law*, (Thomson Reuters, Edinburg, 2011), 481, or according to *U. Magnus*, "Art. 4", in U. Magnus – P. Manowsky (eds.), "European Commentaries on Private International Law –

nominal, fugaz, anecdòtica y aparente".[487] Summarizing all this, the escape clause should only be used when the circumstances are clear or evident to the eye of the interpreter.

In light of this analysis, it must be stressed that a clear and strong reference to the criteria of closest connection is no longer made. As a consequence these criteria should only be residually or rarely applied;[488] on the basis of an approach that can be described as inflexible[489] when set against the already not completely flexible approach adopted by the Convention. Against this backdrop, the "escape clause" can only be applied if the law cannot be determined based on the Article 4 (1) and (2) connection factors; and if having considered all of the cases's circumstances, the contract is found to have the manifestly closest connection with another country.

Finally, having identified in advance the residual nature of the principle in question, the conclusion will be drawn briefly: the closest connection principle can be applied only under exceptional circumstances, such as when the contract requires an exchange of performance of the same type or when the characteristic performer is difficult or impossible to identify[490] such as with letter credit transactions,[491] joint ventures, transfers of shares, or other cooperation contracts.[492]

Commentary, II, Rome I Regulation", (Ottoschmidt, Köln, 2017), 318 some cirmustances must have a significantly prevail over the connecting factors of the regular conflict rules.

487 *A. L. Calvo Caravaca – J. Carrascosa González*, *Derecho Internacional Privado*, (Comares, Granada, 2014), 863.

488 *F. Ferrari*, "Art. 4 Rom I-VO", in F. Ferrari – E.M. Kieninger - P. Mankowski (eds.), *Internationales Vertragsrecht, (VO) EG 593/2008*, (Verlag CH Beck, München, 2012), no. 78; *O. Lopes Pegna*, "Il Rilievo del collegamento più stretto dalla Convenzione di Roma alla proposta di regolamento "Roma I" ", in (2006) *Rivista di diritto internazionale*, 759.

489 *R. Plender - M. Wilderspin*, *The European Private International Law of Obligations*, (Sweet & Maxwell, London, 2009), 197.

490 *R. A. Schütze*, "Internationales Privatrecht", in H. D. Assmann – R.A. Schütze (eds.), *Handbuch des Kapitalanlagerechts*, (Verlag C.H. Beck, München, 2015), § 97; *F.J. Garcìmartin Alferez*, "The Rome I Regulation: Much about nothing?", in (2008) *The European Legal Forum*, 10. Available at http://www.simons-law.com/library/pdf/e/884.pdf.

491 *C. S. A. Okoli - G.O. Arishe*, "The operation of the escape clauses in the Rome Convention, Rome I Regulation and Rome II Regulation", in (2012) *Journal of Private International Law*, 530. In jurisprudence see *High Court of Justice Queen's Bench Division, Habib Bank Ltd v. Central Bank of Sudan* [2006] 1767 (Comm), available at http://www.bailii.org/ew/cases/EWHC/Comm/2006/1767.html . See also *infra* chapter 4.

492 For more see *infra* § 3. IV.

3.III.C The interpretation of the escape clause in Rome I

The above considerations point out the rigidity that characterizes the Rome I Regulation, in particular the structure of Article 4 and the formulation of the "escape clause"[493] that is used as a mere "supplementary"[494] instrument to help the interpreter in the task of identifying the applicable law. This escape clause, as shown, is based on a completely different perspective to that of the Rome Convention, and the court should resort to this instrument only when the contract is not present in Article 4 (1) or when, even with the rule of characteristic performance, the applicable law cannot be identified.

This extremely exceptional nature of the escape clause and the rigid framework of Article 4 leads to the conclusion[495] that the framers of the Rome I Regulation intended, in fact, to reformulate the theory of the "strong presumption approach",[496] on the basis of which the "escape clause" would be "a high hurdle in the way of a party seeking to displace the primary rule",[497] the disregard of which must be clearly justified.[498] This conclusion would be fully substantiated if the actual political goals of Rome I, included promoting "predictability" as a starting point. In this scenario, the interpreter is required to use this clause as a "last resort", i.e. only when the applicable law has not been identified using the principles listed in paragraphs (1) and (2) of Article 4.

493 Recital § 20 of the Rome I Regulation describes literally it as such.

494 *U. Magnus*, "Art. 4", in U. Magnus – P. Manowsky (eds.), "European Commentaries on Private International Law – Commentary, II, Rome I Regulation", (Ottoschmidt, Köln, 2017), 319; *C. S. Okoli - G. O. Arishe*, "The Operation of the escape clauses in the Rome Convention, Rome I regulation and Rome II Regulation", in (2012) *Journal of Private International Law*, 513. In a similar way and on the very restrict application of the escapes clause see *R. Hausmann*, "Le questioni generali nel diritto internazionale privato europeo", in (2015) *Rivista di diritto internazionale privato e processuale*, 512.

495 *C. S. Okoli - G. O. Arishe*, "The Operation of the escape clauses in the Rome Convention, Rome I regulation and Rome II Regulation", in (2012) *Journal of Private International Law*, 531.

496 See for more *supra* § 3.III in Rome Convention and *C.S. Okoli*, "The significance of the Doctrine of Accessory Allocation as a Connecting Factor under Article 4 of the Rome I Regulation", in (2013) *Journal of Private International Law*, 479.

497 *High Court of Justice Queen's Bench Division*, September 25, 2013 - *Bnp paribas sa v anchorage capital europe llp* [64].

498 *M. McParland*, *The Rome I regulation on the law applicable to contractual obligations*, (O.U.P., Oxford, 2015), 432 and 437.

In addition, I have reasoned that the rigid approach of Rome I, and the presence of a list that contains most of the commercial contracts used in EU cross-border transactions, does not give space to the theory of commercial expectations put forward by Fentiman[499] according to whom, as seen,[500] the interpreter in the task of identifying the applicable law must take into account "the gravity of a commercial contract".

Currently the ECJ has not yet had a precise occasion to interpret the escape clause of Article 4 (3). However, a restrictive interpretation of this clause can be supported not only by the inflexible structure of the Rome I Regulation, but also by a well-known much larger project of "communitarization" of p.i.l., or as defined by one scholar[501] the "new Rome regime", and in particular by the same approach adopted by the Rome II Regulation[502] regarding non-contractual obligation, which in Article 4 (3) mentions a clause again pointing out the "manifestly closer connection". According to Dickinson, "as exceptional" this clause [requires] strong clear reasons for displacing the law otherwise applicable under Art. 4 (1) and (2). The addition of the word "manifestly" which does not appear in Art. 4 (5) of the Rome Convention but has been added to the corresponding provision in the Rome I Regulation, suggest a test focusing on objective factors, including outward expressions of the law applicable to the parties' relationship, rather than the subjective intentions or expectations of the parties".[503]

In practice, due to the inflexible nature of the escape clause, the diversity of the category of contracts not expressly listed in Article 4 (1) and the difficulties that the interpreter may also encounter in reference to the contracts listed, the result is that the Regulation looks like a "labyrinth" or "puzzle". In fact the list of contracts and the escape clause as reformulated in Rome I, do not grant the interpreter that margin of discretion to weigh up all the circumstances of the contract against each other, as in the case of

---

499 See also *R. Fentiman*, *International Commercial Litigation*, (O.U.P., Oxford, 2010), *passim*.

500 For more about this theory see *supra* § 3.III.

501 *M. McParland*, *The Rome I Regulation on the law applicable to contractual obligations*, (O.U.P., Oxford, 2015), 4.

502 Regulation (EC) No 864/2007 of the European Parliament and of the Council of July 11, 2007 on the law applicable to non-contractual obligations.

503 In these words, *A. Dickinson*, *The Rome II Regulation – The Law Applicable to non-contractual obligations*, (O.U.P., Oxford, 2008), 340 – 341. In the same way *Dicey & Morris*, *The conflict of laws*, 15th ed. (L. Collins ed.), (Sweet&Maxwell, London, 2012), no. 35-032, 2214 – 2215.

a tacit choice of law.[504] Therefore, working within these hurdles imposed by EU lawmakers, the interpreter could reach a *"résultat injuste"*[505] because the criteria adopted in Article 4 does not always pledge the application of an equitable law closely connected with the reasonable expectations of contractual parties. The consequence, in my opinion, is that the application of an "inequitable" law does not protect the players of the market and can cause harm to the market itself.

3.III.D Critical analysis of article 4 (1) of the Rome I Regulation

The remarks made in the study of individual contracts listed in Article 4 give life to more critiques, starting with the issue that the rigid approach and the presence of a generic list of contracts[506] not only fails to facilitate the task of the interpreter in identifying the applicable law but rather disorientates him.[507] The consequence of this obstacle is that the court may then apply an "inequitable" law.

In this sense, I have argued that the critiques of Article 4 are founded on a standpoint of rigidity and classification. Article 4 (1), appears, from a formal point of view, to have completely lost the flexibility that should be inherent in a p.i.l. instrument that is intended to ensure the application of the most equitable law including a detailed investigation of the problems. In addition Article 4 (1) lists eight different types of contract without a definition, with the result that these omissions can also lead to general problems of interpretation, as in the case of distribution contracts.[508]

---

504 *P. Franzina*, "La scelta tacita della legge applicabile al contratto secondo il Regolamento Roma I", in (2016) *Cuadernos de Derecho Transnacional*, 238.

505 *J. Carrascosa González*, "Règle de conflit et théorie économique", in (2012) *Revue critique de droit international privé*, 529.

506 *F. Ferrari – J. A. Bischoff*, "Article 4", in F. Ferrari (ed.) *Rome I Regulation. Pocket commentary*, (Sellier, Munich, 2014), 129. According to the Authors "there is no one common principle that inspires all the rules contained in Article 4 (1)".

507 At this point I want to rewrite the words of *G. Alpa*, *Competition of Legal Systems and Harmonization of European Private Law. New Paths in a Comparative Perspectives*. (Sellier, Munich, 2013), 54, who famously argues "Legal hermeneutics teaches us that the freedom of the interpreter is not unlimited, but we also know that the interpreter does not tolerate excessive limitations and that, despite the definitions, interpretation overflows, it goes beyond, it adapts, it conforms, it shapes, in other words it 'manipulates' the text. And it should be, because the text has a life of its own".

508 See *supra* about the distribution contracts.

Overall, clearly delineating these contracts is not a a straightforward task as in the case of separating, for example, franchising contracts from distribution contracts[509] and from other closely related contracts such as agency contracts. It is also difficult to distinguish the sale of goods from contracts for the provision of services, especially when the subject matter is intangible. In fact, some service contracts include elements relating to the sale of goods, which some sales contracts include elements relating to the provision of services. To illustrate the reasoning underlying this consideration, let me take the example of a contract for the sale of goods usually includes terms concerning after-sale service. Some sellers also provide instructions and training services for their customers to assist them in the use of their products. These contracts include elements covered by the provision of services, but the predominant obligation in the contract is to transfer ownership of the goods. With this example, even where there are elements common to Article 4 (1) (a) and (b), it is difficult to determine whether or not the contract can be identified as a sale of goods contract.[510] Finally, it is also important to add that the connecting factors for contracts for the sale of goods and contracts for the provision of services are determined on the basis of the characteristic performance rule already realised in the Rome Convention.

These observations suggest that the list of contracts would not appear to be a welcome addition. However, the obvious questions to be posed are: Firstly why did EU lawmakers choose these contracts while leaving out other international commercial contracts? Secondly, with the insertion of a list of contracts, has the aim of improving fairness and the ease of determining the applicable law really been achieved? In all probability, the same result would be achieved by using the characteristic performance rule still governed by Article 4 of the Rome Convention,[511] especially with reference to some contracts. Therefore, starting with this last point, another question presents itself here: Why include an exhaustive list of specific types of contracts, when the choice made in Article 4 (1) (a) (b) is the same

509 About this topic see *S. Marino*, "Nuove forme di contraente debole nel regolamento "Rome I"?", in I Papanicolopulu (ed.), *Atti del V incontro di studio tra giovani cultori delle materie internazionalistiche*, (Giuffrè, Milano, 2008), 287 ss.

510 *U. Villani*, "Il ruolo della prestazione caratteristica dalla Convenzione di Roma al regolamento 'Roma I' sulla legge applicabile ai contratti sulla legge applicabile ai contratti", in (2010) *Studi sull'integrazione europea*, 594.

511 *Z. S. Tang*, "Law applicable in the absence of choice – the new article 4 of the Rome I Regulation", in (2008) *The Modern Law Review*, 790.

as could have been made by applying the "characteristic performance" rule?

Article 4 (1) of Rome I advances little further than its predecessor, the Rome Convention. As it will be illustrated in detail below,[512] it does not improve the situation where characteristic performance cannot be decided. For example, an exchange contract may be a contract for the sale of goods or a contract for the provision of services,[513] depending on the nature of the subject matter. Since both parties are supplying goods or providing services, there are two sellers or service providers in the contract, and it is difficult to decide which law must be applied. Similarly in the case of a joint venture contract,[514] the situation can appear equally confusing because in most cases there is more than one party providing the services.[515]

Finally, the Rome I system fails to take account of the "wide variety of contracts"[516] that exist, and of the variety of frameworks in which these contracts are operative, which is a very important element from an European perspective, considering that there are many countries involved with different legal backgrounds. In addition, the list contained in Article 4 (1) does not seem altogether appropriate in dealing with complex matters. For instance, in contrast to the Rome I Proposal, there is no specific reference to a contract relating to intellectual or industrial property rights, which

---

512 See § 3.III.

513 The case law of some countries (see Italian *Corte di Cassazione Sezioni Unite* March 10, 2000 n. 58, in (2000) *Foro italiano*, VII-VIII, 2226), expressing on the Rome Convention, considered appropriate to exclude the application of the law for the seller's habitual residence, in regard of the relevance of the execution of other obligations related to the sale, as a proof of the existence of a closer connection with the place of execution.

514 See for more *infra* chapter "pros and cons" § 3.IV.

515 *Z. S. Tang*, "Law Applicable in the Absence of Choice – The New Article 4 of the Rome I Regulation", in (2008) *The Modern Law Review*, 792.

516 See Max Planck Institute Comments Rome I, 263 in http://www.mpipriv.de/ww/en/pub/research/research_work/international_private_law_proc/contract_law/opinion_on_greenbook.cfm.

gives rise to serious difficulties for the interpreter[517] when identifying characteristic performance.[518]

In light of the criticisms that have been made, and as the following chapters will show, Article 4 appears a "puzzle" that the interpreter is required to decode. Therefore, the rigid approach will not help the court in the complex task of identifying the applicable law in absence of parties' choice. The result is a limit to the discretionary power of the court that may lead to a "*résultat injuste*" that is certainty detrimental to the contractual parties, the principal players of the internal market.

3.III.E *Special rules for contracts of carriage*

The privileged position that Rome I reserves for contracts of carriage has its source in the Rome Convention,[519] where Article 4 (4) sets forth a special presumption of connection for a contract of carriage of goods. The

---

517 For the criticism about these contracts see *P.A. De Miguel Asensio*, "Applicable law in the absence of choice to contracts relating to intellectual or industrial property rights", in (2008) *Yearbook of Private International Law*, 199. In line with the Author's opinion "Such situations may be frequent in the field of contracts relating to industrial or intellectual property rights to the extent that in some of these contracts the characteristic performance may be impossible to determine. That is the case of so-called reciprocal agreements or license exchange contracts".

518 *F. Ferrari*, "From Rome to Rome via Brussels: Remarks on the law applicable to contractual obligation absent a choice by the parties (Art. 4 of the Rome I Regulation)", in (2009) *RabelsZ*, 762. In line with the Author's opinion "This rule was eliminated due to the criticism it had encountered on the grounds that it was not really capable of appropriately identifying the applicable law to all contracts involving the transfer or assignment of such rights". See also in this way *P. Torremans*, "Licenses and assignments of intellectual property rights", in (2008) *Journal of Private International Law*, 415. According to the Author is important to apply the law of "primary country of protection".

519 Actually, it should not be neglected that the discipline of carriage has always been the subject of harmonisation work by the EU legislator, as demonstrated by frequent legislative production. Consider, too, the Hamburg Conventions of March 31, 1978 or the Montreal Convention on the subject of aircraft transport, or road and rail transport as in the case of the Geneva Convention of May 19, 1956 and the Bern Convention of May 9, 1980. The latter will prevail with respect to the regulation as they require rules provided with exclusive applicability to the case in question. On the point *S. Tonolo*, "La legge applicabile ai contratti di trasporto nel regolamento Roma I", in (2009) *Rivista di diritto internazionale privato e processuale*, 313, according to the Author: "*É infatti generalmente accetta-*

Regulation identifies the applicable law as that of the country where the carrier has habitual residence when concluding the contract, whether this is where loading and unloading takes place or is the main habitual residence of the consignor. This rule, which certainly favours strict criteria of connection to the closest connection principle or characteristic performance, has been the source of a high degree of uncertainty in terms of its application. In fact, the concept of "principal place of business" adopted in the Rome Convention would almost inevitably lead to the application of an inequitable law in particular circumstances, e.g. in relation to maritime carriers operating under a 'flag of convenience'.[520]

Therefore, the analytical discipline provided in the EU instrument must not be regarded as a discounted transposition of the provisions already present in the Convention.[521] This "survival" is the fruit of a bumpy ride through the legislative procedure,[522] something that is perfectly understandable and acceptable, given that this contract is seen as being the international contract par excellence.[523]

However, Rome I separates "contract of carriage of goods" and "passenger transport" respectively as covered by paragraphs (1) and (2). In paragraph (3), there is a clause whereby the rules dictated in the preceding paragraphs do not apply, if from all of the circumstances of the contract,

---

to che, in materia di trasporti internazionali, per gli aspetti sottoposti alle convenzioni di diritto materiale uniforme, le regole di conflitto diventano "permissive conflict rules", *destinate a non ricevere applicazione, anche alla luce della possibile configurazione delle disposizioni contenute in tali convenzioni come disposizioni imperative o norme di applicazione necessaria*".

520 *M. McParland*, *The Rome I regulation on the law applicable to contractual obligations*, (O.U.P., Oxford, 2015), 448. According to the Author "This would frequently be the law of a distant country not linked in any way with the particular transport".

521 *U. Magnus - P. Mankowsky*, "The Green Paper on a future Rome I Regulation – on the road to a renews European Private International Law of Contracts", in (2004) *ZvglRWiss*, 131; *F. Ferrari - S. Lieble*, *Ein neues Internationales Vertragsrecht für Europa - Der Vorschlag für eine Rom I-Verordnung* (Jenaer Wissenschaftliche Verlagsgesellschaft, München, 2007), *passim*; *O. Hartenstein*, "Rom-I Entwurf und Rom II-Verordnung", in (2008) *TranspR*, 143.

522 The Green Paper did not mention the contract of carriage which should not originally have had the current privileged position to date. Only in the last stage of the approval procedure of the Rome I Regulation has been added the current version of the text of article 5.

523 *O. Lando - P. Nielsen*, "The Rome I regulation", in (2008) *Common Market Law Review*, 1706; *P. Zucconelli*, "Il regolamento Roma I e la legge applicabile al contratto di trasporto", in (2011) *Obbligazioni e contratti*, 203.

the case has clearly manifestly closest connection with a country other than those listed in paragraphs (1) and (2).

Before focussing on the structure of the Article, it would seem that the division between transport of goods and people is questionable. In fact, where the contract provides the transport of both people and goods (e.g. the carriage of luggage in the hold of aircraft),[524] the interpretation might easily fall into error considering that both Article 4 (1) (b), and Articles 5 or 6 could be applied.[525] At the same time, there could be difficulties in contracts where the parties are not the passengers, eg. in an agreement between an airline company and a travel agency.[526] In these circumstances, I do not hesitate to say that the absence of choice by the parties does not make it easy to identify the applicable law because the contract could qualify as a provision of services, ruled already by Article 4 (1) (b).

However, where a contract of carriage of goods is concerned, which, in the absence of an exhaustive list, could include carriage by road, rail, air and ship, the EU lawmakers have left in force, as in the Rome Convention, the principle of party autonomy. As a consequence, only in the absence of choice does Article 5 (1) impose a certain hierarchy, stating that the applicable law will be that of the country of residence of the carrier, so long as the following are also in that country:

1. the place of receipt of the goods;
2. the place of delivery of the goods;
3. the habitual residence of the consignor.

According to the framers of Rome I, compared to the Convention rules, these criteria should be helpful in the interpretation of the difficult task of identifying the characteristic performance of the contract of carriage.[527] Neverthless, the interpreter is also required to weigh up the concepts of "carrier" and "consignor" in more detail, as well as the generic notion of habitual residence which may or may not also extend to the branch or agency via which the contract was concluded. This, in turn opens the door

---

524 *Dicey & Morris*, *The conflict of laws*, 15th ed. (L. Collins ed.), (Sweet&Maxwell, London, 2012), no. 33-073.

525 *A. Staudinger*, "Rom I-VO Artikel 6 Beförderungsverträge Handkommentar", in R. Schulze – H. Dörner – I. Ebert – T. Hoeren – R. Kemper – I. Saenger – K. Schreiber – H. Schulte-Nölke – A. Staudinger (eds.), *Bürgerliches Gesetzbuch. Handkommentar,* (Nomos, Baden, 2014), no. 7, in www.beckonline.beck.de .

526 *C. Rudolf*, "Europäisches Kollisionsrecht für vertragliche Schuldverhältnisse – Rom I-VO", in (2011) *Österreichische Juristen-Zeitung*, 154.

527 ECJ C-305/13, *Haeger & Schmidt GmbH v. Mutuelles du assurances IARD and Others*, § 22.

to the well-known phenomenon of "forum shopping". In addition the second sentence of Article 5 (1) contains a "fall-back" rule[528] with an express reference to the "place of the delivery", because in "most international carriage of goods by sea cases, the principal connecting factors are unlikely to be met".[529] This approach demands of the interpreter a careful analysis, and the uniformity of the decisions, in my view, is not always guaranteed. In fact, Rome I provides no guidance on the concept of delivery, and if there has been no specific agreement on it's localization, Article 5 (1) should not apply. As as a consequence, the contract would be governed by the provisions of Article 4 (2) or (3).

The requirements of legal certainty, the roots of which are in the privileged position covered by Article 5, also risk losing meaning when it comes to partial loads[530] or multiple transport,[531] i.e. where a single contract obliges the carrier to distribute the delivery to multiple recipients located in different States, both in the EU and beyond. If it is not possible to identify precisely the main place of delivery, the consequence is the fragmentation of the law.[532] As a consequence, the interpreter[533] must scrupulously work in order to apply the most equitable law.

In addition, it is highly likely that the rigid approach of Rome I and the list of contracts of Article 4 do not constitute an aid for the interpreter in complex categories of contracts such as "charter".[534] To me, this seems to indicate that it is another indication that these rigid criteria do not guarantee the predictability of the outcome of litigation or the legal certainty as to the applicable law.

---

528 *M. McParland, The Rome I Regulation on the law applicable to contractual obligations*, (O.U.P., Oxford, 2015), 474.

529 *Ibid.*

530 *A. Staudinger*, "Art. 5 Rom I-VO", in F. Ferrari – E.M. Kieninger - P. Mankowski (eds.), *Internationales Vertragsrecht, (VO) EG 593/2008*, (Verlag CH Beck, München, 2012), no. 39.

531 *Z. Ringe*, 'Art. 5 Rom-I VO', in *Juris Praxiskommentar BGB, Internationales Privatrecht*, IV (Juris, Saarbrücken, 2009), 6.

532 *P. Zucconelli*, "Il regolamento Roma I e la legge applicabile al contratto di trasporto", in (2011) *Obbligazioni e contratti*, 206.

533 *A. Staudinger*, "Art. 5 Rom I-VO", in F. Ferrari – E.M. Kieninger - P. Mankowski (eds.), *Internationales Vertragsrecht, (VO) EG 593/2008*, (Verlag CH Beck, München, 2012), no. 55. According to the Author "*Zwischenhalte, um etwa lediglich den Zu- oder Ausstieg anderer Kunden bzw. den Wechsel des Transportmittels zu ermöglichen, bilden in der Regel keine weiteren Anknüpfungspunkte im Sinne eines selbständigen Bestimmungs- bzw. neuen Abgangsortes*".

534 See for more § 3. IV.

As regards the transport of persons, this rule is new in comparison to the Convention,[535] which goes no further than establishing a generic provision. The Article 5 (2)[536] is structured as follows: the parties are permitted their choice of law provided that it is "justified" by a connection between the contract and the chosen country. In this framework, the purpose of the framers of Rome I would be, according to one view,[537] trying to avoid both disproportionately favouring the passenger and creating excessive legal uncertainty for the carrier.[538]

Therefore, according to Article 5, the parties may themselves choose the applicable law for a contract for the carriage of passengers only when the law of the country contains the following:

- passenger's habitual residence;
- carrier's habitual residence;
- central administration of the carrier;
- place of departure or the place of destination.

In the absence of parties choice the contract will be governed by the law of the passenger's habitual residence, only if the place of destination or departure is in that same country; otherwise, the law in the country of the carrier's habitual residence will govern the contract.[539] This rule is full of points of connection and could create problems to the interpreter in the task of identifying the applicable law when dealing with a "round trip" (e.g. cruise, or a round the word airline ticket). In this case, by using a more flexible approach Dicey and Morris suggest that the applicable law should

535 *A. La Mattina*, "Il passeggero quale parte debole del contratto di trasporto", in (2012) *Il Diritto Marittimo*, 809. In the Authors' opinion "*La* ratio *di tale disposizione è dichiaratamente quella di garantire un adeguato livello di tutela dei passeggeri. La norma di conflitto, almeno nelle intenzioni del legislatore europeo, sarebbe quindi rivolta a soddisfare il perseguimento di 'considerazioni materiali' ispirate alla tutela della parte debole del contratto di trasporto passeggeri*".

536 Is important to remember that Article 5 (2) shall also apply if the passenger is a consumer, under the provisions of Article 6 (see *infra*) apart from the evaluation of the professional or purely private purpose underlying the purchase of the travel ticket. Package tour contracts evade this rule or transport related to trips organized from the time when the holidays and all inclusive trips are governed by Article 6 of the Regulation.

537 *G. Contaldi*, "Il contratto internazionale di trasporto di persone", in N. Boschiero (ed.), *La nuova disciplina comunitaria della legge applicabile ai contratti (Roma I)*, (Giappichelli, Torino, 2009), 380 – 381.

538 *Ibid*, 377.

539 See also the Opinion of Advocate General Bot in C-133/08 *Intercontainer Interfrigo SC (ICF) v. Balkenende Oosthuizen BV, MIC Operations BV.*

be that of the initial country of departure or place of final destination,[540] which would guarantee a higher level of protection for the passenger, who is more closely connected to the contract.

Finally, in order to tackle the difficulties that the interpreter may well encounter in the contract, Article 5 (3) also closes with an "escape clause" which should assist the interpreter in the crucial task of identifying the applicable law with the principle of the closest connection.[541] Thus, Rome I should call for the interpreter to carry out a detailed assessment, looking at the different aspects of the relationship and the individual connection criteria, such as the nationality of the parties, their residence, the aim of the trip, the language of the contract, the formation of the contract and its execution.[542]

The aim of this provision was an attempt to find the right balance between the needs of legal certainty as required by transport companies and the legitimate expectations of the consignor or passengers,[543] which must be subject to a law that is in some way connected to the contract.[544] The result is that the passenger does not enjoy the same form of protection that is offered by the rules for consumers[545] or employees.

540 *Dicey & Morris*, *The conflict of laws*, 15th ed. (L. Collins ed.), (Sweet&Maxwell, London, 2012), no. 33-077, 1920.

541 Consider the case in which the journey begins in a defined State but then is divided into a series of further stop-overs, not defined a priori.

542 *S. Tonolo*, "La legge applicabile ai contratti di trasporto nel regolamento Roma I", in (2009) *Rivista di diritto internazionale privato e processuale*, 324 - 325.

543 *Z. S. Tang*, *Electronic Consumer Contracts in the Conflict of Laws* (Hart Publishing, Oxford and Portland, 2015), 228. In line with the Author's opinion "the special arrangment in Article 5 intends to achieve a compromise between consumer associations and the transport industry".

544 *I. Pretelli*, "Il regolamento comunitario sulla legge applicabile alle obbligazioni contrattuali (Roma I)", in (2009) *Europa e Diritto Privato*, 1119; *V. Behr*, "Rome I Regulation a mostly unified private international law of contractual relationships within most of the European Union", in (2011) *Journal of law and commerce*, 251.

545 On this point I should remember the words of Symeonides, according to which "[...] in most cases, the contractually chosen law will be applied in the above hypothetical despite depriving the passenger of the protection provided by the mandatory rules of the country whose law would have been applicable in the absence of choice. The resulti is regrettable. For all practical purpose, the passenger is a consumer who chould be protected from the adverse consequences of a contractual choice of law for the same policy and practical reasons for whoich Article 6 protects other consumers". *S. C. Symeonides*, *Codifying Choice of Law Around the World*, (O.U.P., Oxford, 2014), 167. See also *C. Rudolf*, "Inter-

Indeed, though, it is not always easy for the court to identify the carrier's habitual residence or, in particular, the place of departure of the goods. As a result, certainty regarding the applicable law can only be determined once a proper investigation has been undertaken by the interpreter; this will, on the vast majority of occasions, most likely resort to the "escape clause" if the interpreter aspires to apply the most equitable law.

To these considerations must be added that the word "manifestly" inserted also in the escape clause of Article 5 (3) produces the same limits as Article 4[546] to the discretionary power of the interpreter. The consequence is that the escape clause should be applied only rarely or even better with the presence of a plurality of connecting factors listed in Article 5. This circumstance certainly does not guarantee the application of the most equitable law which, within a complex and typical international contract such as transport, may be guaranteed only with the closest connection principle or by the evaluation of all the circumstances of the case. This situation was also pointed out by ECJ in the recent C-305/13 where the Court, enhancing the closest connection principle, held that

> "the contract for the carriage of goods [...], at least in a cross-border context, does not lend itself easily to being connected with the country of residence of the contractual party who effects the characteristic performance, [...] given that the principal purpose of such a contract is the transport of goods and the carrier's habitual residence has no objective connection with that contract".[547]

The court also specified that "in order to ascertain that purpose, it is necessary to take into consideration the objective of the contractual relationship and, consequently, all the obligations of the party who effects the performance which is characteristic of the contract".[548] These considerations must include all relevant circumstances, "including the existence of other contracts connected with the contract in question".[549]

To summarize, I would like to comment as follows. Certainly, for the transport-of-goods contracts, rigid connection criteria and limits to the discretionary power of the interpreter could represent a detriment to the eco-

---

nationales Vertragsrecht – Rom I – Verordnung ab 17.12.2009 maßgebend", in (2009) *ecolex*, 1116.

546 See for more *supra* § 3.I.

547 ECJ C-305/13, *Haeger & Schmidt GmbH v. Mutuelles du assurances IARD and Others*, § 22.

548 *Ibid*, § 26.

549 *Ibid*, § 51.

nomic activities of the parties, in particular of the consignor. Instead, with regard to passengers that can well be described as the "weaker party", even though the applicable law is often pre-chosen in standard contracts, it would be preferable that the EU lawmakers had guaranteed the same protection provided to the consumer[550] when the passenger acts for purposes which are outside his trade or profession, as Basedow's example points out:

> "A German tourist taking a train ride from Madrid to Sevilla should be subject to the same national provisions, regardless of whether he bought the ticket in Madrid or at the office of the Spanish railway company in Germany".[551]

Let me end by noting that, to regulate this type of contract with a more flexible "escape clause", as in the Rome Convention, referring to consumer contracts when the passenger is acting for purposes unrelated to his trade or profession would certainly have allowed not only the application of the most equitable law but would also have assisted the interpreter in not making mistakes in the face of the strict criteria of a multiplicity of connection included in Article 5 of the Rome I Regulation. At this point I want stress that, the complexity of this Article does not simplify the interpreter's task of identifying the applicable law, and consequently the result will not be uniformity of decision-making.

3.III.F Focus on consumer contracts

The Rome I Regulation, just like the Rome Convention, rules contracts concluded by consumers with a *lex specialis*.[552] Article 6 has introduced a detailed framework of rules of p.i.l., containing a multiplicity of connect-

550 *Z. S. Tang*, *Electronic Consumer Contracts in the Conflict of Laws* (Hart Publishing, Oxford - Portland, 2015), 222. The Author, taking as example an online booking of a transport tickets by passenger, held "Depriving the e-passengers of protection is unwelcome and contrary to the policy to protect the weaker party".

551 *J. Basedow*, "Consumer Contracts and Insurance Contracts in a Future Rome I Regulation", in J. Meeusen - M. Pertegás - G. Straetmans (eds.), *Enforcement of International Contracts in the European Union. Convergence and divergence between Brussels I and Rome I*, (Intersentia, Antwerp-Oxford-New York, 2004), 273.

552 For more on the reasons for special rule for the consumers in p.i.l. see *J. Harris*, "Consumer Protection in Private International Law", in F. Mesel - P. Cook (eds.), *Property and Protection: Legal Rights and Restrictions* (Hart Publishing, Oxford, 2000), 245 ss.

ing factors, albeit in recognition of the undoubted importance given to party autonomy and the appropriate safeguards for the consumer,[553] who, as seen, is in a weaker position compared to the sellers or suppliers of goods and services. In fact, the applicable law for contracts between a professional and a consumer is that agreed by the parties or, when such a choice is not made, that of the country in which the consumer habitually resides, provided that the professional - and this is the real innovation compared to the Rome Convention - pursues his/her commercial or professional activities in the country where the consumer habitually resides,[554] or directs his activities to that country and the contract falls within the sphere of the said activity. Therefore the framers of Rome I have defined the consumer as the person who deals with the professional for a purpose which may be regarded as being outside his own trade or profession.[555] Furthermore, compared to the Convention, the framers of Rome I take care to specify that the counterparty of the consumer must be a professional, thus aiming to clarify when the Article 6 can be applied. As a consequence, the interpreter needs to deeply analyse the contract - in fact to be clearer, when a lawyer who buys a series of law reports does so for the purpose of his profession the consumer protection cannot be applied.[556]

However, from among the various innovations, what emerges above all is that, while Article 5 of the Rome Convention limited its operations to contracts for the supply of goods or services to a person and to contracts for financing, the Regulation by contrast, applies equally to contracts of carriage and insurance and to all contracts concluded by consumers, as long as they are not among those mentioned in Article 6. Therefore, the new provision also makes mention of the negotiating figures who were denied the application of Article 5 of the Rome Convention. Consider loan agreements or mortgages not connected to the supply of goods or ser-

553 *G. Passarelli*, "The protection of the European consumer in private international law - Some General Remarks", in (2014) *Contratto e Impresa /Europa*, 209.

554 *C. Rudolf*, "Internationales Vertragsrecht – Rom I – Verordnung ab 17.12.2009 maßgebend", in (2009) *ecolex*, 1117; *P. Cachia*, "Consumer contracts in European private international law: The sphere of operation of the consumer contract rules in the Brussels I and Rome I Regulations", in (2009) *European Law Review*, 483. In line with the Author's opinion "While the concept of pursuing activities in the consumer's state may require some physical presence in that state, the concept of directing activities clearly does not".

555 In general, on the contracts between consumers and professionals see *E. Minervini*, *Dei contratti del consumatore in generale*, (Giappichelli, Torino, 2010), 35.

556 *A. Briggs*, *Private International Law in English Courts*, (O.U.P., Oxford, 2014), 563. See in the same way ECJ C-508/12, *Vapenik v. Thurner*, §§ 30 - 31.

vices;[557] bank contracts not involving the provision of services by the bank (e.g. cash deposits, timeshare transfers, etc.); and contracts relating to real estate property.[558] As a consequence in some cases (eg. when the professional does not conduct his activities in the country where the consumer habitually resides), the law of the "stronger" party (banks, entrepreneurs, provider of services) may be also applied.[559] In addition, the new provision also mentions the category of so-called "active" or "mobile" consumers[560] (i.e. those who travel to a country other than that of their habitual residence to make a purchase and receive a service or those that are parties in relation to e-commerce contracts)[561] who did not previously enjoy adequate protection under Article 5 of the Rome Convention, as it referred only to "tangible goods".[562] In fact, the new rule aims to ensure protection

557 See *Tribunal d'arrondissement* (Luxemburg), March 27, 1990, in (1991) *Rivista di diritto internazionale privato e processuale*, 1097.

558 *F. Ragno*, "The law applicable to Consumer Contracts under Rome I Regulation", in F. Ferrari - S. Leible (eds.), *Rome I Regulation: The Law applicable to Contractual obligations in Europe*, (Sellier, Munich, 2009), 149; *G. Passarelli*, "La legge applicabile ai contratti internazionali conclusi dai consumatori alla luce del regolamento Roma I", in (2011) *Rassegna di diritto civile*, 1152.

559 The Italian *Corte di Cassazione, Sezioni Unite*, May 19, 2010 n. 11532, in reference to the *lex fori* held *"ai fini dell' individuazione del giudice al quale spetta la giurisdizione nei confronti dello straniero, nelle controversie relative a contratti conclusi con i consumatori, è necessario* [...] *che il contratto sia concluso con un professionista le cui attività commerciali o professionali si svolgano nello Stato membro ove è domiciliato il consumatore o siano dirette, con qualsiasi mezzo, verso tale Stato membro o verso una pluralità di Stati che comprendono tale Stato membro. Nella fattispecie la Corte ha escluso la giurisdizione italiana perché la parte che invocava l'applicazione del foro del consumatore, in relazione all' inadempimento del dovere informativo relativo allo* 'jus poenitendi' *in un contratto di mutuo, non aveva neanche allegato che l'impresa bancaria estera dirigesse la propria attività anche verso l' Italia"*. In these words, *G. Alpa*, "Autonomia delle parti e scelta della legge applicabile al contratto "interno"", in (2013) *Nuova Giurisprudenza Civile Commentata*, 574 - 575.

560 *L.E. Gillies*, "Choice of law rules for electronic consumer contracts: replacement of the Rome Convention by the Rome I Regulation", in (2007) *Journal of Private of International Law*, 89; *T. Ballarino*, "Dalla Convenzione di Roma del 1980 al regolamento Roma I", in (2009) *Rivista di diritto internazionale*, 50.

561 *S. Leible*, "Verbesserung des kollisionsrechtlichen Verbraucherschutzes", in S. Leible (ed.), *Das Grünbuch zum Internationalen Vertragsrecht: Beiträge zur Fortentwicklung des Europäischen Kollisionsrechts der vertraglichen Schuldverhältnisse*, (Sellier, Munich, 2004), 142.

562 *M. McParland*, *The Rome I Regulation on the law applicable to contractual obligations*, (O.U.P., Oxford, 2015), 511. According to the Author "The concern was that software did not possess that essential corporeal requirement".

also of so-called "mobile" consumers (e.g. a party in an online contract), but it does not clarify what "mobile" consumer means. An example of a "mobile" consumer might be one who downloads software, music and films via the web or books a trip via email;[563] as well as one who conducts specific financial operations through an internet auction. In these cases, the applicable law will be that of the country where the consumer has habitual residence.[564] In contrast a "passive" consumer might be one who uses an interactive website where it is not possible to conclude a contract or alternatively where the consumer uses a website but the professional does not direct the activities in the country of habitual residence.

The *ratio legis* behind these revisions lies in the fact that e-commerce constitutes certainly one of the most important sales channels in Europe and that the applicable protocol is not entirely clear.[565] In fact in *online* relationships the factors that determine contractual strength and weakness and the critical aspects of a transaction may look different compared to those in the traditional marketplace and it is especially via e-commerce that the propensity toward the phenomenon of so-called standardisation of contracts can be determined. This would suggest that the rules laid down to protect the consumer are also capable of adapting to trading via the internet.[566] As of now, it is known that it is standard contracts, typical of e-

563 *Ibid*, 524; *M. Weller – C. F. Nordmeier*, "Rom I - Art. 6", in G. Spindler - F. Schuster (eds.), *Recht der elektronischen Medien*, (Verlag C.H. Beck, München, 2015), no. 6.

564 *T. D. Czingler – I. Takacs*, "The Quest to Find a Law Applicable to Contracts in the European Union – A Summary of Fragmented Provisions", in (2012) *Global Jurist*, 12 – 13.

565 *E. Minervini – P. Bartolomucci*, "La tutela del consumatore telematico", in D. Valentino (ed.) *Manuale di diritto dell' informatica*, (E.S.I., Napoli, 2011), 348. In line with the Author's opinion "*Il mondo di Internet e quello dei consumatori sono divenuti per il giurista delle realtà complesse da regolamentare, entrambe con le loro definizioni, le loro prassi, i loro meccanismi, e i loro strumenti di tutela*".

566 On the question when a consumer surfing on the internet is active or passive and the applicable law in e-commerce see *C. Riefa*, "Article 5 of the Rome convention on the law applicable to contractual obligations of June 19, 1980 and consumer E-contracts: the need for reform", (2004) *Information & Communications Technology Law*, 59; *Z. S. Tang*, "Parties' choice of law in e-commerce e-consumer contracts", in (2007) *Journal of Private International Law*, 138; *L. E. Gillies*, "Choice-of-Law rules for electronic Consumer contracts: replacement of the Rome Convention by the Rome I Regulation", in (2007) *Journal of Private International Law*, 111; *H. Kronke*, "Applicable law in Torts and contracts in Cyberspace" in K. Boele-Woelki - C. Kessedjian (eds.), *Internet. Which Courts Decides? Which Law Applies?*, (Kluwer Law International, The Hague, 1998), 82.

commerce transactions, that pose delicate problems for the weaker party both regarding the jurisdiction and the applicable law. Therefore, in order to guarantee more protection to the consumer, Rome I ensures that the choice made by the parties cannot deprive the consumer of the protection afforded by the mandatory provisions included in the rules of their country of habitual residence. This reveals that the framers of the Regulation do not want to overturn the protection already guaranteed by the Rome Convention: the only new concern is the necessary connection of contracts involving a professional or commercial activity performed by an "electronic" trader and a specific "connection" of such activities with the country of habitual residence of the "electronic" consumer. Therefore the mere fact that the website is accessible from the domicile of the consumer[567] or that the website is in English language, known to be the lingua franca of the internet,[568] in my opinion is not enough proof that the professional was directing the activities towards that country.

However, the new formulation of the Article compared to the Convention seems to have been inserted to protect the stronger party (eg. multinationals companies), and in some cases it could complicate the task of the interpreter in identifying the applicable law. To be slightly more precise, consider the case of an Italian website (there are a large number of these especially travel websites) which is translated into French and specifically open to the French market and consumers (with the recurrent presence of the French flag within the site, or with links to travel agencies within the French territory that could offer more information to the consumer). In this case, is not clear if a Belgian consumer may be covered by the legal protection of the country of habitual residence. In fact, the Belgian consumer would be purchasing goods (e.g. boat tickets) from the Italian website even though the website does not do any business with the Belgian

567 *M. Weller – C. F. North Meier*, in G. Spindler - F. Schuster (eds.), *Recht der elektronischen Medien*, "Rom I - Art. 6", (Verlag C.H. Beck, München, 2015), no. 13, in www.beckonline.beck.de.

568 *A. Staudinger*, "Rom I-VO Artikel 6 Verbraucherverträge - Handkommentar", in R. Schulze – H. Dörner – I. Ebert – T. Hoeren – R. Kemper – I. Saenger – K. Schreiber – H. Schulte-Nölke – A. Staudinger (eds.), *Bürgerliches Gesetzbuch. Handkommentar,* (Nomos, Baden, 2014), no. 11. In other way *M. Weller – C. F. Nordmeier*, in G. Spindler - F. Schuster (eds.), *Recht der elektronischen Medien*, "Rom I - Art. 6", (Verlag C.H. Beck, München, 2015), no. 13, on www.beckonline.beck.de, according to the Authors "*Sie kann jedoch in der Einzelfallbetrachtung Indiz für die Internationalität der Internetseite sein, wenn sie nicht die Sprache des Landes ist, in dem der Unternehmer seinen gewöhnlichen Aufenthalt hat*".

market, despite there being a French language reference.[569] Therefore, in some cases this rule seems tenous and would not guarantee fair protection to European consumers.

In these cases, the role of the interpreter is fundamental. In fact, in the above example, I believe an important connection tool could be to check both the use of the "domain name" (e.g. .fr; .it; .be),[570] when the website appears in a search made in the country where the consumer has habitual residence,[571] and if there are advertisements of the website in the country where the consumer has habitual residence.[572] In this respect, I believe that this careful interpretation is important in order to adequately protect the consumer, who, besides being the "weaker party", is a central pillar of the European internal market.

In light of this analysis, it is clear that the provision of Article 6 has a hint of compromise; if it is true that the new arrangement persists in limiting protection exclusively for the benefit of those who have suffered from the entrepreneurial initiative of others (so-called passive or sedentary consumer), it is also true that it broadens it (extending it also in principle to the mobile consumer). At this point, the question is: When is it that a professional pursues his commercial or professional activities in the country where the consumer has habitual residence?[573] These circumstances are not

---

569 See ECJ cases C-585/08 *Pammer v. Karl Schlütter GmbH & Co.* and C-144/09 *Hotel Alpenhof GesmbH v. Oliver Heller* [94] where the Court held that the use of a language cannot provide evidence. In the same way *U. Villani*, "La legge applicabile ai contratti dei consumatori nel regolamento Roma I", in (2014) *Studi sull' integrazione europea*, 435. The Author with a restrictive approach states that "*è insufficiente la mera accessibilità del sito, così come la lingua o la valuta del sito*".

570 According to the Opinion of the Advocate General TRSTENJAK, in the cases C-585/08 *Pammer v. Karl Schlütter GmbH & Co.* and C-144/09 *Hotel Alpenhof GesmbH v. Oliver Heller* the "use of domain names not linked to any State", such as '.com', '.net', '.org' or .eu'.

571 *M. McParland*, *The Rome I Regulation on the law applicable to contractual obligations*, (O.U.P., Oxford, 2015), 541; *M. Weller – C. F. North Meier*, "Rom I Art. 6", in G. Spindler - F. Schuster (eds.), *Recht der elektronischen Medien*, (Verlag C.H. Beck, München, 2015), no. 14, in www.beckonline.beck.de.

572 *Ibid*. The Authors take as examples brochures, newspaper advertisements, radio broadcasts and television spots.

573 This question may be answered by reading the decision of ECJ regarding linked cases C-585/08 *Pammer v. Karl Schlütter GmbH & Co.* and C-144/09 *Hotel Alpenhof GesmbH v. Oliver Heller.* Examining these two cases, involving both an Austrian and a German consumer and professional, the Court held that in order to establish if a professional's activity is actually directed toward the State in which

cleary defined in Rome I, and to identify them, the role of the interpreter remains essential, to localize relevant evidence.[574]

Still, it can be argued that Article 6 of the Rome I represents an important innovation by ensuring the right balance between consumer protection and that of the stronger party, and that Article 6's approach to the contract of carriage of passengers, would guarantee the same level of protection for the passengers, who in some cases can be, in my opinion, classified as consumers.

Once again, even for these contracts, especially for those regarding e-commerce, the task of the interpreter must be decisive in order to apply the most equitable law and ensure that consumers are adequately protected. In particular, the court in those contracts where the professional has habitual residence in an industrialized country and the consumer has habitual residence in a Third World country,[575] should use an "escape clause" that is not inserted in Article 6 so that the weaker party is protected. Therefore, the court should apply the law that guarantees more protection to the consumer in compliance with Article 21 "Public policy of the forum" or Article 9 (2) applying the overriding mandatory provisions of the law of the forum.

Let me end by noting that this strong protection of consumers in Rome I, represents surely a valuable result, especially in comparison to the US conflict of laws, which has not adopted over-protective legal tools, although, as Symeonides in his illuminating analysis assumes, "[…] fountunately, American judges can do what legislatures cannot: a study of the nu-

---

the consumer is resident, it is necessary to carry out an overall assessment of the trader's business activities to verify if they are designed to contract with consumers resident in one or more Member States. In fact, the ease of access for the consumer, for example via the internet, to the trader's products is insufficient to declare that the trader carries out his activities in the country of residence of the consumer.

574 In the case C-585/08 *Pammer v. Karl Schlütter GmbH & Co.* § 90 the ECJ held "[…] other evidence, must necessarily be present, such as mention of telephone numbers with the international code, the use of a language other than German or mention of an international clientele composed of customers domiciled in various Member States".

575 *U. Villani*, "La legge applicabile ai contratti dei consumatori nel regolamento Roma I", in (2014) *Studi sull' integrazione europea*, 441. According to the Author "*nella prassi i flussi di beni e servizi si muovono più frequentemente dai Paesi industrializzati verso quelli in via di sviluppo*".

merous American cases involving [...] protection of the weaker parties".[576] Accordingly, it would be in any case advisable that the forthcoming Third Restatement of Conflicts of Laws guarantee a stronger protection to consumers taking ispiration, only in this occasion, from the Rome I Regulation rules.

3.III.G *The "connection system" in insurance contracts*

The introduction of a specific rule for insurance contracts, which is known to play an important role in the market, is certainly one of the most significant changes of Rome I,[577] given that the Convention expressly[578] excludes insurance contracts which cover risks located in the territories of Member States.

Starting by an analysis of Article 7 of Rome I, it is easy to establish a set of rules that have close links with various p.i.l. rules contained in several EU Directives.[579] In particular Rome I specifies various types of insurance contracts, each of which is subject to a different law. The only exception is represented by contracts relating to risks located beyond EU borders and reinsurance contracts that are governed by the general rules of Articles 3, 4

576 *S. C. Symeonides*, *Codifying Choice of Law Around the World*, (O.U.P., Oxford, 2014), 168.

577 *H. Heiss*, "Insurance Contracts in Rome I: Another recent failure of the European Legislature", in (2008) *Yearbook of Private International Law*, 261. In line with the Author's opinion this specific rule has been inserted with the intention of guarantee a simplification.

578 Article 1 (3) Rome Convention provides: "The rules of this Convention do not apply to contracts of insurance which cover risks situated in the territories of the Member States of the European Economic Community. In order to determine whether a risk is situated in these territories the court shall apply its internal law".

579 Council Directive 88/357/EEC of June 22, 1988 on the coordination of laws, regulations and administrative provisions relating to direct insurance other than life assurance and laying down provisions to facilitate the effective exercise of freedom to provide services and amending Directive 73/239/EEC, [1988] OJ L 172; Council Directive 92/49/EEC of June 18, 1992 on the coordination of laws, regulations and administrative provisions relating to direct insurance other than life assurance and amending Directives 73/239/EEC and 88/357/EEC, [1992] OJ L 228; Directive 2002/83/EC of the European Parliament and of the Council of November 5, 2002 concerning life assurance, [2002] OJ 345/1.

and 6, these being beyond the scope of Article 7 but not beyond the scope of Rome I.[580]

Focussing on particular reinsurance contracts, the choice made by the EU lawmakers to exclude these from the scope of application would seem to recognise that in reinsurance contracts it is not easy to identify the "weaker party". Actually, in my opinion, the uncertainty of identifying the "weaker party" in these contracts must be the main element that should lead the interpreter to assert the closest connection principle, thereby avoiding strict rules as complex as that of Article 4, which includes both contracts as provision of services and sale of goods. Consequently, I believe that in these contracts, in order to apply the most equitable law, the interpreter should carefully analyse whether the reinsurance contract has a close relationship with other contracts, whether the reinsurance contract was drafted by any reinsurance brokers, and finally which market the reinsurance was placed in.[581]

The insurance contracts referred to in Directive 73/239/ECC, governed by Article 7 (2) of Rome I, which mentions them as large risks[582] or mass risks located in the territory of the EU,[583] are subject to a general system. In reference to these specific insurance contracts, the problem is that it is not easy to understand what exactly is meant by the expression "large risk" and no definition has been provided. However, in line with learned editors,[584] contracts covering a large risk might include: loss or damage to air-

---

580 *R. Merkin*, "The Rome I Regulation and Reinsurance", in (2009) *Journal of Private International Law*, 74.

581 *M. McParland*, *The Rome I Regulation on the law applicable to contractual obligations*, (O.U.P., Oxford, 2015), 630.

582 Large risks probably refer to the risks related to insuring transportation vehicles and civil liability arising from their use, or risks relating to credit lines and securities, as long as the contractor professionally performs an industrial or commercial or liberal activity, the risk is related to that activity, or the risks involve a contractor whose work meets certain requirements concerning the balance sheet, the volume of business and employees.

583 *C. Rudolf*, "Internationales Vertragsrecht – Rom I – Verordnung ab 17.12.2009 maßgebend", in (2009) *ecolex*, 1117; *P. Stone*, *Private International Law in the European Union*, (Edward Elgar, Northampton, 2018), 496.

584 *P. R. Beaumont - P.E. McEleavy*, *Private International Law*, (Thomson Reuters, Edinburg, 2011), 484 – 549; *A. Staudinger*, in R. Schulze – H. Dörner – I. Ebert – T. Hoeren – R. Kemper – I. Saenger – K. Schreiber – H. Schulte-Nölke – A. Staudinger (eds.), *Bürgerliches Gesetzbuch. Handkommentar*, "Rom I-VO Artikel 7 Versicherungsverträge Handkommentar", (Nomos, Baden, 2014), no.7, in www.beckonline.beck.de.; *P. Stone*, *Private International Law in the European Union*, (Edward Elgar, Northampton, 2018), 517.

craft or, railway stock, and risks relating to credit or surety ship. Further criticism can certainly also be made. In particular, it may be said that the subdivision of categories between insurance contracts (so-called "large risks" and other categories of insurance contracts), not only complicates the task of the interpreter but also does not appear consistent with the traditional differences between commercial contracts or between professional and consumer contracts provided in Rome I. In fact, the large risks category could also include situations that would be protected by Article 6,[585] which, undoubtedly assures greater protection for consumers than Article 7.

Excluding these exceptions when there isn't a choice of law by parties, the applicable law will be that of the country where the insurer has his/her habitual residence. This provision certainly creates an unjustified balance to the detriment of the policyholder and in favour of the insurer, who can, at the same time, take advantage of some national rules in order to limit his/her risks and obligations.

However, Article 7 (2) (2) also inserts an "escape clause" ruling that "Where it is clear from all the circumstances of the case that the contract is manifestly more closely connected with another country, the law of that other country shall apply".[586] In line with the rigid approach of the underlying Article 4, this "escape clause" should be applied only when it is "clear from all the circumstances of the case" that the contract is "manifestly" more closely connected with another country. In the same way, in insurance contracts the interpreter's power to choose the most equitable law is severely limited and the link with the general rule adopted in Article 4 may disorientate him in the complex "puzzle" of the Rome I Regulation.

Article 7 (3) also allows parties to choose the applicable law, provided that one of the connections listed from (a) to (e) is in place between the chosen country and the contract. In the absence of these connecting factors, and in order to assist the interpreter in identifying the applicable law, the Article identifies as a connection criterion also the location of risk,[587] with the application of this governed by Rome I and, in turn, EU Directives on the matter.

---

585 The typical example is that of boat insurance purchased from a private party for tourist purposes. *Contra A. Briggs*, *Private International Law in English Courts*, (O.U.P., Oxford, 2014), 566.

586 Rome I Regulation Article 7 (2) (2).

587 About this principle see *H. Heiss*, "Insurance Contracts in Rome I: Another recent failure of the European Legislature", in (2008) *Yearbook of Private International Law*, 267.

In light of the analysis of Article 7, I want to stress that Rome I further complicates the already complex task of the interpreter in identifying the applicable law in absence of parties choice. In fact almost all of the methods of connection governing p.i.l., such as "closest connection",[588] "*dépeçage*"[589] and "*renvoi*"[590] are present in just one Article. Moreover, the provision in sub-paragraph 3 of Article 7 (3) does not, as Beaumont and McEleavy have observed,[591] contemplate a real "escape clause"; the result is that identifying the applicable law will, for the interpreter, be an uphill struggle. One example is when "the contract has been severed because the risks are in different countries and there is no opportunity to displace the various applicable laws with one law that is manifestly more closely connected".[592]

Similarly, the interpreter might easily be mistaken in the task of identifying the applicable law when the insurer has a branch or agency. In fact, as Dicey and Morris have famously suggested, it might be the case here that direct liability of the branch[593] is regulated by the contract (as is often the case in Germany) even if "the insurer's central administration is located in another country and the last authorisation of the policy is required from the head office, which will coincide (as is often the case) with the place of the central administration".[594] In this circumstance, the learned editors hold the view that, regardless of the contractual terms and conditions, the applicable law is actually in force where the insurer's head office is situated, since it is via that head office that cover is provided.[595]

However, by failing to examine the various forms of insurance contracts present in the Article in detail, it is clear that the developments introduced by Rome I with regard to insurance contracts appear disastrous,[596] or, as

---

588 Article 7 (2) (second paragraph).

589 Article 7 (5).

590 Article 7 (2).

591 *P. R. Beaumont - P.E. McEleavy*, *Private International Law*, (Thomson Reuters, Edinburg, 2011), 551.

592 In these words, *Ibid*, 551.

593 *Dicey & Morris*, *The conflict of laws*, 15th ed. (L. Collins ed.), (Sweet&Maxwell, London, 2012), no. 33-221, 2002.

594 In these words, *Ibid*, no. 33-221, 2003.

595 *Ibid*.

596 *Contra L. Merrett*, "Choice of Law in Insurance Contracts under the Rome I Regulation", in (2009) *Journal of Private International Law*, 66. In the Author's opinion "is clearly a very significant improvement on the current situation. The new system is transparent and ought to be much easier to apply".

some scholars[597] have put it, regulatory "hell". As a consequence a chance to improve the clarity of p.i.l. rules in these contracts has been missed.[598] This is not only because the interpreter in absence of choice by parties, may be confused by a variety of methods of connection[599] and may turn to the classic connecting factors such as "closest connection", but also because many complex insurance contracts, are not regulated. Examples of these are health insurance contracts,[600] life insurance contracts,[601] insurance contracts connected to a bank loan or contracts of insurance which cover non-large risks situated wholly outside the territories of the Member States. The absence of an express reference in Article 7 to these contracts further complicates the interpreter's task which must also comply with the hard-and-fast rules of Article 4,[602] and at the same time the weaker party (the insured) does not have adequate protection in small-risk insurance contracts

---

597 *J. A. Moreno Rodriguez – M. Mercedes Albornoz*, "Reflections on the Mexico Convention in the Context of the Preparation of the Future Hague Instrument on International Contracts", in (2011) *Journal of Private International Law*, 516.

598 *J.J. Kuipers*, *EU Law and Private International Law. The Interrelationship in Contractual Obligations*, (Martinus Nijhoff Publisher, Leiden, 2011), 121.

599 *R. Miquel Sala*, "Los Contractos de Seguro en El Projecto de Ley Modelo Ohadac de Derecho International Privado: Un modelo a Seguir para el Reglamento Roma I", in Anuario Español de Derecho International Privado, 2016, 796 who defines Art. 7 as a "*labeirinto normativo*".

600 On this point see *A. Staudinger*, "Art. 5 Rom I-VO", in F. Ferrari – E.M. Kieninger - P. Mankowski (eds.), *Internationales Vertragsrecht, (VO) EG 593/2008*, (Verlag CH Beck, München, 2012), no. 55. The Author points out that "*Die Rom I-VO entbehrt einer Art. 13 EGVVG aF vergleichbaren Anknüpfung für die substitutive Krankenversicherung. Nach Auffassung des deutschen Gesetzgebers besteht diesbezüglich kein Regelungsbedürfnis, da auf Grund von § 193 Abs. 3 VVG iVm. § 23 Abs. 1 SGB XI mittlerweile ein Versicherungszwang gelte und deshalb Art. 7 Abs. 4 einschlägig sei. Eine solche Einschätzung übersieht jedoch, dass nicht jede Kranken- automatisch eine Pflichtversicherung darstellen muss*".

601 *Dicey & Morris*, *The conflict of laws*, 15th ed. (L. Collins ed.), (Sweet&Maxwell, London, 2012), no. 32-020, 1787. According to the Authors certain kind of insurance contracts are excluded and in particular "insurance contracts arising out of operations carried out by organisations other than undertakings referred to in art. 2 of Directive 2002/83/EC of the European Parliament and of the Council November 5, 2002, concerning life assurance the object of which is to provide benefit for employment or self-employed persons belonging to an undertaking or group of undertakings or to a trade or group of trades, in the event of death or survival or of discontinuance or curtailment of activity, or of sickness related to work or accidents at work".

602 *M. McParland*, *The Rome I Regulation on the law applicable to contractual obligations*, (O.U.P., Oxford, 2015), 627. The Author observes that "Article 4 (1) (b) will probably apply, as an insurance contract is for the provision of services".

because he/she will be deprived of the protection of the mandatory rules of a country that has a closer connection.[603]

In addition, it follows that regulating such a vast and complex field as insurance contracts using rules on a reduced scale and which are strict only by way of outward appearance was probably a pointless task, given that, as already mentioned, not all insurance contracts are regulated. Perhaps here it would have been preferable for the EU lawmakers to have opted out of providing specific rules, thus allowing the interpreter to identify the applicable law for each individual insurance contract, applying only the principles of "closest connection" and "characteristic performance", and therefore ensuring protection under Article 6 to consumers. In fact, it seems that, in practice, Article 7 is not a simple and clear p.i.l. tool to identify the applicable law; rather, it complicates the work of the interpreter in the already chaotic rules of Rome I.

A simple reference to flexible criteria as the closest connection principle or excluding a *lex specialis* for these contracts, as in the Rome Convention, would have simplified the task of the interpreter, assured the localization of an equitable law and, probably, ensured more predictability of the outcome of litigation. In fact, with the "disorder" that characterizes Article 7, in which several connecting factors, different forms of insurance contracts and references to other standards coexist, it is very likely we will notice different decisions in each national court. This "disorder" certainly does not help the European insurance industry which represents an important part of the internal market.[604] What is more, in 2016 the Project Group for a "Restatement of European Insurance Contract Law" proposed to create an option instrument called "Principles of European Insurance Contract Law (PEICL)",[605] that will be applied in all insurance contracts. By this means, learned experts of the insurance market demand more protection and clarity than the Rome I p.i.l. rules provide.

603 *S. C. Symeonides*, *Codifying Choice of Law Around the World*, (O.U.P., Oxford, 2014), 168. The Author defines it as a "regrettable result".

604 *M. McParland*, *The Rome I Regulation on the law applicable to contractual obligations*, (O.U.P., Oxford, 2015), 578. The Author has cited in footnote 2 the study of Insurance Europe, *European Insurance in Figures*, no. 48 (February 14, 2014).

605 See for more *J. Basedow - J. Birds - M. Clarke - H. Cousy - H. Heiss - L. Loacker*, *Principles of European Insurance Contract Law (PEICL)*, (Ottoscmidt, Köln, 2016), *passim*.

3.III.H Focus on individual employment contracts

The Regulation puts in Article 8 a *lex specialis* for individual employment contracts which aims to "modernize" the already thorough Rome Convention rules and to ensure protection for the weaker party, the employee. However, I think that an important opportunity to clarify the concept of "individual employment contract" has been missed, and with the silence on the part of Rome I, it is not easy to understand which contractual categories can be included,[606] especially those closer to employment contracts, like agency contracts.

The EU lawmakers have wanted to allow the parties to choose the applicable law so that the employee, like the consumer, can benefit from the "protection principle",[607] as choices made by the parties cannot deprive the weaker party of the protection afforded by mandatory provisions (the so-

606 *M.A. Sabirau-Perez*, "Changes of the law applicable to an international contract of employment", in (2000) *International Labor Review*, 336; *F. Seatzu*, "La legge applicabile ai contratti individuali di lavoro nel Regolamento Roma I", in N. Boschiero (ed.), *La Nuova disciplina comunitaria della legge applicabile ai contratti (Roma I)*, (Giappichelli, Torino, 2009), 339 that excludes from this field of application employment contracts in public authorities and those which have arisen in family contexts.

607 It is also called "functional allocation" that is common in Dutch p.i.l. see *A. A.H. van Hoek*, "Private International Law: An Appropiate Means to Regulate Transnational Employment in the European Union", in (2014) *Erasmus Law Review*, 163.

called *mandatory rules*).[608] Furthermore, the Recital § 35[609] points out that an agreement to depart from these rules is only valid if has been arranged for the benefit of the employee. This arrangement highlights that the employee quite probably enjoys more regulatory protection compared to the consumer.

In order to identify the law to be applied and hence the mandatory rules of the law that would govern the contract in absence of choice, on similar lines to the Convention, Article 8 (2) refers to some "rigid" criteria which, according to Dicey and Morris, operate as follows:

> "Article 8 (2) (clause 2) specifies the law generally applicable to an individual contract of employment in the absence of choice; Article 8 (3) (clause (3)) contains a default rule which applies only if the applicable law to the contract cannot be determined under Article 8 (2); Article 8 (4) (clause 4) contains a rule of displacement which may, in appropriate circumstances, point to a law other than that indicated in Article 8 (2) or (3)".[610]

These provisions dictate and can be subdivided as follows.

The first provision concerns: "the law of the country in which or, failing that, from which the employee habitually carries out his work in performance of the contract. The country where the work is habitually carried

608 For more about the meaning of mandatory rules in Rome I Regulation see *L. Merrett*, "Posted Workers in Europe from a Private International Law Perspective", in (2011) *Cambridge Yearbook of European Legal Studies*, 219 – 244. According to Article 9 (1) of the Rome I Regulation, in different way compared to Art. 7 of the Rome Convention, the mandatory provisions are defined as "provision the respect for which is regarded as crucial by a country for safeguarding its public interest, such as its political, social or economic organisation, to such extent that they are applicable to any situation falling within their scope, irrespective of the law otherwise applicable to the contract". See also the critical analysis about the territorial scope of the employment legislation in *U. Grušić*, "The Territorial Scope of Employment Legislation and Choice of Law", in (2012) *The Modern Law Review*, 751. The Author, starting from a critical look of decision *Lawson v. Serco*, contends "[…] the Rome I Regulation – and to a certain extent even the Rome Convention – seems to have in effect largely merged contractual and statutory claims into a single category for the purposes of private international law".

609 Recital § 35 "Employees should not be deprived of the protection afforded to them by provisions which cannot be derogated from by agreement or which can only be derogated from to their benefit".

610 In these words, *Dicey & Morris*, *The conflict of laws*, 15th ed. (L. Collins ed.), (Sweet&Maxwell, London, 2012), no. 33-263, 2031.

out shall not be deemed to have changed if he/she is temporarily employed in another country".[611] From a first reading, it is clear that the EU lawmakers have established that this place should be identified on the basis of the centre of gravity of actual performance (so-called *lex loci laboris*)[612] and that this can be localized with reference to the performance of the contract and the place the employee has worked the longest[613] or where the service started,[614] without any temporary work carried out in a different country having any effect.

Certainly, reference to the place of departure is a new rule compared to the rules imposed by the Convention. In so doing, it becomes reasonably easy to predict the applicable law, in particular in complex contracts with mobile performance (think of maritime or airport contracts, airline pilots,[615] international management consultants, and international salesmen[616] or tele-workers).[617] Therefore, this factor helps to solve problems in relation to the crew which were unresolved by the Convention.

The problem, however, is in understanding what the lawmakers meant by "habitually carries out his work", as the Rome I Regulation provides no assistance here. These words might be subject to wide interpretation. In the assessment *Koelzsch v. Luxembourg*, C-29/10, the ECJ held that "the cri-

---

611 Rome I Regulation Art. 8 (2).

612 On this topic see also ECJ C-383/95, *Petrus Wilhelmus Rutten v. Cross Medical Limited.*

613 *P. Stone*, *Private International Law in the European Union*, (Edward Elgar, Northampton, 2018), 496.

614 On this point see also ECJ C-29/10, *Koelzsch v. Luxembourg*, § 48.

615 *M. McParland*, *The Rome I Regulation on the law applicable to contractual obligations*, (O.U.P., Oxford, 2015), 660. In line with the Author's opinion "as regards flight personnel on international flights, three major connecting factors could be found in academic writings, namely the law of the country (a) in which the plane was registered, (b) in which the seat of the business that engaged the personnel was located, and (c) the law of the base from where the employees board the plane and where they returned to." In the same way *A. Staudinger*, "Art. 5 Rom I-VO", in F. Ferrari – E.M. Kieninger - P. Mankowski (eds.), *Internationales Vertragsrecht, (VO) EG 593/2008*, (Verlag CH Beck, München, 2012), no. 20.

616 *P. R. Beaumont - P.E. McEleavy*, *Private International Law*, (Thomson Reuters, Edinburg, 2011), 536.

617 *M. Weller – C. F. Nordmeier*, in G. Spindler - F. Schuster (eds.), *Recht der elektronischen Medien*, "Rom I - Art. 8", (Verlag C.H. Beck, München, 2015), no. 9, in www.beckonline.beck.de. See also *A. Staudinger*, "Article 8", in F. Ferrari (ed.) *Rome I Regulation. Pocket commentary*, (Sellier, Munich, 2014), 303. In line with the Author's opinion "for homeworkers the relevant place is the work-place at home, for tele-work-places it is the habitual place of data entry".

terion of the country in which the work is habitually carried out must be given a broad interpretation and be understood as referring to the place in which or from which the employee actually carries out his working activities and, in the absence of a centre of activities, to the place where he carries out the majority of his activities"[618] towards his employees.[619] According to the ECJ, this principle must be given "a broad interpretation"[620] in order to locate the effective centre of employee working activities.[621] As a consequence, it is important that a legal analysis take place, considering all the circumstances of the case, regardless of the exact place of work, in particular: 1) the place where the employee receives work instructions or where he has an office or organizes all his work;[622] 2) the place where the equipment for the employment is located;[623] 3) the place where the employee habitually lives on work days; and 4) the place from which the employee carries out his transport tasks.[624]

Finally, in order to understand the meaning of "temporarily employed in another country", it is appropriate to look at Recital § 36,[625] to understand which work is classified as temporary, and to establish if the employee is obliged to resume the work that normally takes place in the country of origin after carrying out the work abroad. The applicable law is therefore stable and does not change when the employee is temporarily sent

---

618 ECJ C-29/10, *Koelzsch v. Luxembourg*, § 45.

619 ECJ C-125/92, *Mulox IBC v. Hendrick Geels*, § 24; ECJ C-383/95, *Rutten v. Cross Medical Limited*, § 23.

620 ECJ C-29/10, *Koelzsch v. Luxembourg*, § 34.

621 *J.J. Kuipers*, *EU Law and Private International Law. The Interrelationship in Contractual Obligations*, (Martinus Nijhoff Publisher, Leiden, 2011), 109.

622 In these words, *Dicey & Morris*, *The conflict of laws*, 15th ed. (L. Collins ed.), (Sweet&Maxwell, London, 2012), no. 33-265, 2032.

623 *Ibid.*

624 *A. A.H. van Hoek*, "Private International Law: An Appropriate Means to Regulate Transnational Employment in the European Union", in (2014) *Erasmus Law Review*, 161.

625 § 36 Rome I Recital*:* "As regards individual employment contracts, work carried out in another country should be regarded as temporary if the employee is expected to resume working in the country of origin after carrying out his tasks abroad. The conclusion of a new contract of employment with the original employer or an employer belonging to the same group of companies as the original employer should not preclude the employee from being regarded as carrying out his work in another country temporarily".

abroad provided that the employee has already worked in the country of origin.[626]

At the same time, the framers of Rome I do not give a definition of "temporary or permanent sending". As a consequence, in each individual case the courts should evaluate relevant circumstances in order to identify the place where he habitually works. For example if the employee is expected to resume working in the country where he/she has spent time abroad or the time spent abroad is not for a significant period, then these are relevant circumstances that the courts could take into consideration.[627]

The second provision relates to "the law of the country where the place of business through which the employee was engaged is situated".[628] In order to identify the applicable law, Article 8 (3) introduces the place of hiring, identified as the place where the employee was hired, though this is subordinate to the criterion of habitual place of employment. This provision certainly helps the interpreter to identify the applicable law in international occupations such as transport workers who routinely cross-national borders. However it may present significant problems for work performed on platforms located in international seas or in territories not subject to the sovereignty of any particular country or when the employee is engaged by intermediaries, so called 'hire agencies', based in countries with low minimum standards of employment law and low rates of pay.[629] In the absence of clarity in Rome I, the problem for the courts is how to interpret the terms "place of business" and "engaged". In regards to the "place of business", this can be localized as any place connected to the employer where the employee has permanent and stable work.[630] On the other hand, with reference to the term "engaged", an important connection factor could be the conclusion of the employment contract or the place of recruitment.

---

626 In reference to Article 6 of Rome Convention see Italian *Corte di Cassazione*, January 21, 2013 n. 1302, in (2013) *Rivista di diritto internazionale privato e processuale*, 478.

627 *U. Grušić*, "The international Employment Contract: Ideal, Reality and Regulatory Function of European Private International Law of Employment", (2012) PhD dissertation L.S.E., 161 -162.

628 Rome I Regulation Article 8 (3).

629 *M. McParland*, *The Rome I Regulation on the law applicable to contractual obligations*, (O.U.P., Oxford, 2015), 674.

630 *E. Götzen*, "Contratto di lavoro, criteri di collegamento e legge applicabile: luci e ombre del Regolamento (CE) n. 593/2008", in (2014) *Rivista di diritto internazionale privato e processuale*, 537.

In light of these considerations, the interpreter's task in identifying the applicable law becomes central. Working on different approaches and moving away from rigid connecting factors[631] to those in other rules already examined, the EU lawmakers go on to introduce an element of flexibility with the inclusion of an "escape clause" governed by paragraphs (3) and (4) of Article 8. This is based on the closest connection that the contract has with a country other than the one whose law is identified under paragraphs (1) and (2) of the same Article 8.[632] Similarly to the "escape clause" inserted in the previous Articles which allows the application of a different law only "where it is *clear* from all circumstances of the case that the contract is *manifestly* more closely connected with a country", Article 8 (3) and (4) could guarantee a more flexible approach.

In fact, the structure of the escape clause of Article 8 appears to follow the "weaker presumption approach",[633] allowing the interpreter to analyse in detail all the circumstances of the contract[634] in order to protect the weaker party. In particular, the entire employment relationship before and after this time is considered,[635] to identify the most equitable applicable law. However, it is not made clear what is meant by "where it appears from the circumstances [...]". Therefore, the interpreter has to face a "particular" circumstance to deviate from the rigid rule of Article 8 (2). So although not specified, for 'most closely connected' purposes, the interpreter will be required to assess factors such as the residence or domicile of the

631 *A. Staudinger*, "Art. 5 Rom I-VO", in F. Ferrari – E.M. Kieninger - P. Mankowski (eds.), *Internationales Vertragsrecht, (VO) EG 593/2008*, (Verlag CH Beck, München, 2012), no. 27.

632 For more see *infra* chapter "relevant case law", ECJ C-29/10, *Koelzsch v. Luxembourg*.

633 For more see *supra* § 3.III.

634 ECJ C-64/12, *Anton Schlecker v. Melitta Josefa Boedeker* § 44 "the national court may, under the concluding part of that provision, disregard the law applicable in the country where the work is habitually carried out, if it appears from the circumstances as a whole that the contract is more closely connected with another country".

635 *A. Staudinger*, "Article 8", in F. Ferrari (ed.) *Rome I Regulation. Pocket commentary*, (Sellier, Munich, 2014), 303. In particular, the court with this provision may look at the realities of the relationship on the evidence before it, as in the case of a *de facto* employment. At the same time, it may give weight to evidence that suggest a "resumption of work" or the conclusion of a new contract of employment within the same group of companies.

employee, the language and form of the contract,[636] the employer's administrative headquarters, the place where the company's major subsidiaries are located, or the registration and flag[637] of a ship or aircraft and any particular contracts pertaining to them.

Compared to the other above-mentioned contracts, the flexible escape clause has the merit of enhancing the role of the interpreter in guaranteeing the enforcement of the most equitable law and creating individual justice despite the rigid rules of connection.[638] This is also confirmed by the EU case *Schlecker* (12 September 2013, C-64/12)[639] where the court applied the escape clause of the Rome Convention with the *ratio* that there is a situation in which long-term and permanent employment is present in one country but all other elements are connected with another country. In particular, the court has applied the escape clause and taken into account "key factors" like "the country where the employee's taxes and charges on labour income are paid and the country in which he is affiliated to social security, various pension, health insurance and disability schemes".[640]

As it is structured, Article 8 ensures a fair balance between the protection of the "weaker party" and the employer. In fact, a rigid escape clause such as that of Articles 4, 5 or 7 would have created an imbalance in favour

---

636 *F. Seatzu*, "La legge applicabile ai contratti individuali di lavoro nel regolamento 'Roma I'", in N. Boschiero (ed.), *La nuova disciplina comunitaria della legge applicabile ai contratti (Roma I)*, (Giappichelli, Torino, 2009), 352.

637 *D. Martiny*, "Art. 8 Rom I –VO", in *Münchener Kommentar zum Bürgerlichen Gesetzbuch*, (Verlag C.H. Beck, München, 2010), no. 77-78. In the Author's opinion "*Teilweise wird vertreten, Seearbeitsverhältnisse unterlägen grundsätzlich dem Recht der Flagge, das dem Arbeitsort entspreche (Abs. 2)*". At the same time the Author requires a thorough evaluation by the interpreter, in fact he points out that "*Die Maßgeblichkeit einer „billigen Flagge" selbst dann, wenn keine anderen Verbindungen zum Flaggenstaat ersichtlich sind, stößt freilich auch auf Kritik. Die Vereinbarung des Flaggenrechts wurde bei deutschen Besatzungsangehörigen teilweise als Gesetzesumgehung eingestuft. Die objektive Anknüpfung tendierte hier zum Recht des Reedereisitzes*".

638 *A. Staudinger*, "Article 8", in F. Ferrari (ed.) *Rome I Regulation. Pocket commentary*, , (Sellier, Munich 2014), 315.

639 See also *Cour d'App. Paris* June 7, 1996; *Cour de Cassation* October 23, 2005, in *A. Mattei,* "La legge applicabile al lavoro transnazionale a partire da un caso recente", in (2013) *Lavoro e diritto,* 451. *Contra Bundesarbeitsgericht di Hessen* February 15, 2012 in www.conflictoflaws.net.

640 *V. Van Den Eeckhout*, "The Escape-Clause of Article 6 Rome Convention (Article 8 Rome I Regulation): How Special Is the Case Schlecker?", in (2014) *Tijdschrift Recht en Arbeid*, issue 4. Available in English version at http://papers.ssrn.com/sol3/papers.cfm?abstract_id=2403417.

of the employee and would have given rise to an abuse of his protection. This latter situation could spoil greater economic efficiency and the competitiveness of business, and as a consequence investment abroad. In fact, I believe that, in employment contracts, a flexible "escape clause" is needed not only to focus on the protection of employees as weaker parties and to apply the most equitable law, but also to consider other modern economic objectives such as greater economic efficiency and the competitiveness of business. In today's globalised world employment legislation is one of the factors on the basis of which countries compete for attracting investment and as a consequence provide greater prosperity for their citizens. In light of these considerations, an EU p.i.l. rule should guarantee not only more protection to the employee but also greater economic efficiency and competitiveness of employers so that they would be incentivized to do business abroad knowing that the courts would apply a law that does not create unfair prejudices and as a consequence creates benefits to the internal market.

Concluding, in contrast to the Recital, which held that to limit the interpreter's power with rigid criteria would be a need inherent in the proper functioning of the internal market, I would like to strongly stress that the flexible approach introduced in Article 8's "escape clause", has the merit of ensuring the right balance between protecting the weaker party of the contract and defending the interests of employers, both of which are an important pillar of the internal market. This approach would certainly encourage greater benefits by the enforcement of the most equitable law.

3.III.I Voluntary Assignment of receivables

The continuous evolution of international trade which in the new era of globalisation is currently more concerned with financial flows than with services or goods,[641] dictates that this book also examine voluntary assignment[642] due to the strong impact this contract has on the proper function-

641 *T. C. Hartley*, "Choice of Law regarding the Voluntary Assignment of Contractual Obligations Under the Rome I Regulation", in (2011) *International and Comparative Law Quarterly*, 29.

642 There is abundant literature on the voluntary assignment in private international law. For the most significant see *H. Batiffol*, "Assignment", in *Lectures on the Conflict of Laws and international Contracts*, (Ann Arbor, University of Michigan Law School, 1951), 48 ss.; *P.J. Rogerson*, "The Situs of Debts in the Conflict of Laws—Illogical, Unnecessary and Misleading", in (1990) *Cambridge Law Journal*, 441 ss.; *D. Pardoel*, *Les conflits de lois en matière de cession de créance*, (LGDJ, Paris,

ing of the internal market. In fact assignment is a mechanism widely used, particularly in banking practice, for carrying out various credit or factoring operations.[643]

As is known, there is voluntary assignment of receivables when, in a business activity, the goods or service provider (Creditor/Assignor) defers payments to his/her customer (Debtor) so that the former holds a recovery debt towards the latter until the stipulated deadline. In turn, the creditor (Assignor) can transfer his credit to a third party (Assignee).

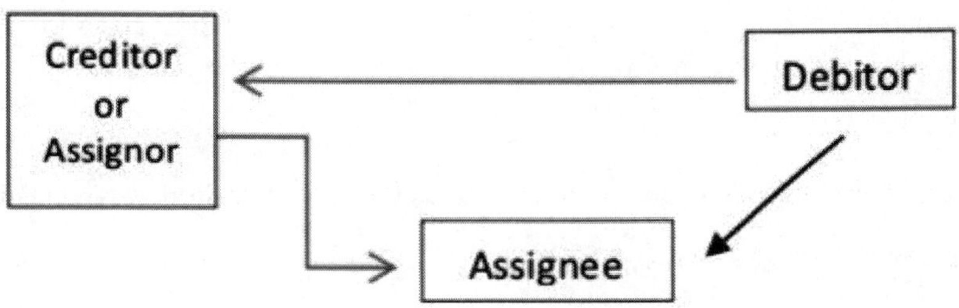

The inconveniences regarding this "hybrid legal institution",[644] which involves elements that belong to the law of obligations and to property

---

1997), *passim*; *T. H.D. Struycken*, "The Proprietary Aspects of International Assignment of Debts and the Rome Convention, Article 12", in (1998) *Lloyd's Maritime and Commercial Law Quarterly*, 345 ss.; *E. Cashin Ritaine*, *Les regles applicables aux transfert internationaux de creance a l'aune du nouveau Règlement Rome I et du droit conventionnel*, in A. Bonomi – E. Cashin Ritaine (eds.), *Le nouveau règlement européen "Roma I" relative a la loi applicable aux obligations contractuelles. Actes de la 20 Journee de droit international privè du 14 mars 2008 a Lausanne*, (Schulthess, Zurich, 2009), 198 ss.; *F.J. Garcimartìn*, *Assignment of Claims in the Rome I Regulation: Article 14*, in F. Ferrari – S. Leible (eds.), *Rome I Regulation: The Law Applicable to Contractual Obligations in Europe*, (Sellier, Munich, 2009), 217.

643 Commission "Green Paper on the Conversion of the Rome Convention of 1980 on the law applicable to contractual obligations into a Community instrument and its modernization", COM (2002) 3.2.13.1; *M. McParland*, *The Rome I regulation on the law applicable to contractual obligations*, (O.U.P., Oxford, 2015), 773.

644 *H. Verhagen – S. van Dongen*, "Cross-border Assignments under Rome I", in (2010) *Journal of Private International Law*, 2 - 3. The Authors underline that "Assignment may be characterised as a hybrid legal institution, involving features belonging to both the law of obligations and the law of property. [...] This hybrid nature of assignment not only creates characterization problems but can also be said to be one of the main causes of the diversity of opinion in the EU

law,[645] are numerous and well-known especially from an international perspective where the credits derive from a contract between parties that have habitual residence in different States.[646] In addition to these problems is the fact that, with voluntary assignment, various different issues come into play (such as amendments, succession, transfer), all of which are governed differently by the legal system in each of the Member States,[647] some of which have not ruled one single independent assignment of a receivables agreement.[648] Furthermore this particular type of contract sets itself apart from others because, as well as the corresponding obligations between assignor and assignee, it results in the transfer of ownership in the receivable assigned.[649]

Member States in respect of the most suitable conflict rule for the assignment of claims".

645 *M. McParland*, *The Rome I regulation on the law applicable to contractual obligations*, (O.U.P., Oxford, 2015), 775.

646 According to *A. J. Bêlohlávek*, *Rome Convention, Rome I Regulation: commentary, new EU conflict-of-laws rules for contractual obligation*, vol. 2, (Juris, New York, 2010), 1728, the assignment is international "[...] if, at the time of conclusion of the contract of assignment, the assignor and the assignee are located in different States". The Author takes in consideration the definition insert in UNCITRAL Convention, and critics this because is considered "relatively narrow and imposes limitations when it connects the international element".The reference is to United Nations Convention on the Assignment of Receivables in International Trade [2004], which has as main goal to support of trans-border movement of goods and services by means of the unification of legal provisions for assignment in international market and assures the harmonisation of national law as well as. For further comments on this Convention see Modern Law for Global Commerce, available also in electronic edition at http://www.uncitral.org/pdf/english/congress/09-83930_Ebook.pdf. See also *L. Radicati di Bronzo*, *La Nuova legge sulla cartolarizzazione e la cessione di crediti a soggetti esteri*, in (1999) *Diritto del Commercio Internazionale*, 1061.

647 *A. Bonomi*, "Il nuovo diritto internazionale privato dei contratti (La Convenzione di Roma del 19 giugno 1980 è entrata in vigore)", in (1992) *Banca borsa e titoli di credito*, 96, according to whom "*Mentre in alcuni ordinamenti l'efficacia della cessione verso il debitore è subordinata al compimento di alcune formalità dirette ad informarlo (ad. es. la notificazione ex art. 1264 cod. civ. italiano) o per lo meno alla conoscenza da parte sua dell'avvenuta cessione, in altri sistemi non sono contenute analoghe norme protettive*".

648 In the same way *G. Passarelli*, "The Voluntary assignment of Receivables in Private International Law", in (2014) *Studi sull' integrazione Europea*, 322.

649 *A. Bonomi*, "Il nuovo diritto internazionale privato dei contratti (La Convenzione di Roma del 19 giugno 1980 è entrata in vigore)", in (1992) *Banca borsa e titoli di credito*, 95.

Considering the importance of this matter in the financial-services industry,[650] in the wake of national legislation as well as on an international level, p.i.l. has consigned the applicable law to voluntary assignment. Recourse is then given to the solutions adopted first by the Rome Convention[651] and then Rome I.

Therefore, in line with the provisions of the Rome Convention,[652] Rome I establishes in Article 14 (1) that the relationship between assignor and assignee is ruled by the proper law of the contract concluded between them;[653] given Article 14's silence on this point, the location would be established on the basis of the criteria aid out in Articles 3 and 4.

In light of these considerations and in contrast to the Convention, in absence of the parties' choice, I believe that the interpreter is firstly required to establish which category the transferred contract belongs in, and then to localize the characteristic performer for mixed and/or complex contracts which give life to a credit transfer, comparing those circumstances with "the concept of assignment" inserted in Article 14 (3).

It seems, however, that voluntary assignment should be qualified as a contract for the provision of services described by Article 4 (1) (b),[654] and therefore be governed by the law of the country in which the service

---

650 *T. C. Hartley*, "Choice of Law regarding the Voluntary Assignment of Contractual Obligations Under the Rome I Regulation", in (2011) *International and Comparative Law Quarterly*, 29.

651 According to Article 12 of Rome Convention "1. The mutual obligations of assignor and assignee under a voluntary assignment of a right against another person ("the debtor") shall be governed by the law which under this Convention applies to the contract between the assignor and assignee. 2. The law governing the right to which the assignment relates shall determine its assignability, the relationship between the assignee and the debtor, the conditions under which the assignment can be invoked against the debtor and any question whether the debtor's obligations have been discharged".

652 *C. Rudolf*, "Internationales Vertragsrecht – Rom I – Verordnung ab 17.12.2009 maßgebend", in (2009) *ecolex*, 1117.

653 *H. LE Verhagen – S. van Dongen*, "Cross-border Assignments under Rome I", in (2010) *Journal of Private International Law*, 13.

654 *Contra A. Bonomi*, "Il nuovo diritto internazionale privato dei contratti (La Convenzione di Roma del 19 giugno 1980 è entrata in vigore)", in (1992) *Banca borsa e titoli di credito*, 99. In line with the Author's opinion "*La cessione del credito non è, infatti, riconducibile alle ipotesi di fornitura di beni mobili materiali e di prestazione di servizi*".

provider (in this case the assignee) has habitual residence.[655] Where the contract goes beyond the "outright transfers of claims" for payment due, it can be considered both a sale and a contract not included in the list, and the law to be applied is the one in force at the grantor's residence.[656]

In contrast, where the transfer acts as a *datio in solutum*,[657] i.e. according to the Italian doctrine "*estinzione definitiva del rapporto obbligatorio anche dal punto di vista sostanziale con una prestazione di vero soddisfacimento*",[658] or in general the extinction of a previous obligation between the assignor and assignee,[659] consequently it is the law of the previous contract that applies.[660] Therefore, it will be the interpreter, starting from the national legal system, who will have the task of qualifying the previous contract and assessing whether it falls within one of those categories on the list referred to in Article 4 (1).[661]

Furthermore, where claims by way of security and pledges are being transferred, and although the assignor might be seen as being the "characteristic performer", the "escape clause" inserted in Article 4 (3) should be applied, with the result that the obligation must be granted rather than the

655 *T. C. Hartley*, "Choice of Law Regarding the Voluntary Assignment of Contractual Obligations Under the Rome I Regulation", in (2011) *International and Comparative Law Quarterly*, 39.

656 In the same way see *A. Leandro*, "Legge applicabile alle obbligazioni contrattuali – reg. CE n. 593/2008, Art. 14", in (2009) *Nuove Leggi Civili Commentate*, 845.

657 According to *T. C. Hartley*, "Choice of Law Regarding the Voluntary Assignment of Contractual Obligations Under the Rome I Regulation", in (2011) *International and Comparative Law Quarterly*, 32, the assignment is distinguished from novation "Novation is a contract to which Debtor, Creditor and Assignee are all parties, in which they agree that A will take the place of C in his relationship with D. It differs from assignment in that the assent of D is necessary. Since the new contract replaces the old one, the parties are free to agree whatever terms they wish; normally, however, A will take over C's liabilities towards D as well as C's claims against him. As far as conflict of laws is concerned, the normal choice of law rules will apply to determine the validity of the new contract. Article 14 is not relevant".

658 In Italian legal system see *M. Martorana*, *La novazione nel diritto civile italiano*, (Palermo, 1924), 18. In the same way *C.M. Bianca*, *Diritto civile*, IV – *L'obbligazione*, (Giuffrè, Milano, 1993), 430 – 431.

659 *M. McParland*, *The Rome I Regulation on the law applicable to contractual obligations*, (O.U.P., Oxford, 2015), 780. According to the Author Article 14 will not apply also to a novation.

660 *A. Leandro*, "Legge applicabile alle obbligazioni contrattuali – reg. CE n. 593/2008, Art. 14", in (2009) *Nuove Leggi Civili Commentate*, 845.

661 In the same way *G. Passarelli*, "The Voluntary assignment of receivables in Private International Law", in (2014) *Studi sull' integrazione europea*, 329.

assignment.[662] In this context I think that the "escape clause" should be applied even outside of this specific hypothesis, in particular with recourse to the theory of "accessory allocation".[663] It is applicable "in situation where the court uses a law governing one or more contract(s) to govern or infect another closely related contracts, where the parties have not made an express choice of law to govern all the contracts they have entered into a commercial transaction".[664] Indeed, in the case where the credit assigned finds his/her own source in a previous contract between the debtor and the assignor (in which the applicable law was chosen), I begin by assuming that the court should evaluate if the same law might be applied also to the contract between assignor and assignee, when the latter has not chosen the applicable law.[665] This theory finds its source not only in some European

662 On this point emerge the theory of the Accessory Allocation as connecting factor. For more see *C.S.A. Okoli*, "The significance of the doctrine of accessory allocation as a connecting factor under article 4 of the Rome I Regulation", in (2013) *Journal of Private International Law*, 449 ss.

663 This doctrine was recognised and applied as important connecting factor under English, French and German domestic private international law rules in contractual obligations. It was defined "doctrine of infection" in England, "*caractère accessoire*" in France and "*akzessorische Anknüpfung*" in Germany. For the English approach see cases *Wahda Bank v. Arab Bank Plc* (1996) CLC 408. For the French approach see *S. Corneloup*, "Choix de loi et contrats lies", in S. Corneloup – N. Joubert (eds.), *Le reglement communautaire 'Rome I' et le choix de loi dans les contrats internationaux*, (LexisNexis, Dijon, 2011), 285. For the German approach see *E. Jayme*, "Komplexe Langzeitverträge und Internationales Privatrecht (Ein Tagungsbericht)", in (1987) *IPRax*, 63.

664 In these words, *C.S.A. Okoli*, "The significance of the doctrine of accessory allocation as a connecting factor under article 4 of the Rome I Regulation", in (2013) *Journal of Private International Law*, 449. The Author not has expressly inserted the voluntary assignment in the list of contracts where is possible apply this particular theory. However, it may be applied also in voluntary assignment. In different way *U. Magnus*, "Art. 4", in U. Magnus – P. Manowsky (eds.), "European Commentaries on Private International Law – Commentary, Rome I Regulation", (Ottoschmidt, Köln, 2017), 277 who, instead, in the case of two separates contracts closely connected, the law applicable for each of these contracts has to be determined separately.

665 *P. Lagarde*, "The European Convention on the Law Applicable to Contractual Obligations: An Apologia", in (1981) *Virginia Journal of International Law*, 97 – 98. In line with the Author's opinion "A subcontractor, for example, might be governed by the same law governing the principal contract between the contractor and the employer rather than the law of the country in which the subcontractor has his place of business".

doctrines,[666] but also in Rome I, where Recitals §§ 20 and 21 invite the interpreter to consider the presence of a close relationship between that contract and other contracts.

In light of the foregoing considerations, I want to emphasize that the framework of Article 14 of Rome I could confuse the interpreter in a "hybrid" contract such as that of voluntary assignment, where a flexible rule with the criterion of the closest connection certainly would facilitate the task of identifying the most equitable applicable law in absence of parties' choice.[667] In fact, the presence in Article 4's list of contracts such as provision of services, the difficulty of determining the characteristic performance of the contract[668] under Article 4 (2), and the existence of a rigid "escape clause" (3) certainly lead to the application of an "inequitable" law. Therefore, for voluntary assignment it is not appropriate to assume a "renvoi", albeit indirect, to a rigid rule as those of Article 4 of Rome I.

Finally, it remains necessary to point out that an important opportunity to shed some clarity on a current and complex subject was lost during the drafting of the Rome I and also after the Report that Article 27 imposed on the Commission came into force on June 17, 2010. In this respect, I believe that a reasonable rule is necessary given that this contract is nowadays still governed differently in the various Member States and plays an important role for the proper functioning of the internal market.

---

666 *Ex multis C.S.A. Okoli*, "The significance of the doctrine of accessory allocation as a connecting factor under article 4 of the Rome I Regulation", in (2013) *Journal of Private International Law*, 465 - 466. According to the Author "[...] the utilization of AA under Article 4 is that it reconciles the requirements of legal certainty and flexibility. In other words, the doctrine of AA ordinarily operates as an exception to the main rule(s) to do justice in individual cases, but also leads to legal certainty, since a single law is applied to contracts that have a very close relationship in a commercial transaction".

667 See on this point English *Court of Appeal* January 26, 2001 - *Raiffeisen Zentralbank Österreich AG v. An Feng Steel Co. Ltd.* In this case, in reference to the applicable law in a voluntary assignment, the Lord Justice Mance confirmed that identifying the applicable law requires careful evaluation of the scope of the Rome Convention.Therefore according to the court this evaluation is important in understanding that "the conflict of laws does not depend (like a game or even an election) upon the application of rigid rules but upon a search for appropriate principles to meet particular situations".

668 *M. McParland, The Rome I regulation on the law applicable to contractual obligations*, (O.U.P., Oxford, 2015), 789. According to the Author in this contract is "impossible to determine the characteristic performance".

3.IV Pros and Cons of rigid rules: Practical implications

Before a practical analysis is made a question ought to be posed: Was it necessary to transform the Rome Convention into an EU Regulation? Several French jurists have asked this.[669] However, the conversion of the Rome Convention into an EU instrument, surely has represented great progress towards the creation of "(quasi)-constitutionalization" of EU p.i.l. It is my belief that the methods used can be criticized for their lack of flexibility. In fact, excessive preference has been given to "predictability" and "legal certainty" as opposed to "legal congruence" and to the in-depth study of the underlying legal institutions, causing a disproportionate rigidity, which probably does not lead to a truly reforming regulation.

The analysis of previous pages shows that the major change introduced by Rome I was to replace the flexible approach of Article 4 of the Rome Convention with hard-and-fast rules. Therefore, after a flexible structure which characterised the "conflict of laws" of the EU and US at least in the second half of the twentieth century, Europe has returned to a strongly rigid mechanism[670] that could have been described as "less rigid" by reference to the Proposal.[671] In fact the "escape clause" that was replaced in the Proposal has been reinserted with a "strong presumption approach".[672]

However, as seen, comparing the framework of the two rules, Article 4 of the Rome Convention shows quite an opposite structure, starting with the general principle of the closest connection and then showing general presumptions. On the contrary, Article 4 of Rome I leads with a list of spe-

669 The debate has been developed in France following the publication of an open letter to the President of the French Republic with which the transformation is questioned, and it is reported by the Italian jurist *T. Ballarino*, "Dalla Convenzione di Roma del 1980 al Regolamento Roma I", in (2009) *Rivista di diritto internazionale*, 40 and 46.

670 *A. Bonomi*, "Conversion of the Rome Convention on contracts into an EC instrument: some remarks on the Green Paper of the EC Commission", in (2003) 5 *Yearbook of Private International Law*, 73.

671 Commission, Proposal for a Regulation of the European Parliament and the Council on the law applicable to contractual obligations (Rome I), COM (2005) 650 final, art 4 (f). In reference to the Proposal, one of the most authoritative doctrine has criticized "[...]*la suppression malheureuse de la clausole d'exception*" that leads to "[...] *toute flexibilitè au nom de la sècuritè juridique*". In these words *P. Lagarde*, 'Remarques sur la proposition de règlement de la Commission europèeene sur la loi applicable aux obligations contractuelles (Roma I)', in (2006) *Reveu Critique de Droit International Privè*, 338 and 349.

672 See *supra* § 3.III.

cific contracts for which the applicable law is determined, and the classical p.i.l. instruments with their very rigid criteria are only inserted in subsequent paragraphs.

By using an inflexible structure, it is clear that the framers of the Rome I Regulation have attempted to solve, at least with reference to the list of contracts which are inserted in paragraph (1), the problem of the diversity of interpretation around Article 4 of the Rome Convention. Therefore, according to Recitals §§ 6 and 16, the legal certainty is "highly foreseeable"[673] in that it would be a support to the EU internal market "in order to improve the predictability of the outcome of litigation, certainty as to the law applicable and the free movement of judgments".[674] Indeed, the Recital's provision that the "foreseeable" legal certainty apparently coexist with "a degree of discretion"[675] is not borne out in the Rome I Regulation because the inflexible approach of the Article 4, in particular of the escape clause,[676] undermines the discretionary power of the court and as a consequence legal congruence.

In fact, it is evident that the aim of the framers of Rome I was to reduce drastically the discretionary power of the court in applying the "escape clause", which they believe should be used only if strong reasons point to a more closely connected law[677] as well as a 'derating' of the characteristic performance.[678] This circumstance is also confirmed by the differences in the wording of Article 4 of Rome Convention and Article 4 of Rome I. In

673 Recital § 16 of Regulation (EC) 593/2008 of the European Parliament and of the Council, of June 17, 2008 on the law applicable to contractual obligations (Rome I) [2008] OJ L177/6.

674 Recital § 6 of Regulation (EC) 593/2008 of the European Parliament and of the Council, of June 17, 2008 on the law applicable to contractual obligations (Rome I) [2008] OJ L177/6.

675 Recital § 16 of Regulation (EC) 593/2008 of the European Parliament and of the Council, of June 17, 2008 on the law applicable to contractual obligations (Rome I) [2008] OJ L177/6.

676 See *supra* § 3.III about the "strong presumption approach".

677 *P. Mankowsky*, "Der Vorschlag für die Rom I – Verordnung", in (2006) *IPRax*, 101.

678 According to some Authors in Rome I the characteristic performance should be declassified to a "merely descriptive approach". In these words, *P. Piroddi*, "Between Scylla and Charybdis. Art. 4 of the Rome I Regulation Navigating along the Cliffs of Uncertainty and Inflexibility", in G. Venturini - S. Bariatti (eds.), *Liber Fausto Pocar "New Instruments of Private International Law"* (Giuffrè, Milano, 2009), 831 and in the footnotes nr. 44 where the Author describes "It has been asserted that the characteristic performance, insofar as it bases on the concept of national economy of the State where it is located, is conceptually con-

fact, starting from a formal comparison of the two rules, it is clear that Article 4 of the Regulation begins with a list of specific contracts for which the applicable law is always indicated. Then the rule of "characteristic performance" is stressed and finally the "escape clause". At the same time, Article 4 of the Convention shows a completely different structure, starting with paragraph (1), where the rule of the principle of "closest connection" is immediately clear. It then adds the principles of "rebuttable presumptions" and of "characteristic performance".

According to Magnus,[679] there is a precise logical rationale rather than a mere formal difference in these changes. The intention of the framers of the Regulation to overturn the order already indicated in the Convention would seems intended to reduce drastically the interpreter's discretionary power and to create more certainty over the identification of the applicable law.

This choice of the framers of Rome I has been criticised from many points of view, not only for the excessive rigidity. In fact, some authors[680] have criticised the choice to include a list of contracts in Article 4 (1) given that EU lawmakers would be limited in defining the simplest contractual assumptions, thus leaving the interpreter the complex task of determining characteristic performance in contractual situations that present the most difficulty. This occurs in the case of contracts with reciprocal performance where it is not easy to identify which of the two performances should be chosen to locate the country of residence of one of the contracting parties. Consider the case of "a plumber resident in Italy who sells an apartment located in Switzerland and who, in the sales contract will also repair the

flicting with the fundamental assumptions of the European Community internal market, as an area without internal frontiers, characterised by the abolition of obstacles, as between Member States, to the free movements".

679 *U. Magnus*, "Article 4 Rome I Regulation. The applicable law in absence of choice", in F. Ferrari - S. Leible (eds.), *Rome I Regulation the law applicable to contractual obligations in Europe*, (Sellier, Munich, 2009), 30.

680 *Ex multis U. Villani*, "Il ruolo della prestazione caratteristica dalla Convenzione di Roma al Regolamento Roma I", in (2010) *Studi sull'integrazione europea*, 593. According to the Author "*Sembra, invero, che il legislatore europeo abbia 'comodamente' isolato le ipotesi più semplici quali la vendita e la prestazione di servizi, e per questi contratti abbia elevato a criterio di collegamento quello desunto dalla prestazione caratteristica (del venditore, del prestatore), lasciando poi all' interprete l'arduo compito di ricercare la prestazione caratteristica nelle situazioni più complesse. Ma, in realtà, più la fattispecie contrattuale è complessa, più difficile, se non impossibile (o arbitraria), è l'individuazione della prestazione caratteristica*".

broken taps".[681] In this specific case, hard-and-fast rules certainly do not help the interpreter in the "puzzle" of Rome I. It would appear that the *ratio legis* behind Article 4 (2) or (3) is to establish the applicable law only if it is not determinable in accordance with paragraph (1), placing it in more than one contractual category.[682] In addition, some contracts, even ones listed in Article 4 of Rome I often appear deeply ingrained in the socio-economic context of the country where the monetary performance debtor resides as opposed to the country of the other contracting party. Consider, for example, a sale payable in instalments where it is the purchaser who takes on the performance of the service with a longer duration.

The principle of closest connection, despite being a consolidated principle of p.i.l., and despite its ability to ensure the most equitable law in complex cases such as the one above, is not sufficiently recognized in Rome I except for in employment contracts. The rigid approach of the "escape clause" inserted in Article 4, as well as in Articles 5 and 7, minimizes the function of this principle and as a consequence undermines legal congruence. In fact, an escape clause that can only be applied rarely, in particular only when the contract is "manifestly more closely connected with a country", is tantamount to not having it at all since to date no clear definition has been given to the meaning of "manifestly". This word carries an "all or nothing" implication, and could confuse rather than assist the court during the task of identifying the applicable law.[683] In addition I believe that it diminishes the important function that should be inherent in the nature of an "escape clause", that is, citing Carrascosa Gonzàlez[684]

> "[…] *garantir que le réglé de conflit s'applique conformément à ce ratio. En effet, la clause d'exception évite l'application d'un rattachement qui conduit,*

681 Author's translation. The example is taken verbatim by *U. Villani*, "Il ruolo della prestazione caratteristica dalla Convenzione di Roma al Regolamento Roma I", in (2010) *Studi sull'integrazione europea*, 594.

682 *Ibid*, 594 - 595. In the Author's opinion the abovementioned contract would be governed by the Swiss law of the location of the property since the prevalence of the obligation of the seller with respect to that concerning the repair of the taps is without doubt, a prevalence that would lead to qualify the contract as a right in rem in immovable property.

683 On the other hand, with reference to the Rome II Regulation, there are criticisms raised by *R. J. Weintraub*, "Rome II and the tension between predictability and flexibility", in (2005) *Rivista di diritto internazionale privato e processuale*, 570.

684 *J. Carrascosa González*, "Règle de conflit et théorie économique", in (2012) *Revue critique de droit international privé*, 529.

> *à l'égard d'un rapport de droit spécifique, à un « résultat injuste », incompatible avec l'objet et la finalité de la même règle de conflit*".

The lesson to be drawn from this is straightforward: the rigid criteria inserted in Rome I have certainly made a drastic change in the EU p.i.l. system of contractual obligations. According to the framers of Rome I, this innovation would have the objective of improving the predictability of the outcome of litigation and certainty of the applicable law, but in reality it imposes on the interpreter highly detailed and lengthy work in the "labyrinth" of the Rome I rules, characterized by the examination of a long series of contracts, connecting factors and the protection of "weaker" parties. In addition, I have reasoned that the hard-and-fast rules do not necessarily result in less work for the interpreter especially when it comes to complex contracts, which could fall into more than one category of those indicated in the list of Article 4. Consequently, this complex work is unlikely to guarantee the predictability of the outcome of litigation called for in the Recital and could act as a brake on the EU internal market rather than a benefit.

However, to these considerations, which already point out the failure of Rome I's rigid criteria, in my view it is important for the court to concentrate on the interpretation of the contracts and their relation with these rigid rules. In fact, the judicial duty of the court to analyse every single contract in careful detail, with the aim of ensuring the application of the most equitable law, has also a central role within some national legal systems,[685] such as § 914 of the ABGB[686] or Article 1362 of the Italian Codice

---

685 In France *Cour de Cassation* (1 Ch. civ.) May 22, 2007 and *Cour de Cassation* (Ch.com.) December 19, 2006 - *Soc. Danzas GmbH et Soc. Westra c. Soc. Tapiola et autre*, in (2007) *Revue critique droit international privé*, 59. The Court held "*le juge saisi doit procéder à une comparaison des liens existant entre le contrat et, d' autre part, l' autre pays en cause, et rechercher celui avec lequel il présente les liens les plus étroits'*. Moreover these two rulings highlight the requirement asked of the judge to give a detailed explanation on the choice made. In particular as Lagarde authoritatively stated in a comment on the decisions "*Le juge devrait alors procéder à la recherche d' una pluralité d'indices, dont aucun ne serait décisif par lui-même, mais dont la somme pourrait avoir un effet sur la détermination de la loi applicable* [...]" . In this way *P. Lagarde*, in (2007) *Revue critique droit international privé*, 3, 602.

686 The § 914 Austrian civil code provides: "*Bei Auslegung von Verträgen ist nicht an dem buchstäblichen Sinne des Ausdrucks zu haften, sondern die Absicht der Parteien zu erforschen und der Vertrag so zu verstehen, wie es der Übung des redlichen Verkehrs entspricht*". In line with *H. Hausmaninger*, *The Austrian Legal System*, (Manz,

Civile.[687] This public duty ("*dovere di ufficio*")[688] forces the judge to establish the country in which the contract actually has closest connection on the basis of the "*nationalité des contractants, la langue du contrat, la monnaie, le lieu de conclusion du contrat et celui de son exécution, etc.*".[689]

The point, however, is that this judicial duty, which should provide the court with broad investigatory powers, is certainty irreconcilable with the Rome I Regulation, as is clearly shown by the list of the hard-and-fast rules and the "degree of the discretion"[690] forced by the Recital.

What is more, it is rightly noted that the rigid approach of Rome I contrasts also with a fundamental principle of arbitration law: the freedom of the tribunal to determine an applicable law that is a principle recognized by the laws of almost all the Member States.[691] In addition, it is well known that in absence of agreement, an arbitral tribunal when determining the applicable law uses arbitration rules[692] and most of them (see i.e.

Wien, 2003), 263, "bilateral contracts that fail to employ unequivocal language must be interpreted according to the 'true intention' of the parties. The true meaning of a declaration of intent must be established by evaluating what the addressee could have recognized as being the intention of the person making the declaration. If doubts remain, the 'costums of fair dealing' must be considered [at the same time] certain factual behavior expresses a legally relevant intent".

687 The Article 1362 c.c. provides: "*Nell'interpretare il contratto si deve indagare quale sia stata la comune intenzione delle parti e non limitarsi al senso letterale delle parole. Per determinare la comune intenzione delle parti, si deve valutare il loro comportamento complessivo anche posteriore alla conclusione del contratto*". In reference to the interpretation of the contract and the discretionary power of the court, the Italian *Corte di Cassazione* in the decison August 20, 2015 n. 17020 helds: "*Le clausole del contratto devono essere considerate non unitariamente ma complessivamente per poter ricostruire il contenuto dell'accordo*". See on this point also *G. Alpa*, *Competition of Legal Systems and Harmonizazion of European Private Law. New paths in a Comparative Perspectives* (Sellier, Munich, 2013), 154.

688 In these words *U. Villani*, "Il ruolo della prestazione caratteristica dalla Convenzione di Roma al Regolamento Roma I", in (2010) *Studi sull'integrazione europea*, 587.

689 In these words *F. Ferrari*, "La Loi applicable a défaut de choix par les parties selon l'article 4 de la proposition de règlement Roma I", in *Droit International Prive – annees 2006 – 2008* (A. Pedone, Paris, 2009), 121.

690 Recital § 16 of Regulation (EC) 593/2008 of the European Parliament and of the Council, of June 17, 2008 on the law applicable to contractual obligations (Rome I) [2008] OJ L177/6.

691 *D. Babić*, "Rome I Regulation: binding authority for arbitral tribunals in the European Union?", in (2017) *Journal of Private International Law*, 73.

692 *Ibid*, 75.

Art. 21 of International Chamber of Commerce) are rules that strongly enhance the role of the arbitrator to choose the applicable law.

Moreover, the Rome I Regulation hampers this "degree of the discretion" also with the absence of a reference to data theory,[693] which, as seen,[694] allows the court to examine carefully the presence of foreign elements for the application of a foreign rule. This limit to the analysis of local and moral data not only inhibits the application of the most equitable law but also conflicts with the central rule that some national legal systems give to these data.[695]

Furthermore, the Regulation has resolved very few current issues with the Rome Convention. In particular, it continues to leave many uncertainties and problems for non-nominated contracts and for the identification of characteristic performance. In addition, the rigid "escape clauses" inserted in Rome I certainly do not help the interpreter in the crucial task of identifying the applicable law. On this point, it should be added that it is unclear why the framers of Rome I have protected "weaker parties" such as employees and consumers with a flexible connecting factor, and yet have not provided the same kind of protection to other parties who may also be considered "weaker parties", such as tenants; franchisees; commercial agents.[696] The lack of a *ratio legis* behind this choice, concedes the assumption that the rigid criteria adopted by Rome I lack consistency and conceptual vision.[697]

Many of these problems, some of which have been highlighted above, are heightened when the interpreter is faced with specific contracts, many of which are typical of the new era of globalisation, such as:

– *"arbitration agreements"*: It is well known that the vast majority of disputes in commercial arbitration arise from contractual obligations. In this very common contract, the arbitrators become private judges by an

---

693 *Contra* for a *"partielle sogar Eingang in Art. 12 Abs. 2 Rome - I"* of the *"Datumtheorie" M.P. Weller, Die Grenze der Vertragstreue von (Krisen-) Staaten*, (Mohr Siebeck, Tübingen, 2013), 45. Actually, I believe that criticisms of this last view can be based on the clear reference to data theory in Art. 3 of the Rome Convention as well as in Art. 17 of the Rome II Regulation.

694 See *supra* § 3.II.

695 On this topic see for more *E. Jayme, Internationales Privatrecht: Ideengeschichte von Mancini und Ehrenzweig zum Europäischen Kollisionsrecht*, (C.F. Muller, Heidelberg, 2009), 200 – 204.

696 *G. Rühl*, "The Protection of Weaker Parties in the Private International Law of the European Union: a Portrait of Inconsistency and Conceptual Truancy", in (2014) *Journal of Private International Law*, 342 – 343.

697 *Ibid*, 358.

agreement with the parties. When the contract is broken and the parties have not choosen the applicable law, the role of the interpreter is not easy. In fact, according to Art. 4 (1) (b), the applicable law in these cases will be that of the country where the arbitrator has habitual residence. Actually, applying the above-mentioned "accessory allocation"[698] approach, which qualifies the arbitration as a clause of the main contract, the applicable law could be different. In addition, according to some academics and judicial theories, what will be applied is the law that governs the arbitration procedure[699] or the law of the place in which the award is to be made or the law of arbitral seat.[700] From a pragmatic standpoint, these circumastances show - in very common and international contracts such as arbitration agreements – that the hard-and-fast rules complicate the already complex task of choosing the applicable law and at the same time do not guarantee uniformity of decisions or certainty of the applicable law.[701]

– *"attorney contracts":* In these contracts, with the issue of professional services concluded with a law firm with multiple branches in many EU countries,[702] the applicable law, according to Article 4 (1) (b), is that of the country where the service provider has his/her habitual residence. This law is not always the most equitable and most connected to this particular contract. In fact, I think the interpreter should analyse all the circumstances of the contract and, in particular, factors such as the conclusion of the contract, the principal place of business of the law firm, and the competent court. As a consequence, in an attorney contract the

---

698 See § 3.III C.

699 See in this vein OGH (Austrian), RdW, 1998, 551 mentioned by *U. Magnus*, "Art. 4", in U. Magnus – P. Mankowsky (eds.), "European Commentaries on Private International Law", (Ottoschmidt, Kölm, 2017), 389.

700 In this way see *Rotterdam Rechtbank v. Netherlands*, 24 November 1994, in (1996) *Yearbook Commercial Arbitration*, 638. See for more *L. Silberman – F. Ferrari*, "Getting to the law applicable to the merits in international arbitration and the consequences of getting it wrong", in F. Ferrari - S. Kröll (eds.) *Conflict of Laws in International Arbitration*, (Sellier, Munich, 2011), 282 ss.

701 *L. Graffi*, "The law applicable to the validity of the arbitration agreement: a practioner's view", in F. Ferrari – S. Kröll (eds.) *Conflict of Laws in International Arbitration*, (Sellier, Munich, 2011), 43. The Author, mentioning some opinions, observes that "[…] it has been suggested that international arbitration calls for greater flexibility".

702 *F. Ferrari*, "Art. 4 Rom I-VO", in F. Ferrari – E.M. Kieninger - P. Mankowski (eds.), *Internationales Vertragsrecht, (VO) EG 593/2008*, (Verlag CH Beck, München, 2012), no. 105.

applicable law should be localized with the closest connection principle in order to apply the most equitable law. Certainly, the rigid escape clause and the presence of the services contract in the list of Article 4 do not help the interpreter to apply the most equitable law.

- *"barter transactions":* These contracts make the task of localizing the applicable law by the interpreter more difficult, not only for their relationship with "sale of goods"[703] of Article 4 (1) (a) but also with Article 4 (1) (c) when the subject of the contract is an immovable property. According to learned editors,[704] in these contracts characteristic performance is absent, with the result that the court must apply the closest connection principle in absence of choice by parties. In a different way, according to some accounts,[705] the applicable law will be that of the country where the transaction is notorized. Therefore, to localize the centre of gravity for these contracts, it remains indispensable to have a very flexible rule that permits the interpreter to identify the most equitable law. However, considering the inflexible approach of Rome I, it is better for the court to force the parties to choose the applicable law.
- *"bond":* These are special loans made by a bond holder (investor) to a borrower. These types of contracts have been created for the purpose of raising capital and nowadays are largely used by companies, municipalities, states, and sovereign governments to finance projects and operations. Usually, the relationship between the bond holder and the debtor of the bond is governed by an expressly or implicitly chosen law. In case of the absence of parties' choice, learned editors assume that the applicable law will be chosen according to the criteria of Art. 4 (1) (b), Art. 4 (2) or Art. 4 (4).[706] The interpreter in this nowadays widely-used contract, in my opinion, needs a deep understanding of the circumstances of the case. In particular, the interpreter needs to focus on the quality of the investor as well as of the borrower. In fact, I believe that in cases in which the lender is a government body or a consumer,

---

703 In fact, in line with *M. McParland, The Rome I regulation on the law applicable to contractual obligations*, (O.U.P., Oxford, 2015), 372 "barter contracts will not fall within Article 4 (1) (a)".

704 *Dicey & Morris, The conflict of laws*, 15th ed. (L. Collins ed.), (Sweet&Maxwell, London, 2012), no. 33-008, 1884; *P. R. Beaumont - P.E. McEleavy, Private International Law*, (Thomson Reuters, Edinburg, 2011), 469.

705 *F. Ferrari – J. A. Bischoff*, "Article 4", in F. Ferrari (ed.), *Rome I Regulation. Pocket commentary*, (Sellier, Munich, 2014), 132.

706 *U. Magnus*, "Art. 4 – Rome I", in U. Magnus – P. Mankowsky (eds.), "European Commentaries on Private International Law", (Ottoschmidt, Kölm, 2017), 365.

the applicable law must be that of the country where the government body or the consumer has the seat or habitual residence. In my opinion, only in this way will it avoid that a specific choice contrast with mandatory rules.

- *"brokerage contracts":* It is well known that a broker is an individual or firm that arranges a contract between two o more parties. In absence of choice of law by parties, according to Art. 4 (1) of Rome I, the applicable law will be that of the country where the broker has his/her seat.[707] In my opinion, this process cannot be taken for granted, because this type of contract is very complex and Art. (1) (b) cannot always be applied. In fact, in the case of contracts of real estate brokerage, I believe that Art. 4 (1) (c) should apply because it concerns a right in rem. At the same time, take the example of a contract of brokers who exchange stock on behalf of their clients. In this case, I believe it is important to focus on the type of client. In fact, in the case in which the client is acting for private or personal purposes, the investor can be considered a consumer,[708] so Art. 6 will be applied. In addition, in some broker contracts, such as those concerning ship and medical trade, the broker can be qualified as an agent and as a consequence, according to some national laws, as employees.[709] Therefore, in this cases art. 8 could be applied. After this analysis, I do not hesitate to say that from a pragmatic standpoint, the puzzle of Rome I rules aggravates the complex role of the interpreter to choose the applicable law and at the same time does not guarantee uniformity of decisions or certainty of the applicable law.
- *"buy-back contracts":* These are contracts where a contracting party undertakes to transfer a production facility and to purchase the products that will leave from it. This takes place when a contracting party commits to transferring a cost-effective plant and buys the products manufactured by it. It is clear that it is not easy for the interpreter to localize the characteristic performer in this type of contract. Therefore, the court should firstly determine if the characteristic performance is the

707 *Ibid*, 365.

708 See on this topic *ex multis G. Vettori, Il contratto dei consumatori, dei turisti, dei clienti, degli investitori e delle imprese deboli. Oltre il consumatore.* (Cedam, Padova, 2013), *passim*; *U. Magnus*, "Art. 4 – Rome I", in U. Magnus – P. Mankowsky (eds.), "European Commentaries on Private International Law", (Ottoschmidt, Kölm, 2017), 416.

709 *U. Magnus*, "Art. 4 – Rome I", in U. Magnus – P. Mankowsky (eds.), "European Commentaries on Private International Law", (Ottoschmidt, Kölm, 2017), 375.

production or the purchase of the products and then apply appropriately the law of the habitual residence of either the purchaser or the manufacturer. In such cases, I assert that the rigid rules of Article 4 do not help the court. As a consequence, a more flexible rule would have the merit of ensuring the application of the most equitable law, which would not create unfair economic balance between the parties.

- *"charter contract":* These contracts are very common in the EU internal market, where they are used to hire a vessel for the carriage of goods. I believe that in this category can be included "time charter" contracts, as they represent a provision of services to be rendered to the charterer by a shipowner through the use of the vessel by the ship-owner's own employess; "voyage charters", which are contracts of carriage of goods under which the charterer pays for the use of a ship's cargo space; and C.I.F. (cost, insurance and freight) contracts, where a vessel is chartered to carry the goods to destination. Certainly, this overview proves that in these contracts the applicable law can be identified both by Article 4 (1) (b) where the owner of the vessel is the service provider and by the criteria of Article 5. Therefore, I have reasoned that, depending on the p.i.l. rule used by the interpreter, a different law could be applied. As a consequence, in order to determine the applicable law, the interpreter should identify the principal obligation of the characteristic performer, and if this entails the obligation to carry goods, then Article 5 (1) will be engaged.[710] Alternatively the applicable law will be identified by Article 4 (1) (b).[711] This analysis of charted contracts provides evidence, once again, the numerous contracts and rigid criteria inserted in Rome I complicate the interpreter's task and as a consequence might not guarantee either the predictability of the outcome of litigation or the legal certainty as to the applicable law.
- *"donation":* The difficulties of the interpreter increase when he/she has to classify a measure of which the legal nature is different in individual

710 In this way *A. Staudinger*, "Rom I-VO Artikel 5 Beförderungsverträge Handkommentar", in R. Schulze – H. Dörner – I. Ebert – T. Hoeren – R. Kemper – I. Saenger – K. Schreiber – H. Schulte - Nölke – A. Staudinger (eds.), *Bürgerliches Gesetzbuch. Handkommentar,* (Nomos, Baden, 2014), no.13, in www.beckonline.beck.de; *A. Spickhoff*, "VO (EG) 593/2008 - Art. 5", in H.G. Bamberger – H. Roth (eds.) *Beck'scher Onlinekommentar BGB*, (Beck, München, 2013), no. 2, in www.beckonline.beck.de.

711 In this way *M. McParland*, *The Rome I regulation on the law applicable to contractual obligations*, (O.U.P., Oxford, 2015), 464. The Author reports the case ECJ C-305/13 *Haeger & Schmidt GmbH*.

Member States. A typical case is that of a donation, which in some EU Member States is classified as a contractual obligation and in others as a unilateral act. For example the qualification of donation as a "contractual obligation" is not accepted by the English doctrine.[712] In particular it is not is recognized as a type of contract, which is required to be supported by mutual consideration in order to be valid, but a mere gift that is by definition gratuitous. Therefore, the beneficiary has no contractual right to demand anything from the donor. On the contrary, in other European countries, such as Austria, Germany or Italy, the donation is classified as a contract. In light of these considerations, it is clear that an interpreter who encounters a donation and who has points of contact with different Member States should proceed to analyse some preliminary issues, such as the nature of the donation for the country of reference. He/she must then decide if the donation is bound by "contractual obligation", if it touches on the system of succession, and if the object of the donation is also the right of immovable property. In reference to the applicable law in absence of parties' choice some learned scholars[713] affirm that the donation has the closest connection with the country where the donor, at time of completion of the donation,[714] has habitual residence.[715] Although this cannot be considered a general rule, according to this doctrine, the donor should be the characteristic performer. I should also take into account that, in a case where the donation is made conditionally,[716] it is necessary for the interpreter to weigh up carefully what is the characteristic performance of the donee or the donor and then apply the law of habitual residence of the characteristic performer. To illustrate the reasoning underling this conclusion, let me use the case in which a wealthy Italian donor makes the donation of a small house in a boarder town in Germany to his young

712 *W. Morrison*, *Blackstone's Commentaries on the Laws of England*, (Cavendish Publishing Limited, London, 2001), § 442.

713 *Dicey & Morris*, *The conflict of laws*, 15th ed. (L. Collins ed.), (Sweet&Maxwell, London 2012), no. 33-008, 1884. In the same way also *A. J. Bêlohlávek*, *Rome Convention, Rome I Regulation: commentary, new EU conflict-of-laws rules for contractual obligation*, (Huntington, N.Y., Juris, 2010, 2 v), 244.

714 *L. Fumagalli*, "La Convenzione di Roma e la Legge regolatrice delle donazioni", in (1993) *Rivista di Diritto Internazionale Privato e Processuale*, 599.

715 On this point with reference to Italian case law see *Tribunale di Venezia* February 28, 2003, in (2004) *Rivista di diritto internazionale privato e processuale*, 272 ss.

716 This type of donation is in force in German legal system (§ 525 BGB) and Italian jurisdiction with the "*onere*", that was called "*modus*" in Roman law.

Polish housekeeper (beneficiary) with the 'obligation later' to assist his three children for a lifetime. In this particular case it appears fair to consider that the "non-monetary performance"[717] (*Nicht-Geldleistung*) is that of the donee who is the characteristic performer. Therefore, the applicable law should be that of the habitual residence of the donee. Indeed in this example where the object of the donation is an immovable property the court should also apply the hard-and-fast rule of Article 4 (1) (c) of the Rome I where the connection factor is one of the *lex rei sitae,*[718] so that as a consequence a law not closest to the contract could be applied. In light of these considerations the interpreter in the task of identifying the law applicable to the donation, especially when it has implications for the rights of immovable property, must consider carefully the complexities of all the circumstances in order to apply the most equitable law. Otherwise, I believe that the inflexible escape clause and the rigid criteria of the Rome I could come to inequitable outcomes.[719]

- *"engineering contracts":* At a glance, in this type of contract the characteristic performer may be identified as the engineering firm that handles the design, construction, administration and maintenance of the work. Actually, the contractor may not be limited to paying out a sum of money, but may also have an active role in the development of the project, acting as supervisor of the works and handling the necessary authorization requirements. In such cases, a detailed study of the contract by the interpreter and the subsequent identification of the applicable law with the closest connection principle could ensure the application of the most equitable law, i.e. one that does not adversely affect the engineering firm or the other parties of the contract.
- *"exchange contracts":* In these contracts, no services have a monetary character. Therefore, it is clear that the characteristic performance rule can easily break down and the application of the closest connection criterion becomes the mandatory solution in identifying the applicable

717 *J. Hill*, "Choice of law in contract under the Rome Convention: the approach of the UK Courts", in (2004) *International Comparative Law Quarterly*, 334. The Author mentioned the Scottish case *William Grant & Sons International Ltd vs. Marie Brizard Espana SA*, [1998].

718 *G.P. Calliess*, *Rome Regulations. Commentary on the European rules of the conflict of laws*, (Kluwer Law International, Alphen a/d Rijn, 2011), 92.

719 In the same way *G. Passarelli*, "Donation: short notes between Italian civil law and EU private international law", in (2015) *Cuadernos de Derecho Transnacional*, 476 – 482.

law. Moreover, in this contract the hard-and-fast rule of Article 4 (1), in particular (a) (c) (f), may lead the court to apply an inequitable law, and does not guarantee the predictability of the decisions desired by the Rome I Recital. Therefore, in light of these considerations, I arrived at the conclusion that it is better for the court to force the parties to choose the applicable law.

- *"joint venture contracts":* This is one of the most common types of international contract[720] because it represents a collaboration between companies located in different Member States. In the case of the Italian *Corte di Cassazione – Sezioni Unite* with the decision May 3, 2005 n. 9107,[721] on a contract where two industries exchange quantities of chemicals in order to produce a certain material, the court upheld the decision that it is impossible to apply the characteristic performance rule considering the fact that each party is obliged to put up capital, technology and personnel. As a consequence of this interpretation, the Italian *Corte di Cassazione* held that the applicable law can be identified solely with the closest connection principle. In light of this case, I want to stress that, when a court is faced with a joint venture contract, it should break up the hard-and-fast rules and use the closest connection principle to identify the applicable law. Certainly, the rigid approach of the Rome I does not guarantee the localization of the most equitable law in joint venture contracts, especially when the partnership between the companies is also related to provision of services, distribution, sale of goods or insurance contracts. The result, in my opinion, is that the complexity of these contracts and the hard-and-fast rules will lead to different case-by-case decisions, which might not improve the predictability hoped for by the Rome I Recital.
- *"loan contracts":* In these contracts, it is not clear which party (the leader or the borrower) is the characteristic performer.[722] In the absence of choice the escape clause and the scrupulous work of the interpreter should play an important role in identifying the applicable law to ensure case-by-case the most equitable law. I believe that the list of Article

720 These contracts are especially used on the petroleum market as joint operating agreements in oil and gas transactions, and also in large-scale projects in the building trade.

721 Available at http://www.unalex.eu/Judgment/Judgment.aspx?FileNr=IT-466&FixLng=it.

722 *P. R. Beaumont - P.E. McEleavy, Private International Law*, (Thomson Reuters, Edinburg, 2011), 468 have mentioned the case *Atlantic Telecom GmbH v. Noter*, (2004).

4 and the rigid escape clause do not help the already complex task of the interpreter when he/she is faced with contracts such as "leasing" or "rent to buy". In fact, these two contracts are very common in international practice, and the complexity that characterizes them, does not help the interpreter in the task of identifying the applicable law, since considerations on a case-by-case basis may lead to a contracts qualified as "provision of services", "sale of goods", "consumer contract", or "contract relating to a right *in rem*" when the subject is a real-estate property.[723]

- *"medical and hospital contracts":* The choice of the applicable law by the interpreter could be faulty also when she/he is faced with a contract between a patient and an international hospital or a foreign physician, or in the case of "telemedicine", a medical treatment by a doctor via the internet. Now suppose the case of a German patient who undergoes a delicate surgical intervention by a French physician in an internationally owned hospital based in Britain. This contract could meet the conditions of Article 4 (1) (b) for provision of services by a hospital. But the surgical operation performed by the French physician could equally qualify as the provision of a service. Finally in several EU countries[724] the patient is described as a consumer,[725] therefore Article 6 may be applied or Article 7 when there is health insurance involved. Consequently, the task of the interpreter becomes complicated considering the numerous types of contracts that can be taken into consideration. Therefore, this task should focus on the importance of the service or of the patien's country.
- *"pledge":* When a contract involves pledge on movable property, the task of the interpreter is further complicated due to the presence of pro-

723 *A. Spickhoff*, "VO (EG) 593/2008 - Art. 4", in H.G. Bamberger – H. Roth (eds.) *Beck'scher Onlinekommentar BGB*, (Beck, München, 2013), no. 68, in www.beckonline.beck.de; *D. Martiny*, "Art. 4 Rom I –VO", in *Münchener Kommentar zum Bürgerlichen Gesetzbuch*, (Verlag C.H. Beck, München, 2010), no. 211.

724 In Italy for example the patient is cualified as a consumer. On this opinion see *ex multis M. Pennasilico*, "L' interpretazione dei contratti del consumatore", in P. Perlingieri – E. Caterini (eds.), *Il diritto dei consumi*, (E.S.I., Napoli, 2004), 145 ss.; *S. Rodotà*, *"Persona-consumatore"*, in P. Stanzione (ed.), *La tutela del consumatore tra liberismo e solidarismo, Atti del Convegno di Salerno, 21 e 22 ottobre 1994*, (E.S.I., Napoli, 1999), 19 ss.; *E. Gabrielli, Il consumatore e il professionista*, in E. Gabrielli - E. Minervini (eds.), *I contratti dei consumatori*, (Utet, Torino, 2005), 6.

725 For the application of the consumer law see also *A. Spickhoff*, "VO (EG) 593/2008 - Art. 6", in H.G. Bamberger – H. Roth (eds.) *Beck'scher Onlinekommentar BGB*, (Beck, München, 2013), no. 13, in www.beckonline.beck.de.

vision of services contracts in Article 4 (1). In fact, compared to other types of contract, it is certainly not easy for the interpreter to identify who is the "service provider". According to Dicey and Morris,

> "If the pledge is given as part of a transaction in which credit is provided simultaneously to the pledger by the pledge in the course of the latter's business, it is considered that the pledgee should be regarded as the service provider even if the loan is separately documented. Otherwise, it is possible that a contract for the pledge of a movable may be governed by the law of the country where the party required to effect the characteristic performance of the contract has his habitual residence. If that approach is taken, the law of the country of the pledger's habitual residence may apply, for the reasons given above. It is suggested that it is most unlikely that a contract for the pledge of a movable will be regarded as a contract where the applicable law cannot be determined on the basis of Article 4 (1) (b) or 4 (2) so as to lead to the conclusion that, pursuant to Article 4 (4), the contract will be governed by the law of the country with which it is most closely connected".[726]

To the above remarks should be added that the pledge on movable property may be connected to another contract, as a sale of goods or supply of goods, with the result that only a careful analysis by the interpreter, supported by a flexible p.i.l. tool, could identify the most equitable law without creating unfair economic prejudices to contractual parties.

- *"publishing contracts":* The complexity of these contracts has already been the subject of studies within the Rome Convention.[727] In fact, in many countries (e.g. Italy), publishing companies often adopt specific practices. For example, when a contract is signed for the publishing of a University text for students, the publisher will agree to pay the author, but contrarily, if a treatise is written for scientific purposes and the author does not hold prestigious academic standing, the author must agree to pay the publisher. In the latter case, the applicable law could be that of the country in which the publisher has the central headquar-

---

726 In these words, *Dicey & Morris*, *The conflict of laws*, 15th ed. (L. Collins ed.), (Sweet&Maxwell, London, 2012), no. 33-013, 1886.

727 *K.F. Juenger*, "The E.C.C. Convention on the Law Applicable to Contractual Obligations: An American Assessment", in P. North (ed.), *Contract Conflicts*, (North-Holland Publ. Co., Amsterdam, 1982), 301. The Author gives this question: "what, for instance, should be the characteristic performance of a contract to publish and distribute a literary work?".

ters[728] because the characteristic performace is the product of the publication and its best possible marketing by the publisher.[729] Consequently, in the first example the applicable law may be that of the country where the author has habitual residence.[730] This explains why, in these contracts, using only the closest connection principle would favour the application of the most equitable law, since disregarding the hard-and-fast rules of Article 4 (1) (b), it would not only lead to different applicable laws on a case-by-case basis, but also cause harm to the weaker party, i.e. the author. On this point, it should be noted that, for this type of contract, the consequences regarding an unequitable applicable law should not be underestimated, given the strong connection of these contracts with copyright rules, plagiarism, etc.

- most *"trade finance obligations":* These contracts involve letters of credit, current accounts, venture capital, credit transfers but especially interbank contracts, for example mutual financial obligations, where both services have financial characteristics.[731] According to learned editors,[732] these contracts pertain to the provision of services[733] and therefore the applicable law is that of the country where the bank (investor)

728 *A. Spickhoff*, "VO (EG) 593/2008 - Art. 4", in H.G. Bamberger – H. Roth (eds.) *Beck'scher Onlinekommentar BGB*, (Beck, München, 2013), no. 77, in https://beck-online.beck.de/. According to the Author *"Für den Verlagsvertrag ist die Verbreitungsverpflichtung des Verlegers kennzeichnend, so dass gemäß Abs 2 das Recht an seinem Sitz gilt"*.

729 *U. Magnus*, "Article 4 Rome I Regulation. The applicable law in absence of choice", in S. Leible - F. Ferrari (eds.), *Rome I Regulation the law applicable to contractual obligation in Europe*, (Sellier, Munich, 2009), 424.

730 *Ibid*, The Author take also the case in which a publisher engages with an author to write a book. In this case according to the learned editor the law of the principal place of business will be applied only if the contract implied an obligation of the publisher to publish and market the book. In contrast the law of the author habitual residence will be applied.

731 See also the decision of *Tribunale di Milano*, December 4, 1997 – *Banca Agricola Milanese s.p.a. v. Commerzbank AG*, in (1999) *Rivista di diritto internazionale privato e processuale*, 63.

732 *Dicey & Morris*, *The conflict of laws*, in L. Collins (ed.), (Sweet&Maxwell, London, 2012), no. 33-305, 2062.

733 See for more the national decisions cited in *M. McParland*, *The Rome I Regulation on the law applicable to contractual obligations*, (O.U.P., Oxford, 2015), 530. *Contra A. Bonomi*, "Il nuovo diritto internazionale privato dei contratti" (La Convenzione di Roma del 19 giugno 1980 è entrata in vigore), in (1992) *Banca borsa e titoli di credito*, 99. According to the Author *"La cessione del credito non è, infatti, riconducibile alle ipotesi di fornitura di beni mobili materiali e di prestazione di servizi"*.

- has its habitual residence according to Article 4 (1) (b) of Rome I. Actually, according to case law in some nations,[734] certain financial services and investments are transactions concluded by consumers (see for example money market instrument),[735] so Article 6 may be applied. Finally, as often is the case in international bank transactions, (i.e. those that p.i.l. must regulate), the contract between a business and a bank is negotiated with a branch that has headquarters in another country. Consider the case where an Austrian company signs a bank contract with an Italian branch of the "Deutsche Bank" or the case where in a venture capital investment there are multiple investors, one of whom is an institutional body. In this case, the interpreter must carefully analyse the contract and he/she needs a flexible escape clause. In light of these observations, I believe that only a flexible "escape clause" and therefore the use of the principle of closest connection should be applied on a case-by-case basis to provide the most equitable law, in order to avoid harms to the contractual parties.

– *"virtual enterprises contracts":* Criticism could be made in reference to disputes over virtual enterprises. By their very nature, these contracts are characterised by numerous international points of contact (see geographical location), and it has been difficult, first with the Convention and then with Rome I, for the interpreter to identify the applicable law in the absence of parties' choice.[736] Consequently, I believe that in this

734 *Ex multis Queens Bench Division - Standard Bank London Ltd. v Apostolakis (No2)* [2002] 2 CLC 933 – 936.

735 In this way *M. McParland, The Rome I Regulation on the law applicable to contractual obligations*, (O.U.P., Oxford, 2015), 567.

736 For more see *E. M. Weitzenboeck*, "Determining applicable law and jurisdiction in contractual disputes regarding virtual enterprises", in K. Pawar - F. Weber - K. Thoben (eds.), *Proceedings of the 8th International Conference on Concurrent Enterprising: Ubiquitous Engineering in the Collaborative Economy. Rome, Italy, 17-19 June 2000* (ICE, 2002), 32. According to the Author: "Image a virtual enterprise made up a group of talent creative freelancers that was contracted by a French firm to design and production of the brochure by VE. The proper law, according to Article 4 (2), is the principal place of business of the VE. Is, as is often the case in practice, the VE has not been set up as a separate legal person, but its members are based in the same country, say Italy, then Italian law would be the applicable law. However, if the VE members are situated in different countries (e.g. Italy and Austria) and the different stages of the design and production are being carried out in these countries, then, although the characteristic performance of the contract is identifiable, it points to two different countries. Such a situation makes the application of Article 4 (2) difficult, if not impossible. One

type of contract resorting to the flexible "escape clause" is the only one way to apply the most equitable law.

3.V Outline in context

In light of the above considerations, it is clear that in many contracts used in international practice, even for some of those listed in Article 4, the court should use the principle of closest connection and of characteristic performance. In fact, I have reasoned that only by using these instruments could the court apply the most equitable law and thereby avoid harm to the reasonable expectations of contractual parties.

However, even if the court wanted to observe this "public duty", in some cases imposed by national standards,[737] the rigid approach of Rome I does not allow use of these traditional instruments. The result is that the court faced with inflexible criteria and with only a "degree of discretion",[738] cannot apply the most equitable law because a hard-and-fast rule is incompatible with this process. Consequently, the process can result in the application of "inequitable" law with all the problems this could create.

It is important to remember that famous scholars,[739] have held that the narrow and inflexible application of legal concepts, results is not in legal certainty or convenience but rather in unequal treatment and inconsistent justice. These drawbacks in Rome I are amplified not only by the need for predictability pointed out in the Recital, but also because in the murky "labyrinth" (or as defined by some Authors[740] "jungle") of connection tools and contracts, the interpreter's task it is made significantly more

---

would here try to see whether the contract is severable and whether part of it has a closer connection with another country".

737 Cfr. *ex multis supra* § 3.IV Austrian and Italian legal systems.

738 Recital § 16 of Regulation (EC) 593/2008 of the European Parliament and of the Council, of June 17, 2008 on the law applicable to contractual obligations (Rome I) [2008] OJ L177/6.

739 *Ex multis G.C. Cheshire – P.M. North*, *Private International Law*, (Butterworths, London, 1970), 34; *R. Jukier*, "Flexibility and Certainty as Competing Contract Values: A Civil Lawyer's Reaction to the O.L.R.C.'s Recommendations on Amendments to the Law of Contract", in (1988) *Canadian Business Law Journal*, 38.

740 In these words, *J. A. Moreno Rodriguez – M. Mercedes Albornoz*, "Reflections on the Mexico Convention in the Context of the Preparation of the Future Hague Instrument on International Contracts", in (2011) *Journal of Private International Law*, 516; *M. Mercedes Albornoz*, "Choice of Law in International Contracts in

complicated. As a consequence she/he cannot unravel the complexity of a case or comprehend the real "nature" of the contract,[741] with the risk that the result will not only be an applicable law not in line with the reasonable expectations of the contractual parties but also a lack of uniformity in the decisions. Therefore, according to this judicial duty, a good solution may be that when the litigation has begun the judges or a mediation body compels the parties to choose the applicable law especially in complex contracts, such as barter, exchange, joint ventures, smart contracts, etc., where it is impossible to identify characteristic performance.[742]

These considerations can be used to demonstrate that a reasonable legal instrument that combines certainty with flexibility, could guarantee more discretionary power to the interpreter in localizing the legal relationship and at the same time would facilitate the task of identifying the applicable law.[743] Instead, the rigid and untidy structure of Rome I complicates the court task and does not guarantee the application of the most equitable law producing problems that could hinder international transactions and weaken the EU internal market.

On the latter point, contrary to the Rome I Recital, it is important to emphasize that to date there are no field studies that show that the rigid rules, intended to ensure predictability, certainty and uniformity, bring any benefit to the internal market. Rather, the risk is that legal certainty and predictability, respectively declared also in a recent study[744] as unrealistic concepts and as illusions in real life, can produce with hard-and-fast

Latin American Legal Systems", in (2010) *Journal of Private International Law*, 26.

741 *A. Saydé*, *The Abuse of EU Law and Regulation in the Internal Market*, (Hart Publishing, Oxford, 2014), 207.

742 See for more *infra* § C.V on mediation body.

743 *G. Rühl*, "Method and Approach in Choice of Law: An Economic Perspective", in (2006) *Berkeley Journal of International Law*, 825.

744 *L.C. Wolff*, "Flexible choice-of-law rules: Panacea or oxymoron?", in (2014) *Journal of Private International Law*, 440.

rules inequitable outcomes[745] that are detrimental to the internal market.[746]

To conclude, my contention is that rigid rules, particularly in the field of such p.i.l. which also involve economic aspects, do not improve the ease of business transactions because they do not reflect the fast social and economic changes of the market, which require an individual evaluation and not an automatic process.[747] On this basis, the economic theories which underpin the normative guidance through hard-and-fast rules, do not encourage economic players by facilitating international business transactions.[748] Paradoxically, according to a drastic and extreme view of many academics,[749] international transactions often seem to thrive most where each legal form is missing.[750]

In light of these observations, I suggest that the maximization of profits for companies and therefore presumably greater benefits for the internal market would be facilitated not only by promoting party autonomy[751] but

745 On this topic and in particular on the eternal struggle between certainty and equity in p.i.l. see *P. H. Neuhaus*, "Legal Certainty Versus Equity in the Conflict of Laws", in (1963) *Law and Contemporary Problems*, 800. According to the Author in the beginning of the twentieth century p.i.l. had the objective to pursue the legal certainty. After several years it has come to the conclusion that mechanical application of rule often came to inequitable outcomes.

746 In this way *A. Saydé*, *The Abuse of EU Law and Regulation in the Internal Market*, (Hart Publishing, Oxford, 2014), 172.

747 On this point see *H. E. Yntema*, "The Objectives of Private International Law", in (1957) *The Canadian Law Review*, 736.

748 *V. Gessner*, "Contractual certainty in International Trade", in V. Gessner (ed.), *Towards a Theoretical Framework for Contractual Certainty in Global Trade*, (Hart Publishing, Oxford, 2009), 5.

749 *Ex multis W. Scheuerman*, "Globalization and the Fate of Law", in D. Dyzenhaus (ed.), *Recrafting the Rule of Law: The Limits of Legal Order* (Hart Publishing, Oxford, 1999), 262; *P.S. Atiyah*, *The Rise and Fall of Freedom of Contract* (Clarendon Press, Oxford, 1979), 713. With an extreme view, on the absence of economic benefits of a system of p.i.l. see *H.J. Schmidt-Trenz*, *Aussenhandel und Territorialität des Rechts: Grundlegung einer neuen Institutionenökonomik des Aussenhandels*, (Nomos, Bade, 1990), *passim*.

750 Curries, in his famous aphorism said that "we are better without choice of law rules". See for more *B. Currie*, *Selected Essay on the Conflicts of Laws*, (Duke University Press, Durham, 1963), *passim*.

751 *H. Hoyer*, "Der Anwendungsbereich des Einheitlichen Wiener Kaufrechts", in H. Hoyer – W. Posch (eds.) *Das Einheitliche Wiener Kaufrecht. Neues Recht für den Internationalen Warenkauf* (Orac, Wien, 1992), 41.

also by reasonable and flexible rules rather than by fast, hard and uniform ones.[752]

752 *B. R. Dorbeck – Jung*, "Global Trade: Changes in the Conceptualisation of Legal Certainty?", in V. Gessner (ed.), *Towards a Theoretical Framework for Contractual Certainty in Global Trade*, (Hart Publishing, Oxford, 2009), 297.

4. Implementation and Conclusion

Introduction

The arguments advanced in the previous pages are not whole new. As seen, many authors have pointed to the internal market's need for rigid or flexible rules of contractual obligations in all its ramifications. This book attempts to contribute to this debate, which is much more timely in the new era of globalisation.

The critical analysis of the changes introduced by the Rome I Regulation, particularly those that concern the applicable law in absence of choice, may not be equally persuasive for all readers. However, this will not affect the assessments presented in the foregoing pages in relation to the need not only to enhance party autonomy without harming their reasonable economic expectations, but above all for the need to codify a rule of contractual obligations that combine certainty with flexibility in order to guarantee a central rule to aid the interpreter in identifying the applicable law.

These considerations are based not only on the negative effects that, as seen, rigid rules have on the market but also on the necessity to ensure greater respect for the differing legal cultures[753] of Member States and to enhance the role of the interpreter. In fact, a foreseeable risk is that the EU bodies' attempt to encourage legal certainty, thereby limiting national judges' discretionary powers of interpretation with hard-and-fast rules, will not comply with the judges' duty to make a judgement of equivalence considering all the circumstances of the contract, but also that this attempt will disorientate the court in the complex "puzzle" of Rome I. As a consequence, a lack of uniformity of decisions and/or a "*résultat injuste*"[754] may occur, with serious consequences prejudicial also to the players of the internal market.

---

753 According to *G. Comparato*, *Nationalism and private law in Europe*, (Hart Publishing, Oxford, 2014), 147, the cultural pluralism is also a value to be safeguarded rather than an obstacle to efficiency of the market.

754 *J. Carrascosa González*, "Règle de conflit et théorie économique", in (2012) *Revue critique de droit international privé*, 529.

Therefore, this analysis attempts to reach conclusions, divided into short sub-paragraphs on the basis of the studies carried out. The aim is to introduce into the discussion some new proposals considering that, as seen, the rigid approach of rules of contractual obligations (in all its ramifications) actually does not contribute to the ambitious European project of improving the predictability and certainty of the outcome of litigations and the applicable law, which according to EU bodies would facilitate more reliable intra-EU transactions and economic outcomes.

4.1 Legal congruence versus legal certainty: Which legal tool for an efficient market?

As noted, EU bodies hold a well-established belief that for SME the European market does not guarantee the security needed to encourage these businesses to make cross-border investments. In consideration of these problems and in order to increase intra-Community transactions, as seen, the EU bodies decided to work to harmonise the rules[755] using rigid criteria such as those of Rome I, in order to improve the "proper functioning of the internal market".

With reference to the subject of this chapter, it is not necessary to dwell on the harmonisation of EU rules, but rather on the rigid criteria used to ensure legal certainty. As is known, the choice to adopt hard-and-fast rules has been taken by politicians and bureaucrats, motivated by mainly political reasons.[756] These choices, as seen, have totally changed the EU p.i.l. system of contractual obligations with the adoption of inflexible criteria in Rome I. This drastic and poorly explained choice can be criticized considering that the problems of the connecting factors is one the most delicate in the field of p.i.l. In fact, as Schwind notably observed, these factors require "deep theoretical understanding combined with experience regarding the probabilities of certain fact situations".[757]

755 *H. Ofner*, "Rom bis Rom V das Haager Unterhaltsprotokoll – Das Internationale Privatrecht zwischen Rechtsvereinheitlichung und Rechtszersplitterung", in (2012), *ecolex*, 573; *A. Luminoso*, "Dall' America Latina un messaggio per l'Unione europea sul diritto dei contratti", in (2012) *Contratto e Impresa/ Europa*, 577.

756 For more see *G. Rühl*, "The Problem of International Transactions: Conflict of Laws Revisited", in (2010) *Journal of Private International Law*, 81.

757 *F. Schwind*, "Problems of codification of Private International Law", in (1968) *International and Comparative Law Quarterly*, 435.

In addition, the politicians being the architects of these rules have failed to recognize the dynamics and needs of the internal market. Therefore, the risk is that wrong choices may undermine the market or protect only the interest-group lobby,[758] who may possibly seek regulation as a weapon in business competition.[759] In fact, in the case of Rome I the rigid rules will protect the interests of only the stronger contractual parties (seller, service provider, distributor, and insurer) or those who, in contrast to SME, do not need to be encouraged to make cross-border investments.

Moreover, considering that, once again, there are no field studies on the benefits that "legal certainty" and contract law rigid rules bring, it is still possible that "legal congruence", reasonable rules and an "incomplete contract" might encourage SME that are a big market share, and also affect the international transactions of big companies.[760] Indeed, I should remember that "legal certainty" finds it's roots in Weber's theory, according to which this certainty might stimulate investment currently hampered by economic uncertainty in the global market. In this respect, my argument is that at present there is no basis for this theory for two reasons. Firstly, this theory is contrary to the "varieties of capitalism" literature[761] according to which single and targeted solutions might not improve economic growth;[762] and secondly, I believe that in the new era of globalisation, the market uncertainty that should generate the need to improve the predictability of the outcomes and the legal certainty, is greatly reduced by technological and social innovations.[763]

---

758 *G. Rühl*, "The Problem of International Transactions: Conflict of Laws Revisited", in (2010) *Journal of Private International Law*, 84.

759 *J. W. Hurst, Law and Markets in United States History. Different Modes of Bargaining among interests*, (The University of Wisconsin Press, Madison, 1982), 32.

760 *Supra* § 1.III.

761 *J. Hollingsworth – R. Bayer, Contemporary Capitalism: The Embeddedness of Institutions*, (C.U.P., Cambridge, 1999), *passim*.

762 A similar way was that of P.S. Mancini, according to whom "*la comunanza di diritto era impossibile di esistere tra individui di diverse nazioni*", continuing "*si è ritenuto che una certa competizione tra le leggi degli Stati potesse favorire il progresso. Vediamo per esempio, negli Stati Uniti d' America, più di 50 sistemi diversi di diritto civile che cercano di sperimentare vie diverse per raggiungere mete uguali*". With these words P.S. Manicini, "Della nazionalità come fondamento del diritto delle genti", in *E. Jayme* (ed.) *Della nazionalità come fondamento del diritto delle genti. Ristampa riveduta e corretta della prima edizione,* (Giappichelli, Torino, 2000), 12 and 17.

763 *B. R. Dorbeck – Jung*, "Global Trade: Changes in the Conceptualisation of Legal Certainty?", in V. Gessner (ed.), *Towards a Theoretical Framework for Contractual Certainty in Global Trade*, (Hart Publishing, Oxford, 2009), 297.

Finally, to these considerations must be added the experience of the US, which still enjoys the largest trade in the world. In fact, the conflict of laws Revolution teaches us not only that the courts need more guidance rather than a mere list of factors[764] but also that contract law rules, in all their ramifications, should not be mechanistic because they have to deal with many private as well as public interests and considerations.[765] As a consequence, my argument is that the rules must not disregard legal sociology,[766] the level of political-cultural integration[767] inherent to each system and the nature of the market itself.[768]

In light of these considerations and in addition to the previous analysis, the predictability of the outcomes of litigation with the hard-and-fast rules seems to give rise to harmful effects in the internal market, contrary to the claims of the Rome I Recital.

Therefore, in order to benefit the internal market there seems to be a need for rules of contract law in all its ramifications, so as to provide more power to the court in the task of enhancing the reasonsable expectations of contractual parties. At the same time, flexible rules – not rules that create different interpretations but rather ones that ensure a reasonable and fair interpretation - seem to be of considerable importance not only by enhancing the interpreter's role, but also by adapting to the different legal traditions[769] that there are especially relevant in the EU, and by remaining open simultaneously to the political, social and even economic and cultural changes,[770] involved in international commerce in the new era of globali-

764 *S.C. Symeonides*, "The Choice-of-Law Revolution Fifty Years after Currie: An End and a Beginning", in (2015) *University of Illinois Law Review*, 78.

765 *Ex multis H. E. Yntema*, "The Objectives of Private International Law", in (1957) *The Canadian Law Review*, 722; *A. Mills*, "The Identities of Private International Law: Lessons from the U.S. and EU revolutions", in (2013) *Duke Journal of Comparative & International Law*, 458.

766 *P. Šarčević*, *International Contracts and Conflicts of Laws*, (Graham&Trotman/ Martinus Nijhoff, London/Dordrecht/Boston, 1990), 22.

767 *A. Malatesta*, "Cultural diversity and Private International Law", in G. Venturini - S. Bariatti (eds.), *Liber Fausto Pocar "New Instruments Of Private International Law"* (Giuffrè, Milano, 2009), 643 ss.

768 In similar way *P. Perlingieri*, *Il diritto civile nella legalità costituzionale nel sistema italo-comunitario delle fonti*, (E.S.I., Napoli, 2006), 477 – 478.

769 See on this topic *U. Mattei*, "Three Patterns of Law: Taxonomy and Change in the World's Legal Systems", in (1997) *American Journal of Comparative Law*, 17.

770 *P. Šarčević*, *International Contracts and Conflicts of Laws*, (Graham&Trotman/ Martinus Nijhoff, London/Dordrecht/Boston, 1990), 21- 22; *F. Schwind*, "Problems of codification of Private International Law", in (1968) *International and Comparative Law Quarterly*, 431.

sation. Hard-and-fast rules such as those of Rome I clearly do not conform to this requirement, and it is difficult to imagine a modern government body rejecting such innovative changes only to limit the discretionary power of the interpreter.

4.II Rome I: Learning from the mistakes

This book intends to enter into the discussion of the eternal "struggle between predictability and flexibility" also of the rules of p.i.l. of contractual obligations.[771]

Considering the findings of the above political-economic analysis and the benefits for the internal market, it appears necessary to examine in more detail the consequences of limiting the power of the interpreter through the rigid rules laid down in Rome I, which among many projects on contract law seems to have the most direct impact on the EU internal market.

As is known, p.i.l. rules are not self-contained or self-sufficient[772] and are therefore not able alone to easily locate the centre and the nature of the legal relations.[773] As a consequence, as notably illustrated also by Savigny,[774] the risk is that a rigid rule may lead to inequitable outcomes. To these considerations must be added that the hard-and-fast rules of Rome I are also supported by a rigid escape clause[775] that limits strongly the discretionary power of the interpreter. Having an "escape clause" that can only be applied rarely when the contract is "manifestly more closely connected with a country", is tantamount to not having one at all.[776] Such a term ap-

---

771 See also *ex multis F. Schwind*, *Aspects et sens du droit international privé* [electronic resource] *: cours général de droit international privé*, in (1984) *Recueil des cours*, electronic resource available at https://books.google.at/, 25 and more recently also *J. Suderow*, "Nuevas normas de litispendencia y conexidad para europa: ¿el caso del torpedo italiano? ¿Flexibilidad versus previsibilidad?", in (2013) *Cuadernos de Derecho Transnacional*, 184 – 198.

772 *E. B. Crawford – J.M. Carruthers*, "Connection and Coherence Between and Among European Instruments in the Private International Law of Obligations", in (2014) *International and Comparative Law Quarterly*, 28.

773 *A. Mills*, "The Identities of Private International Law: Lessons from the U.S. and EU revolutions", in (2013) *Duke Journal of Comparative & International Law*, 449.

774 *F. C. v. Savigny*, *System des heutigen Römischen Rechts*, (Berlino, 1849), *passim*.

775 As seen the only one exception is for the employment contracts.

776 See *supra* § 3.I.

pears as "all or nothing", and could confuse rather than assist the court[777] in the already murky "labyrinth" or, as called by some Authors, veritable "jungle"[778] of Rome I.

In this regard, it should be emphasised that rigid mechanisms - such the ones provided in Articles 4, 5 and 7 of Rome I imposing hard-and-fast rules and a strict "escape clause" without any *ratio legis*, only limit the discretionary power of the court and can lead to internal contradictions.[779] Additionally rigid mechanisms should be regarded as a failure because in a democratic society no system can "mechanize judgment"[780] through the implementation of hard-and-fast rules that prevent the court from being the final arbiter of the law.[781] In the same way, Grechenig and Gelter,[782] reporting on the theories of the legal realism school, founded during 1920s and 1930s, emphasise that these schools rejected the idea that law could be an autochthonous, judgment-free science, whereby the lawmaker could activate at predetermined solutions for all possible cases through objective methods (such as analogies) within a closed logical system.

In my opinion, these last observations deserve greater attention when evaluating p.i.l. of contractual obligations. The difficulties faced by the interpreters "are so complicated that it is impossible to draft general rules in

---

777 See also, regarding the Rome II Regulation, the criticism raised by *R. J. Weintraub*, "Rome II and the tension between predictability and flexibility", in (2005) *Rivista di diritto internazionale privato e processuale*, 570.

778 *J. A. Moreno Rodriguez – M. Mercedes Albornoz*, "Reflections on the Mexico Convention in the Context of the Preparation of the Future Hague Instrument on International Contracts", in (2011) *Journal of Private International Law*, 516; *M. Mercedes Albornoz*, "Choice of Law in International Contracts in Latin American Legal Systems", in (2010) *Journal of Private International Law*, 26.

779 In this way notably *S.C. Symeonides*, "The Choice-of-Law Revolution Fifty Years after Currie: An End and a Beginning", in (2015) *University of Illinois Law Review*, 80. According to the Author "Uncritical, undigested, and uncoordinated 'picking and choosing' can lead to internal contradictions and incoherence".

780 *S.C. Symeonides*, "Rome II and Tort Conflicts: A Missed Opportunity", in (2008) *American Journal of Comparative Law*, 180. In the same way *R. M. Dworkin*, "The Model of Rules", in (1967) *The University of Chicago Law Review*, 16; *S.C. Symeonides*, "Codification and Flexibility in Private International Law", in K.B. Brown -D.V. Snyder (eds.), *General Reports of the XVIIIth Congress of the International Academy of Comparative Law*, (Springer, Washington, 2012), 167 ss.

781 See also on this point *R. M. Dworkin*, "The Model of Rules", in (1967) *The University of Chicago Law Review*, 32 ss.

782 *K. Grechenig - M. Gelter*, "The Transatlantic Divergence in Legal Thought: American Law and Economics vs. German Doctrinalism", in (2008) *Hastings International and Comparative Law Review*, 314.

anticipation of conflicts".[783] Therefore, when a conflict of law problem arises, according to a learned editor as is Yntema, "it should be resolved with a detailed investigation of these problems, with reference to their actual and vital context".[784] Certainly, these difficulties are amplified especially in the specific matter of contractual obligations, where it is not possible to create a single rule that is perfectly suited for every case.[785] On this last point, Leible, in his illuminating analysis, assumes

> "[...] *en las obligaciones contractuales no existe un centro de gravidad unìvoco.* [...] *ningun criterio de connexion resulta adecuado para brindar una soluciòn vàlida para todos los casos en el derecho internacional de los contractos. Con puntos de conexiòn rigidos no se logra la armonia de decisiones, ni la previsibilidad y planeabilidad de las transacciones.* [...] *Por otro lado, sin embargo, es imposible establecer una regla fija que se adecue a los multiples supuestos de hecho y a los diferentes intereses de las partes.*"[786]

In light of these considerations, it seems evident that the "revolutionizing" of the Rome I Regulation is actually a return[787] to old and unproductive criteria that according to some scholars[788] give life to the "European crisis of the conflict of laws". This is the approach that I have adopted in this

783 *P. H. Neuhaus*, "Legal Certainty Versus Equity in the Conflict of Laws", in (1963) *Law and Contemporary Problems*, 800. The Author has rewritten the words of Georg Cohn in (1955) *Existenzialismus und Rechtswissenschaft*. See more recently on this topic also *S. Marino*, "Le legittime aspettative delle parti nel diritto internazionale privato", in (2015) *Contratto e Impresa / Europa*, 340. In line with the Author's opinion "*il diritto internazionale privato è un settore sempre più elevato all'universalismo per cui è difficilmente giustificabile la prevalenza aprioristica di una legge su un'altra*".

784 *H. E. Yntema*, "The Objectives of Private International Law", in (1957) *The Canadian Law Review*, 726.

785 *K. Kagami*, "The Systematic Choice of Legal Rules of Private International Law: An Economic Approach", in J. Basedow – T. Kono (eds.), *An Economic Analysis of Private International Law*, (Mohr Siebeck, Tüebingen, 2006), 32; *H Batiffol*, *Aspects philosophiques du droit international privè*, (Dalloz, Paris, 1956), 245.

786 In these words *S. Leible*, "La importancia de la autonomia conflictual para el futuro del Derecho de los contractos internacionales", in (2011) *Cuadernos de Derecho Transnacional*, 219 – 220.

787 *P. Lagarde*, "Remarques sur la proposition de règlement de la Commission européenne sur la loi applicable aux obligations contractuelles (Roma I)", in (2006) *Revue critique droit international privé*, 339.

788 *M. F. Fogt*, "Private International Law in the Process of Harmonisation of International Commercial Law: The 'Ugly Duckling'?", in M. F. Fogt (ed.) *Unification and harmonisation of international commercial law: interaction or deharmonisation?* (Wolters Kluwer Law and Business, The Netherlands, 2012), 63; *J.J.*

book. In fact, this radical change from rather flexible criteria to rigid ones represents a countertrend because the formalistic and obsolete approach not only was developed going against historical p.i.l. theories (*ex multis* Currie and Huber) but also reduces the economic benefits[789] that the principle of closest connection secures in several European and non-European national legal systems.[790]

In fact, as seen, the flexible mechanism adopted by the framers of the Rome Convention was taken as an example by many other lawmakers. So it is appropriate to ask: Why were the flexible rules of the Rome Convention not appreciated by the framers of the Rome I Regulation? These not only promote legal congruence, thus reducing inequitable outcomes, but at the same time, could be adapted to cover the multiple differences of varying legal institutions and definitions[791] found among EU Member States. Consequently, a reasonable legal tool must be made available in order to ensure the application of the most equitable law and to be responsive to the continually evolving contemporary society,[792] principally in Europe, which is characterised by different legal cultures, business practices and lifestyles.[793]

Kuipers, "Bridging the Gap. The Impact of the EU on the Law Applicable to Contractual Obligations", in (2012) *RabelsZ*, 576. The Author held: "The PIL approaches that the European Union has adopted in secondary law are rather medieval from the point of view of a conflict of laws".

789 *G. Rühl*, "Method and Approach in Choice of Law: An Economic Perspective", in (2006) *Berkeley Journal of International Law*, 834 ss.

790 *S.C. Symeonides*, "The American Revolution and the European Evolution in Choice of Law: Reciprocal Lessons", in (2008) *Tulane Law Review*, 1799. See *supra* § 3.III.

791 *R. Sacco*, "Legal Formants: A Dynamic Approach to Comparative Law (Instalment II of II)", in (1991) *The American Journal of Comparative Law*, 390; *G. Alpa*, *Competition of Legal Systems and Harmonizazion of European Private Law. New paths in a Comparative Perspectives* (Sellier, Munich, 2013), 53; *R. Cafari Panico*, "Traduzione di atti stranieri notificati in Italia e prospettive di riforma", in *La Convenzione giudiziaria di Bruxelles del 1968 e la riforma del processo civile italiano*, (Giuffrè, Milano, 1985), 105 ss.

792 *P. H. Neuhaus*, "Legal Certainty Versus Equity in The Conflict of Laws", in R. Fentiman (ed.) *Conflict of Laws* (New York University Press, New York, 1996), 537; *M. F. Fogt*, "Private International Law in the Process of Harmonization of International Commercial Law: The 'Ugly Duckling'?", in M. F. Fogt (ed.) *Unification and harmonization of international commercial law: interaction or deharmonisation?*, (Wolters Kluwer Law and Business, The Netherlands, 2012), 66.

793 *Ex multis M. F. Fogt*, "Private International Law in the Process of Harmonization of International Commercial Law: The 'Ugly Duckling'?", in M. F. Fogt (ed.) *Unification and harmonization of international commercial law: interaction or dehar-*

In this regard, a consequence of reasonable rules is that it would become the task of the court to determine who should take upon themselves the delicate duty of identifying the most equitable law. As history teaches us, the role of the jurist (in particular the court) is an important one because it gives life to "*ars boni et aequi*", using the single term present in the contract[794] to proceed in searching for a plurality of connecting indices.[795] This work of interpretation becomes more important when the court is faced with an international contract and the parties have different nationalities, and thus different legal traditions.[796] In this case the interpreter should rely on a reasonable legal instrument to successfully apply the most equitable law in order to avoid inequitable outcomes and to facilitate adaptation to general tendencies through judicial decisions.[797] This implies that the court holds a moral and professional obligation to take into consideration not only the legal aspects and the language of the contract but also its underlying economic, cultural and inner aspects, without forgetting the importance that some legal systems give to trade customs and commercial usages.[798]

In short, this careful analysis of all the circumstances of the contract and of the real intention of the parties appears incompatible with the "mechanized judgment" and hard-and-fast rules as in Rome I, which in my opinion also causes damages to the internal market.

---

monization?, (Wolters Kluwer Law and Business, The Netherlands, 2012), 59; *R. Sacco*, "Legal Formants: A Dynamic Approach to Comparative Law (Instalment II of II)", in (1991) *The American Journal of Comparative Law*, 388. The Author regarding comparative law, states also that "Law, language and culture break down into cultural, linguistic and legal morphemes".

794 *P. Perlingieri*, "Interpretazione e qualificazione: profili dell'individuazione normativa", in (1975) *Diritto e Giustizia*, 827. According to the Author "*Il contratto va non soltanto interpretato ma anche qualificato alla luce dei princípi dell'ordinamento. Il problema sta nell'individuazione della funzione pratico-giuridica, socio-giuridica di ogni singolo atto*".

795 *P. Lagarde*, in (2007) *Revue critique de droit international privé*, 602.

796 *G.C. Cheshire*, "International contracts" (Jackson, Son&company, Glasgow, 1948), 76. According to the Author "It must be inferred from the language of the contract and its attendant circumstances what law the parties had in mind when they made the contract".

797 *F. Schwind*, "Problems of codification of Private International Law", in (1968) *International and Comparative Law Quarterly*, 434.

798 See *supra* § 2.V. In particular, on the importance of "commercial usages" in p.i.l. as "alternative to international legislation" see *P. Šarčević*, *International Contracts and Conflicts of Laws*, (Graham&Trotman/Martinus Nijhoff, London/Dordrecht/Boston, 1990), 18.

4.III Suggestions for future

Critically, the foregoing pages arrive at the conclusion that there is no reason to believe that political choice, often influenced only by well-organised interest groups, is the best instrument to guarantee harmonisation and as a result create benefits for the market. In fact, the present book argues that rigid rules create two significant risks: the over-application of some national laws (in particular where the stronger contractual parties are located) in international contract cases, and unfairness, which may develop from power imbalances during the resolution of economic conflicts. Therefore, the aim of a good legislator, whose scope extends to economic considerations, is to avoid the majority of international transactions, as they are controlled by the economic interests of fewer players. In fact I think that this approach does not benefit the EU internal market.

In addition, my argument is that the risk in adopting a strong approach with hard-and-fast rules may also compromise legal certainty as well as offers no obvious welfare gains.[799] These critiques are not directed to technocrats, because a project of harmonisation, unification and indentification of the economic needs of the market, must by necessity depend on a meticulous technocratic legal process.

My argument is that the Rome I Regulation represents a lost opportunity and that its failure, particularly in relation to the criteria adopted by Articles 4, 5, 7 and 14, derives from the EU lawmakers' inclusion of hard-and-fast rules to resolve the assumption that the flexible rules of the Rome Convention would harm the proper functioning of the internal market. Actually, the EU lawmakers have also failed to recognize that it is not the legal certainty or the harmonisation of the rules[800] with rigid criteria that creates benefits for the internal market, but rather the "harmonisation"

799 See on this point *P. Stephan*, "The Futility of Unification and harmonisation in international commercial law", in (1999) *Virginia Journal of International law*, 1999, 33.

800 For a critical approach on the harmonisation and "*universalles Kollisionrecht*" of EU p.i.l. rules see *G. Kühne*, "Internationales Privatrecht im 20. Jahrhndert. Der Einfluss von Gerhard Kegel und Alexander Lüderitz auf das Kollisionrecht", in (2015) *ZVglRWiss*, 359; *P. Perlingieri, Il diritto dei contratti tra persona e mercato*, (E.S.I., Napoli, 2003), 484, according to which "*per realizzare la armonizzazione auspicata non pare opportuno adottare soluzioni di carattere puramente tecnico*".

and "rationality" of the decisions.[801] The latter could also be provided with rules based on "reasonable criteria",[802] that do not undermine the main function of the p.i.l. of contractual obligations, which is to select, interpret and apply in each case the law that will best promote suitable conditions for international commerce.[803] In fact, the harmonisation process needs to confront the real world of day-to-day decision-making in legal matters and disputes and must take into account the different legal cultures. Here I want still stress that the harmonisation process must be spontaneous and voluntary, not forced by lawmakers with rigid and messy rules. In other words, uniformity of law and benefits for the market, cannot be created by just imposing rules through public policy.[804] I believe this process requires the understanding of the legal culture of all participating countries as well as "experienced integration".[805] Only in this way will there be no fear of the EU market by SME. It would be equally unacceptable to force parties to choose an applicable law or to impose irrational rigid rules that could also collide with the will of the parties. In my view, this will unquestionably stifle the growth of the internal market!

The previous pages have shown that harmonisation is not a legislative issue but a cultural issue, and as a consequence it needs an approach that can stimulate market actors and not impose rigid rules on them. It is impor-

801 In general on the subject of harmonising international decisions as aim fixed by p.i.l. see *H. Hoyer*, *Die Anerkennung ausländischer Ehescheidungen in Österreich* (Manz, Wien, 1972), 35-39; *Id.*, "Some remarks on Art. 1, 2 and 20 of the EC Draft Convention", in O. Lando – B. von Hoffmann – K. Siehr (eds.) *European Private International Law of Obligations*, (Mohr, Tübingen, 1975), 116; *P.H., Neuhaus*, *Die Grundbegriffe des Internationalen Privatrechts*, 2, (Mohr, Tübingen, 1976), 46 - 63, *F. Schwind*, *Handbuch des Österreichischen Internationalen Privatrechts*, (Springer, Wien, 1975), 13 and 54.

802 *G. Rühl*, "Method and Approach in Choice of Law: An Economic Perspective", in (2006) *Berkeley Journal of International Law*, 840; *J. Basedow*, "Lex mercatoria and the Private International Law of the Contract", in J. Basedow – T. Kono (eds.), *An Economic Analysis of Private International Law*, (Mohr Siebeck, Tüebingen, 2006), 92.

803 *H. E. Yntema*, "The Objectives of Private International Law", in (1957) *The Canadian Law Review*, 741.

804 According to *J. W. Hurst*, *Law and Markets in United States History. Different Modes of Bargaining among interests*, (The University of Wisconsin Press, Madison, 1982), 27: "the market need protection not only against private invasion but also against abuses of public power".

805 I would like to comment as follows: with every problem comes an opportunity. Therefore, even resolving single cases in international contract law could be seen as an opportunity for harmonising the law and decisions.

tant that, especially in Europe, institutions start by adopting a realistic approach that considers the complexity of the effort and that enhances the interests of the market players. All this suggests an interactive and gradual process. Here I investigated how this process can be structured to also achieve the economic goals of the market.

In this regard, the difficult question remains of how the judicial apparatus can be developed, restablished or maintained. I believe that the first step is to create rules that support and enhance the party autonomy rather than restrain it,[806] for example, adopting flexible EU legal principles on contract law (not as an optional instrument) for cross-border transactions. Secondly, I believe that the market needs a reform of EU p.i.l. with reasonable rules and the creation an external mediation body for EU trans-border transactions.

I would like to point out that it is important to avoid a total politicization of the process and to adopt a new logical and innovative legal solution. The way forward is to start a new process of harmonisation based on a European pathway that also enhances the cultural differences between Member States, and utilizes the skills of learned international lawyers and judges that have the ability and experience to deal with EU cross-boarders cases. Naturally, this is a long and progressive path but one that can attain harmonisation and also assure uniformity of decisions, thereby avoiding alarm for the market players and as a consequence creating benefits for the internal market.

Let me conclude by mentioning that between the two extremes represented by strict criteria and a general rule, can be found a middle ground that could offer simple "guiding criteria" which, while safeguarding the reasonable expectations of the parties, could identify the most relevant points of the contract.[807]

---

806 On the same way see *S. Grundmann - F. Möslein - K. Riesenhuber*, *Contract Governance: Dimensions in Law and Interdisciplinary Research*, (O.U.P., Oxford, 2015), 22; *F. Böhm*, 'Privatrechtsgesellschaft und Marktwirtschaft', in (1966) 17 *Jahrbuch für die Ordnung von Wirtschaft und Gesellschaft*, 85, 88, 138; *D. Kennedy*, "A Transnational Genealogy of Proportionality in Private Law", in R. Brownsword - H. Micklitz - L. Niglia - S. Weatherill (eds.) *The Foundations of European Private Law* (Hart Publishing, Oxford, 2011), 185–220.

807 Kagami, from an economic perspective, notes that p.i.l. rules must be very simple, because more sophisticated is the rule, the more costly it is in practice. See *K. Kagami*, "The Systematic choice of Legal Rules for Private International Law: An Economic Approach", in J. Basedow – T- Kono (eds.), *An Economic Analysis of Private International Law*, (Mohr Siebeck, Tübingen, 2006), 18.

Therefore, in order to make the present study something more than a mere critique, the following points offer some potential solutions regarding this topic. These could be not only a contribution to the future development of Third Restatement of Conflict of Laws in the US, but could also be applied to European perspective where, as is known, some scholars are studying the steps to a future p.i.l. codification with an idea labelled as "Rome 0 Regulation".[808]

The first point originates from the belief that it is preferable to maintain special rules only for contracts involving particular social-political interests where public interests come together with private interests and where there is a need to protect the weaker party, as in the case of consumer and employment contracts. The latter have a *lex specialis* in Rome I that already allows the court to apply the most equitable law and at the same time ensure adequate protection to the weaker party. Therefore, with the exception of these contracts, it is appropriate to suggest a rule[809] that is clear and easy to implement. In particular, it should outline clear and objectives points of contact within the contract that the interpreter must take into account in order to ensure the application of the most equitable law. This rule should have the aim of guiding the interpreter with an approach that could be defined as "contacts-evaluation",[810] requiring him to justify his choice, taking into consideration the variety of circumstances in his analysis, and identifying the various "contacts" also "by counting".

In general terms, the rule should impose on the interpreter, in absence of choice of law by the parties, the requirement to evaluate of the following relevant points of contact with which the contract might have the stronger connection: a) the place where the contract was concluded; b) the place where negotiations were held; c) the place where the contract was performed or the place of payment; d) the place where the offer was made; e) the language used in the contract; f) the connection of the contract with some other previous contract; g) the legal status of the parties and in particular whether one of the parties is a government body; h) the place of ha-

808 See for more *S. Leible – M. Müller*, "A General Part for European Private International Law? The Idea of a 'Rome 0 Regulation'", in (2013) *Yearbook of Private International Law*, 137 – 152.

809 See also *S.C. Symeonides*, "The Choice-of-Law Revolution Fifty Years after Currie: An End and a Beginning", in (2015) *University of Illinois Law Review*, 79.

810 In a similar way *Y. Shunhong - X. Yongping - W. Baoshi*, "The Closest Connection Doctrine in the Conflict of Laws in China", in (2009) *Chinese Journal of International Law*, 438. The Authors have suggested an approach called "integrated contacts-evaluation", referring to the Chinese private international law.

bitual residence or place of business of the contracting parties; i) the place of loading and unloading of goods; l) the nationality of the parties; n) the currency used; and o) the references to foreign law or customs and commercial usages. The applicable law should be that with which the contract reveals the most points of contact among those listed.

This "new approach", called "contacts evaluation", would be easy to ascertain and partially discretionary, with the aim to combine certainty and flexibility. As such, it might ensure the application of the most equitable law which in turn would have the merit of having a positive impact on EU business transactions and promoting the proper functioning of the internal market. It might also encourage objective decision making because it requires the court to give reasons for its application of criteria of reasonableness and good faith to the majority of "points of contacts" with a country. At the same time, this new "breed" of p.i.l. rule might easily resolve more difficult cases, such as when the court is faced with an unknown legal institution. Last but not least, it would put an end to the current debates on rigid or flexible criteria, characteristic performance and the interpretation of the escape clause.

4.IV *Can an external mediation body meet the needs of the market?*

Previously it has been illustrated how the Rome I Regulation provides an untidy rule where the court, in the absence of parties' choice, must identify "mechanically" the applicable law from the complex "puzzle" of rules. This mechanistic approach degrades the important task of the interpreter and in particular of the court.[811] In support of this argument, it would be wise to acknowledge the contributions made by several national judges in relation to judicial decisions, arbitral awards,[812] legal advice,[813] and practice in general.

811 *S.C. Symeonides*, "The Choice-of-Law Revolution Fifty Years after Currie: An End and a Beginning", in (2015) *University of Illinois Law Review*, 63. According to the Author "judges are not stupid, just busy. Most of them encounter conflicts cases only infrequently and thus they do not have the opportunity or the incentive to develop the necessary expertise".

812 In this vien *D. P. Fernández Arroyo*, "Private adjudication without Precedent?", in H. Muir Watt – D. P. Fernández Arroyo (eds.), *Private International Law and Global Governance* (O.U.P., Oxford, 2014), 119 ss. who suggests that the arbitration could be seen as a private transnational rule-making.

813 *P. Pichonnaz*, "Harmonization of European Private Law: What Can Roman Law Teach Us; What can It Not?" in M. F. Fogt (ed.) *Unification and harmonization of*

Personally, I believe that the market can also have benefits when judges rely on an economic argument in order to justify a result. For certain, the rigid rules do not allow this result. In order to pursue this objective, I believe that it is essential to train the court in both the economic and social aspects of the cases they will encounter. It is necessary to promote a form of international and business culture and the idea that judges are also part of a wider harmonisation process and that all the cases they work on represent an opportunity to pursue this goal.

In fact, emphasizing these elements during the various stages of the development of the law[814] would enhance a process that cannot be determined exclusively by members of a Parliament or by EU institutions.[815]

Rather, the EU should adopt a step-by-step approach starting with a procedural device, in particular with an external mediation body, mandatory for all cross-border transactions and with an expert in legal mediation in international transactions. Through this device, all the actors of the market (contractual parties and lawyers) should participate in the process of harmonisation. Out-of-court settlements (or conciliation agreements), could be published in a database that everyone can access so that court decisions could also be influenced by similar cases. Building on the experience gathered, one could turn to full harmonisation at a later stage if that should turn out to be advisable.

Therefore, the final "decision" of the external body could also function as "guideline concepts" namely: legal consequences associated with such concepts established on the basis of balancing the needs of all the parties and starting by the different legal culture or simply choice the law applicable to the contract. As a consequence, these "guideline concepts" could also pave the way for creating legal and trade practices. All these considerations can be used to demonstrate that avoiding to draft a contract and cre-

---

international commercial law: interaction or deharmonization? (Wolters Kluwer Law and Business, The Netherlands, 2012), 35.

814 *R. Sacco*, "Legal Formants: A Dynamic Approach to Comparative Law (Instalment II of II)", in (1991) *The American Journal of Comparative Law*, 347. See also *R. Baratta*, "General Issues of Private International Law in the Europe System - Reflections by Italian Scholars. The Process of Characterization in the EC conflict of Laws: Suggesting a Flexible Approach", in (2004) *Yearbook of Private International Law*, 169; *G. Gorla*, "Lo studio interno e comparativo della giurisprudenza e i suoi presupposti: le raccolte e le tecniche per l'interpretazione delle sentenze", in (1964) *Foro italiano*, IV, c. 73 ss.

815 *P. Šarčević*, *International Contracts and Conflicts of Laws*, (Graham & Trotman/ Martinus Nijhoff, London/Dordrecht/Boston, 1990), 27.

ating an external mediation body could avoid giving courts discretion so that the risk of arbitrary action by judges will be reduced and so that the parties could be encouraged to have an out-of-court settlement. This may avoid sending courts on missions that often they cannot carry out because of the very real capability problem.[816]

In addition, my point is that an external mediation body may not only facilitate agreement between parties[817] but also reduce the transaction costs compared to litigation or arbitration.[818] In this sense, I believe that Posner's analysis can support these arguments. In fact, Posner famously observes that

> "transaction costs in a broad sense are incurred at only two stages: the negotiation and drafting of the contract, and the legal dispute that propels the interpretive issue into court or arbitration. Actually, there is an intermediate stage. When a dispute over the contract's meaning arises, the parties will first try to resolve it themselves. They will do this not only because of the costs of litigation, but also because of the reputation factor [...] the party demonstrably in the wrong on the interpretive issue will hesitate to force the issue to litigation".[819]

Therefore, starting by these observations, it is a clear that resolving the dispute during the stage prior to the litigation, with the support of a mediation body could be a good aim for both the parties also for economical reasons. In fact, this can avoid costs of negotiation, of drafting the contract, and of paying lawyers for the litigation (which is surely more costly than

816 *S. Macaulay*, *The Real and the Paper Deal: Empirical Pictures of Relationships, Complexity and the Urge for Transparent Simple Rules*, in (2003) *Modern Law Review*, 79. According to *M. J. Bonell*, "The law governing international commercial contracts and the actual role of the Unidroit Principles", in (2018) *Uniform Law Review*, 17: "also if a judge was prepared to apply a foreign law, it is far from granted that he or she will be in position to interpreter it properly".

817 An external mediation body could also bring out the will of the parties, in absence of a written contract, to appeal for an international arbitrator commitee or a competent court.

818 Commercial arbitration is neither available in every dispute nor achievable by medium-sized litigation, and parties often have difficulties in finding arbitrators specialized in international commercial disputes. In this way see *J. Basedow*, *Lex Mercatoria and Private International Law of Contracts*, in J. Basedow – T. Kono (eds.), *An Economic Analysis of Private International Law*, (Mohr Siebeck, Tübingen, 2006), 65.

819 In these words, *R.A. Posner*, "The Law and Economics of Contract Interpretation", in (2005) 83 *Texas Law Review*, 1614.

mediation), and it can also avoid damage to the parties' reputation by avoiding appearance in a public court.

In short, it is reasonable to conclude, on the basis of existing evidence, that a thorough reform of the system of civil justice is needed to initiate the unification/harmonisation process and secure real benefits for the EU market.

4.V Concluding remarks

The lesson to be learned from this book is that in the new era of globalisation, the market requires a law of contracts that enhances the role of the interpreter guiding and balancing intersubjective contractual relationships.[820] In particular, the market needs norms of contract law that orients the interpreter to find parties' economic contractual intentions and that can adapt to the requirements of the new era of globalisation, not norms that arbitrarily "impose a choice".

In fact, I have tried to prove that the needs of the global economy invite legislators to abandon the position of "market guardian",[821] seeking a self-regulation of exchanges and looking for rules that enhance party autonomy without creating imperative and rigid legal instruments that can harm the "Supreme Will" of contractual parties. In fact, as Macaulay assumes, "formal thought in law may actually defeat the intent of transacting parties, and benefit those with power and wealth".[822] From the perspective just outlined, every forced law creates tension with values and instills fear in enterprises, the principal actors of the market.

---

820 In this respect see *G. Alpa*, "Il contratto in generale. Fonti, teorie e metodi", in P. Schlesinger (ed.), *Trattato di diritto civile e commerciale* (Giuffrè, Milano, 2014), according to which "*Il compito del giurista odierno consiste appunto nel misurare la distanza tra il contratto come tradizionalmente concepito e il contratto come disegnato dall'esperienza del diritto vivente e dalla realtà sovranazionale. Continuare a leggere le regole del codice nella prospettiva originaria, magari con qualche aggiornamento, non è solo diventato impossibile, è diventato inutile*". For a deeply analysis see also *L. Gatt*, "Il Contratto nella storia e nel pensiero giuridico", in L. Gatt (ed.), *Il contratto del terzo millennio. Dialogando con Guido Alpa*, (Editoriale Scientifica, Napoli, 2018), 17.

821 In this way *U. La Porta*, *Globalizzazione e diritto. Regole giuridiche e norme di legge nell'economia globale.* (Liguori Editore, Napoli, 2005), 139, Author traslation.

822 *S. Macaulay*, "The Real and the Paper Deal: Empirical Pictures of Relationships, Complexity and the Urge for Transparent Simple Rules", in (2003) *The Modern Law Review*, 57-58.

Therefore, a central point is that market protection also takes the form of preventing economic power from gaining strength and substituting political power,[823] as has been in the case of the Rome I Regulation. In fact, my argument is that, the regression towards the rigid rules of Rome I is represented by invoking new and rigid criteria which produce a lack of coherence and conceptual vision that are not only unhelpful for the interpreter and do not ensure an efficient solution to the problem of the cross boarder transactions but also may damage the basic principles of p.i.l.[824] In addition, I have reasoned that this European "attack" and its strong and direct "orders" also on single national legal cultures not only frighten SME into avoiding cross-border transactions but also increase the populism phenomenon that is taking over.

But exactly for these reasons I believe that, in a democratic and pluralistic society such as Europe, the rules, in particular that of contract law, cannot be rigid, irrational and liable to protect only one contractual party. What is more, the interpreter must be guided by generally recognized rules capable of rational interpretation[825] and that do not lead to inequitable outcomes which may in turn affect the proper functioning of the internal market.

Quite definitely, the book has aimed to demonstrate that the EU p.i.l. of contractual obligations would be concerned not with resolving private disputes "quickly" and with automatic operation, but it seeks to argue that it should have an important systemic function that will encourage a careful analysis by the court searching for a "just decision in the case"[826] in order to avoid harm to the reasonable expectations of the parties, who represent the principal players of the market.

In conclusion, the study conducted in these pages has the merit of highlighting that the benefits for the internal market are not achieved by limit-

---

823 *N. Irti*, *L'ordine giuridico del mercato*, (Laterza Editore, Bari, 2009), 131.

824 For the latest schools of thought on p.i.l. in the 20th century and for a critical approach to KLAUS SCHURIG's views see *G. Kühne*, "Internationales Privatrecht im 20. Jahrhndert. Der Einfluss von Gerhard Kegel und Alexander Lüderitz auf das Kollisionrecht", in (2015) *ZVglRWiss*, 366. According to the Author "*Insgesamt durfte das Fundament des uberkommen IPR zwar im Wesentlichen (noch) unerschuttert sein. Aber die seismischen Wellen, die es bedrohen, sind deutlicher zu spuren, als Schuring es uns glauben machen will*".

825 *P. H. Neuhaus*, "Legal Certainty versus Equity in the Conflict of Laws", in (1963) *Law and Contemporary Problems*, 802.

826 *H. E. Yntema*, "The Objectives of Private International Law", in (1957) *The Canadian Law Review*, 727.

ing the discretionary power of the interpreter. Rather, the attention must be directed to the promotion of a more long-term process of sustainable wealth formation rather than to the idea of wealth-maximization.[827] This aim can be guaranteed with "reasonable" criteria and the time to ensure that the jurisprudence and the doctrine of different Member States, also with the support of an external mediation body, can be harmonised[828] without disregarding the legal, cultural and economic differences among them.

No doubt, I believe that to fulfil this purpose, it is to necessary focus on the previous suggestions as well on the creation of a contract "Law and Economic" theory adaptable to the new era of globalisation.[829] This topic could be examined not only by the EU bodies but also by the ALI that nowadays is drafting the Third Restatement of Conflicts of Laws.

827 *R. P. Malloy*, *Law in a Market Context. An Introduction to Market Concepts in Legal Reasoning*, (C.U.P., Cambridge, 2004), 61.

828 Wagner argues that the EU must use a step-by-step approach. See *H. Wagner*, "Economic analysis of cross border Legal uncertainty", in J. Smits (ed.), *The need for a European Contract Law. Empirical and Legal Perspectives*, (Europa Law Publishing, Amsterdam, 2005), 44.

829 See *supra* § 2.VI. On this topic is important to point out the words of *M. Gelter - K. Grechenig*, *History of Law and Economics*, (Preprints of the Max Planck Institute for Research on Collective Goods Bonn 2014/5), 6 available at https://www.coll.mpg.de/pdf_dat/2014_05online.pdf , according the Author's opinion "However, it is certainly fair to say that the influence of Law & Economics on the mainstream legal discourse is still much larger in the U.S. than in Europe. Scholars continuously argue that courts outside the U.S. rarely take economic consequentialist arguments and empirical evidence into account".